Rust Web Programming

A hands-on guide to developing fast and secure web apps with the Rust programming language

Maxwell Flitton

BIRMINGHAM—MUMBAI

Rust Web Programming

Group Product Manager: Aaron Lazar
Publishing Product Manager: Richa Tripathi
Senior Editor: Rohit Singh
Content Development Editor: Rosal Colaco
Technical Editor: Gaurav Gala
Copy Editor: Safis Editing
Project Coordinator: Deeksha Thakkar
Proofreader: Safis Editing
Indexer: Priyanka Dhadke
Production Designer: Roshan Kawale

First published: February 2021
Production reference: 1250221

Published by Packt Publishing Ltd.
Livery Place
35 Livery Street
Birmingham
B3 2PB, UK.

ISBN 978-1-80056-081-9

www.packt.com

To my mother, Allison Barson, who has always had my best interests at heart throughout my journey with unconditional support.

– Maxwell Flitton

Contributors

About the author

Maxwell Flitton is a software engineer who works at a medical engineering AI company called Monolith AI, and was an R&D software engineer in financial tech before. In 2011, Maxwell achieved his Bachelor of Science in nursing from the University of Lincoln, UK. While working 12 hours shifts in the A&E departments of hospitals, Maxwell obtained another degree in physics from The Open University in the UK, and then moved on to another milestone, obtaining a postgrad diploma in physics and engineering in medicine from UCL in London. He has developed an open source machine learning deployment software called DeployML, which can be downloaded via `pip`, and he teaches computational medicine at Imperial College London every now and then.

I want to thank my academic supervisor, Christos Bergeles, who went above and beyond in supporting me in academic pursuits. I also owe thanks to the staff of Charing Cross Hospital, Accident and Emergency department, London, who helped me grow as a person. I also want to thank my colleagues at Auto Service Finance, Rimes, and Monolith AI, who have supported me to grow as a developer.

About the reviewer

Roman Krasiuk is an R&D software engineer who has worked on industry-leading products in trading, blockchain, and energy markets. Having started his professional career at the age of 18, he loves to dispel the myth that young people cannot occupy lead roles.

His areas of expertise include large-scale infrastructure development, the automation of financial services, and big data engineering. Roman is a firm believer in coding as a form of art and his biggest desire is to create a masterpiece that will show people just how gorgeous code can be.

Table of Contents

Section 2: Processing Data and Managing Displays

3
Handling HTTP Requests

4
Processing HTTP Requests

5
Displaying Content in the Browser

Section 3: Data Persistence

6
Data Persistence with PostgreSQL

7
Managing User Sessions

8
Building RESTful Services

Section 4: Testing and Deployment

9

Testing Our Application Endpoints and Components

10

Deploying Our Application on AWS

11
Understanding Rocket Web Framework

Appendix A
Understanding the Warp Framework

Assessments

Other Books You May Enjoy

Index

Preface

Rust is a new and fast-growing programming language that provides memory safety without a garbage collector. With its low memory footprint, it allows web developers to build high-performing and secure web apps with relative ease. This book will help web developers to adopt Rust for web app development, while addressing safety and high-performance issues.

Rust Web Programming will take you through each stage of the web development process, showing you how to combine Rust and modern web development principles to build supercharged web apps. This book tries to keep dependencies at a minimum and will avoid leaning too heavily on advanced Rust concepts while keeping modules isolated. As a result, you will be able to build fully functioning web apps and modules that can be plugged into a range of different web frameworks with confidence. This will give you a solid foundation to learn advanced concepts in Rust in the future while applying it to an already functioning web application.

You'll start with an introduction to Rust and understand how to avoid common pitfalls when migrating from traditional dynamic programming languages. The book will show you how to structure Rust code for a project that spans multiple pages and modules. Next, you'll explore the Actix Web framework and get a basic web server up and running. As you advance, you'll learn how to process JSON requests and display data from the web app via HTML, CSS, and JavaScript.

You'll be able to structure scalable web apps in Rust in Rocket, Actix Web, and Warp. You'll also be able to apply data persistence to your web apps using PostgreSQL. We'll also build login, JWT, and config modules for your web apps, and serve HTML, CSS, and JavaScript from the Actix Web server.

We'll also build unit tests and functional API tests in Postman and Newman, and deploy the Rust app with NGINX and Docker onto an AWS EC2 instance.

You'll also learn how to persist data and create RESTful services in Rust. Later, you'll build an automated deployment process for the app on an AWS EC2 instance and Docker Hub. Finally, you'll play around with some popular web frameworks in Rust and compare them.

By the end of this Rust book, you'll be able to confidently create scalable and fast web applications with Rust.

Who this book is for

This book on web programming with Rust is for web developers who have programmed in traditional languages such as Python, Ruby, JavaScript, and Java and are looking to develop high-performance web applications with Rust. Although no prior experience with Rust is necessary, a solid understanding of web development principles and basic knowledge of HTML, CSS, and JavaScript are required if you want to get the most out of this book.

What this book covers

Chapter 1, Quick Introduction to Rust, focuses on what's different about Rust. It covers the strong typing and ownership of variables in relation to memory management as this could trip up a developer from a dynamic language. It also covers structs and how behavior is added to them with impl blocks. Finally, macros are introduced as these are heavily utilized in web development with Rust, making processing such as JSON serialization straight forward.

Chapter 2, Designing Your Web Application in Rust, covers the basic Cargo tools for managing a Rust project which include running, documenting, and managing dependencies. With this, we'll run code that has been structured in different files and directories (modules) to build some user structs with traits and manage configuration parameters in a config struct from a config JSON file. We'll finally parse parameters into Cargo to determine whether a development or production config file is parsed in.

Chapter 3, Handling HTTP Requests, introduces the Actix Web framework to get a basic web server up and running. With this, we'll manage multiple routes from different modules to host a range of different views in a structured approach. We'll also explore the async and await concepts that are behind the views of Actix.

Chapter 4, Processing HTTP Requests, explains how we pass through params, bodies, headers and forms to the views and process them returning JSON. We'll then build a response struct that enables us to add a code and an optional message.

Chapter 5, Displaying Content in the Browser, displays data from the web app via HTML through different methods using the Actix Web framework and typed crate. We'll then build on this and utilize CSS and JavaScript to enable the HTML page to interact with the web app API.

Chapter 6, Data Persistence with PostgreSQL, explains how we build a database and define user models using structs. We use the methods we learned about in *Chapter 4, Processing HTTP Requests*, to develop a create/delete use API.

Chapter 7, Managing User Sessions, helps us to build a login system that manages sessions and enforces expiration time frames for these login sessions, utilizing JWT and datetime.

Chapter 8, Building RESTful Services, helps us to create TODO data models that link to the user data model. We'll then build a RESTful CRUD API that manages the TODO tasks around the user.

Chapter 9, Testing Our Application Endpoints and Components, helps us to build unit tests in Rust for the structs that have functionality. We'll then test the API endpoints with Postman and then automate these tests with Newman.

Chapter 10, Deploying Our Application on AWS, helps us to build an automated deployment process for the app on an AWS EC2 instance with NGINX using docker hub.

Chapter 11, Understanding Rocket Web Framework, covers the Rocket framework. We'll explore the main differences between Rocket and Actix. We'll also build a basic server using Rocket and define the routes, and reuse code and modules that we have built before that worked in the Actix Web framework.

Appendix A, Understanding the Warp Framework, explores the main differences between Warp and Actix. We'll also build a basic server using Warp and define the routes.

Assessments, contains the answers to the questions from all the chapters.

To get the most out of this book

You will need to know some basic concepts around HTML and CSS. You will also need to have some familiarity with JavaScript. However, this is just for displaying the data to the user. If you are reading this book to just build purely backend API servers then this is not needed.

Some basic understanding of web development and coding in another language is also desired as this book does not cover programming basics like functions, loops, and so on. Instead, this book focuses on the quirks that Rust introduces, which you need to understand to code like you would in other languages.

Software/hardware covered in the book	OS requirements
Rust	Windows, macOS, and Linux (any)
Docker	Windows, macOS, and Linux (any)
Docker-compose	Windows, macOS, and Linux (any)
Postman	Windows, macOS, and Linux (any)

If you are using the digital version of this book, we advise you to type the code yourself or access the code via the GitHub repository (link available in the next section). Doing so will help you avoid any potential errors related to the copying and pasting of code.

After reading this book, you will be able to build fully functioning web applications that can be deployed without having to lean too heavily on advanced Rust concepts. However, this is just a solid foundation. It is advised that you improve your Rust web programming ability by reading up on more advanced Rust concepts, which will enable you to solve more complex problems.

Download the example code files

You can download the example code files for this book from GitHub at `https://github.com/PacktPublishing/Rust-Web-Programming`. In case there's an update to the code, it will be updated on the existing GitHub repository.

We also have other code bundles from our rich catalog of books and videos available at `https://github.com/PacktPublishing/`. Check them out!

Code in Action

Code in Action videos for this book can be viewed at `http://bit.ly/3jULCrw`.

Download the color images

We also provide a PDF file that has color images of the screenshots/diagrams used in this book. You can download it here: `https://static.packt-cdn.com/downloads/9781800560819_ColorImages.pdf`.

Conventions used

There are a number of text conventions used throughout this book.

`Code in text`: Indicates code words in text, database table names, folder names, filenames, file extensions, pathnames, dummy URLs, user input, and Twitter handles. Here is an example: "The template for our application image can be defined in a `Dockerfile` file in the root of our application next to our `Cargo.toml` file."

A block of code is set as follows:

```
RUN apt-get update -yqq && apt-get install -yqq cmake g++

RUN cargo install diesel_cli --no-default-features
                              --features postgres
```

Any command-line input or output is written as follows:

```
echo DATABASE_URL=postgres://username:password@postgres/to_do >
.env
```

Bold: Indicates a new term, an important word, or words that you see onscreen. For example, words in menus or dialog boxes appear in the text like this. Here is an example: " We can see that it has been updated (**PUSHED**) in the last 2 minutes."

> **Tips or Important Notes:**
> Appear like this.

Get in touch

Feedback from our readers is always welcome.

General feedback: If you have questions about any aspect of this book, mention the book title in the subject of your message and email us at `customercare@packtpub.com`.

Errata: Although we have taken every care to ensure the accuracy of our content, mistakes do happen. If you have found a mistake in this book, we would be grateful if you would report this to us. Please visit www.packtpub.com/support/errata, selecting your book, clicking on the Errata Submission Form link, and entering the details.

Piracy: If you come across any illegal copies of our works in any form on the Internet, we would be grateful if you would provide us with the location address or website name. Please contact us at copyright@packt.com with a link to the material.

If you are interested in becoming an author: If there is a topic that you have expertise in and you are interested in either writing or contributing to a book, please visit authors.packtpub.com.

Reviews

Please leave a review. Once you have read and used this book, why not leave a review on the site that you purchased it from? Potential readers can then see and use your unbiased opinion to make purchase decisions, we at Packt can understand what you think about our products, and our authors can see your feedback on their book. Thank you!

For more information about Packt, please visit packt.com.

Section 1: Setting Up the Web App Structure

Rust is a memory safe programming language. However, new developers can feel intimidated when picking up Rust. This does not help when Rust is described as a systems language, as if this tag instantly disqualifies Rust for web development.

However, we have to remember that Rust is memory safe. If we, as experienced web developers in other memory safe languages, understand the quirks of Rust such as borrow checking and lifetimes, we can code in Rust in a productive way. If we get to grips with package management (known as crates) and modules, there is nothing stopping us from building structured and safe applications in Rust in a fast paced manner.

This section gets the experienced web developer up and running with the basics of Rust and covers concepts that will enable you to structure a web app.

This section comprises the following chapters:

- *Chapter 01, Quick Introduction to Rust*
- *Chapter 02, Designing Your Web Application in Rust*

1
Quick Introduction to Rust

Rust is growing in popularity, but it is described as having a *steep learning curve*. By covering the basic rules of Rust, as well as how to manipulate a range of data types and variables, we will be able to write simple programs in the same fashion as dynamically typed languages with close to the same lines of code.

In this chapter, we will cover the main differences between Rust and generic dynamic languages to provide you with a quick understanding of how to utilize Rust. Installation and project management will be covered in the next chapter. Therefore, it's advised that you code the examples covered in this chapter using the online Rust playground.

In this chapter, we will cover the following topics:

- Reviewing data types and variables in Rust
- Controlling variable ownership
- Building structs
- Metaprogramming with macros

Let's get started!

Technical requirements

For this chapter, we only need access to the internet as we will be using the online Rust playground to implement all the code. The code examples provided can be run in the online Rust playground at `https://play.rust-lang.org/`.

For detailed instructions, please refer to the README file at `https://github.com/PacktPublishing/Rust-Web-Programming/tree/master/Chapter01`. You will also find all the source code used in this chapter at the preceding link.

The CiA videos for this book can be viewed at: `http://bit.ly/3jULCrw`

Reviewing data types and variables in Rust

If you have coded in another language, you will have used these data types already. However, Rust has some quirks that can throw developers, especially if they come from dynamic languages. In order to see the motivation behind these quirks, it's important that we explore why Rust is such a paradigm-shifting language.

Why Rust?

With programming, there is usually a trade-off between speed/resources and development speed/safety. Low-level languages such as **C/C++** can give the developer fine-grained control over the computer with fast code execution and minimal resource consumption. However, this is not free. Manual memory management can induce bugs and security vulnerabilities. On top of this, it takes more code and time to solve a problem in a low-level language. As a result of this, C++ web frameworks do not take up a large share of web development. Instead, it made sense to go for high-level programming languages where developers can solve problems safely and quickly.

However, it has to be noted that this memory safety comes at a cost. Languages such as **Python**, **JavaScript**, **PHP**, and **Java** keep track of all the variables defined and their references to a memory address. When there are no more variables pointing to a memory address, the data in that memory address gets deleted. This process is called **garbage collection** and consumes extra resources and time.

With Rust, memory safety is ensured without the costly garbage collection process. Instead, the compiler maps the variables, enforcing rules to ensure safety via a mechanism called the **borrow checker**. Because of this, Rust has enabled rapid, safe problem solving with truly performant code, thus breaking the speed/safety trade-off. As more data processing, traffic, and complex tasks are lifted into the web stack, Rust, with its growing number of web frameworks and libraries, has now become a viable choice for web development.

Before we get into developing a web app in Rust, we're going to briefly cover the basics of Rust. All of the code examples provided can be run in the online Rust playground at `https://play.rust-lang.org/`.

In the Rust playground, you may have the following layout:

```
fn main() {
    println!("Hello, world!");
}
```

The `main` function is the entry point where the code is run. If you're coming from a JavaScript or PHP background, your entry point is the first line of the file that is directly run, and the whole code block is essentially a `main` function. This is also true of Python; however, a closer analogy would be the `main` block that would be run if the file is directly run by the interpreter:

```
if __name__ == "__main__":
    print("Hello, World!")
```

This is often used to define an entry point in something such as a **Flask** application.

Using strings in Rust

Rust, like other languages, has typical data formats such as strings, integers, floats, arrays, and hash maps (dictionaries). However, because of the way in which Rust manages memory, there are some quirks we have to look out for when using them. These quirks can be easily understood and handled but can trip up experienced developers from dynamic languages if they are not warned about them.

In this section, we will cover enough memory management that we can start defining and using various data types and variables. We will dive into the concepts of memory management in more detail in the *Controlling variable ownership* section, later in this chapter.

We will start off with strings. We can create our own `print` function that accepts a string and prints it:

```
fn print(input_string: String) {
    println!("{}", input_string);
}

fn main() {
```

```
        let test_string = String::from("Hello, World!");
        print(test_string);
}
```

Here, we defined a string using the `from` function in the `String` object, and then passed it through our own `print` function to print it using Rust's built-in `println!` function. (Technically, this is a macro; `!` denotes that we can put multiple parameters inside the parentheses. We will cover macros later.)

Notice that the `print` function expects the `String` object to be passed through. This is the minimum amount of typing that's needed for a function. Now, we can try something a bit more familiar for a dynamic language. We don't call a `String` object function; we just define the string using quotation marks:

```
fn print(input_string: str) {
    println!("{}", input_string);
}

fn main() {
    let test_string = "Hello, World!";
    print(test_string);
}
```

What we have done here is defined a string literal and passed it through the `print` function to be printed. However, we get the following error:

error[E0277]: the size for values of type `str` cannot be known at compilation time

In order to understand this, we have to have a high-level understanding of stack and heap memory.

Stack memory is fast, static, and allocated at compile time. Heap memory is slower and allocated at runtime. String literals can vary in size as they are the string data that we refer to. String objects, on the other hand, have a fixed size in the stack that consists of a reference to the string literal in the heap, the capacity of the string literal, and the length of the string literal. When we pass a string literal through our own `print` function, it will have no idea of the size of the string literal being passed through. String literals can be converted into strings with `to_string`:

```
fn print(input_string: String) {
    println!("{}", input_string);
```

```
}
```

```
fn main() {
    let test_string = "Hello, World!";
    print(test_string.to_string());
}
```

Here, we converted the string literal just before passing it through the `print` function. We can also get the `print` function to accept a string literal reference by *borrowing* it using the & operator:

```
fn print(input_string: &str) {
    println!("{}", input_string);
}
```

```
fn main() {
    let test_string = &"Hello, World!";
    print(test_string);
}
```

Borrowing will be covered later in this chapter. What is essentially happening here is that `test_string` is merely a reference to the string literal, which is then passed through to the `print` function. One last thing we must note about strings is that we can get the string literal from the string with the `as_str` method.

Understanding integers and floats

Rust has signed integers (denoted by `i`) and unsigned integers (denoted by `u`) that consist of 8, 16, 32, 64, and 128 bits. The math behind binary notation is not relevant for the scope of this book. What we do need to understand, though, is the range of numbers allowed in terms of bits. Because binary is either 0 or 1, we can calculate the integer range by raising two to the power of the number of bits. For example, for 8 bits, 2 to the power of 8 equates to 256. Considering the 0, this means that an `i8` integer should have a range of 0 to 255, which can be tested by using the following code:

```
let number: u8 = 255;
```

Let's take a look at the following code:

```
let number: u8 = 256;
```

It's not surprising that the preceding code gives us the following overflow error:

```
literal `256` does not fit into the type `u8` whose range is
`0..=255`
```

What's not expected is if we change it to a signed integer:

```
let number: i8 = 255;
```

Here, we get the following error:

```
literal `255` does not fit into the type `i8` whose range is
`-128..=127`
```

This is because unsigned integers only house positive integers and signed integers house positive and negative integers. Since bits are memory size, the signed integer has to accommodate a range on both sides of zero, so the modulus of the signed integers is essentially half.

In terms of floats, Rust accommodates f32 and f64 floating points, which can be both negative and positive. Declaring a floating-point variable requires the same syntax as integers:

```
let float: f32 = 20.6;
```

It has to be noted that we can also annotate numbers with suffixes, as shown in the following code:

```
let x = 1u8;
```

Here, x has a value of 1 with the type of u8. Now that we have covered floats and integers, we can use vectors and arrays to store them.

Storing data in vectors and arrays

Rust stores sequenced data in vectors and arrays. Arrays are generally immutable and don't have push functions (append for Python). They also only accommodate one data type. This can be managed using structs and traits, but this will be covered later on in this chapter. You can define and loop through arrays and vectors with fairly standard syntax:

```
let int_array: [i32; 3] = [1, 2, 3];

for i in int_array.iter() {
    println!("{}", i);
```

```
}
```

```
let str_vector: Vec<&str> = vec!["one", "two", "three"];
```

```
for i in str_vector.iter() {
  println!("{}", i);
}
```

```
let second_int_array: [i32; 3] = [1, 2, 3];
let two = second_int_array[1];
```

Let's try and append "four" to our str_vector:

```
str_vector.push("four");
```

Here, we get an error about how we cannot borrow as mutable. This is because, by default, variables defined in Rust are not mutable. This can be easily remedied by putting a mut keyword in front of the variable's name:

```
let mut str_vector: Vec<&str> = vec!["one", "two",
    "three"];
```

This also works for strings and numbers. While it might be tempting to define everything as a mut variable, this forced immutability not only has performance benefits, but it also improves the safety. If you are not expecting a variable to change in a complex system, then not allowing it to mutate will throw up the error right then as opposed to allowing silent bugs to run in your system.

Mapping data with hash maps

In some languages, **hash maps** are referred to as **dictionaries**. In order to define a hash map in Rust, we must import the hash maps from the standard library. Once we've defined a new hash map, we can insert an entry, get it out of the hash map, and then print it:

```
use std::collections::HashMap;
```

```
fn main() {
    let mut general_map: HashMap<&str, i8> =
        HashMap::new();
    general_map.insert("test", 25);
    let outcome: i8 = general_map.get("test");
```

```
        println!("{}", outcome);
}
```

With this, we get the following error for defining the outcome variable:

expected `i8`, found enum `std::option::Option`

Here, we can see that the `get` method does not actually return an `i8` type, despite us inserting an `i8` type into the hash map. It's returning an `Option` enum instead. This is because the `get` method could fail. We could pass in a key that does not exist. Therefore, we have to unwrap the option to get the value we're aiming to get:

```
let outcome: Option<&i8> = general_map.get("test");
println!("here is the outcome {}", outcome.unwrap());
```

However, directly unwrapping the result can result in an error being raised. Because `Optional` is either `Some` or `None`, we can exploit Rust's `match` statement to handle the outcome:

```
match general_map.get("test") {
    None => println!("it failed"),
    Some(result) => println!("Here is the result: {}",
        result)
}
```

Here, if the result is `None`, then we print that it failed. If the result is `Some`, we access the result in the `Optional` wrapper and print it. The arrows in the `match` statement can have their own code blocks. For instance, we can nest a `match` statement within a `match` statement. For instance, we can perform another lookup if the original lookup fails. In the following code, we can check to see if there's an entry under the `"testing"` key. If it's not there, we can then check to see if there's an entry under the `"test"` key. If that fails too, we must give up:

```
match general_map.get("testing") {
    None => {
        match general_map.get("test") {
            None => println!("Both testing and test
                failed"),
            Some(result) => println!("testing failed but
                test is: {}", result)
        }
```

```
        },
        Some(result) => println!("Here is the result: {}",
            result)
}
```

Calling the `insert` function again with the same key will merely update the value under that key. Calling the `remove` function from the hash map with the desired key will remove the entry if it exists. There are some experimental functions such as reserve allocations, capacity, and more that will move to the stable build of Rust in time. Be sure to check the official Rust documentation for more functions for the hash map at `https://doc.rust-lang.org/beta/std/collections/struct.HashMap.html`.

Crates, tooling, and documentation will be covered in *Chapter 2, Designing Your Web Application in Rust*. Note that the hash map in this example can only accept `i8` integers. We will cover how to enable different data types so that they can be stored with structs later in this chapter.

Handling results and errors

Like other languages, Rust throws and handles errors. It manages errors through two different types: `Option` and `Result`. We saw `Option` in action in the hash map, where we had to unwrap the `get` function to access the data in the hash map. Since `Option` only returns `None` or `Some`, `Result` returns `Err` or `Some`.

This is fairly similar, however, if `Err` is exposed, as the Rust program *panics* and the program crashes with what is in the outcome of `Err`. While there will be plenty of opportunities to throw errors, we will also want to throw our own when needed. When systems become more complex, it can be handy to purposefully throw errors if there is any undesired behavior. A good example is inserting data into a **Redis cache**.

Technically, there is nothing stopping us from inserting a range of keys into Redis. In order to prevent this, if the key is not an expected variant of what we want, we should throw an error. Let's demonstrate how to throw an error, depending on the data:

```
fn error_check(check: bool) -> Result<i8, &'static str> {
    if check == true {
        Err("this is an error")
    } else {
        Ok(1)
    }
}
```

```
fn main() {
    let result: i8 = error_check(false).unwrap();
    println!("{}", result);
}
```

Note that there is no `return` keyword. This is because the function returns the final expression in the function when there is no semicolon at the end of the expression. In our function, if we set the input to `true`, we get the following error:

```
thread 'main' panicked at 'called `Result::unwrap()` on an
`Err` value: "this is an error"'
```

This `Result` wrapper gives us a lot of control of the outcome. Instead of throwing `try` and `except` blocks, we can wait until we're ready to handle the error. We can build a simple error handling function with a `match` statement:

```
fn error_check(check: bool) -> Result<i8, &'static str> {
    if check == true {
        return Err("this is an error")
    } else {
        return Ok(1)
    }
}

fn describe_result(result: Result<i8, &'static str>) {
    match result {
        Ok(x) => println!("it's a result of: {}", x),
        Err(x) => println!("{}", x)
    }
}

fn main() {
    let result: Result<i8, &'static str> =
        error_check(true);
    describe_result(result);
}
```

In the wild, this comes in useful when we must roll back a database entry or clean up a process before throwing an error. We also have to note the typing for `Result`. In this result, we return an `i8` integer (we can return other variables), but we can also return a reference to a string literal that has the `'static` notation. This is the lifetime notation. We will cover lifetime notation in more detail later in this chapter, but for now, the `'static` notation is telling the compiler that the error string will stay around for the entire runtime of the program.

This makes sense, as we would hate to lose the error message because we moved out of scope. Also, it's an error, so we should be ending the program soon. If we want to tolerate an outcome, we should be reaching for the option and handling `None`. We can also signpost a little more with the `expect` function as opposed to using `unwrap`. It still unwraps the result, but adds an extra message in the error trace:

```
let result: i8 = error_check(true).expect("this has been
    caught");
```

We can also directly throw errors with the `panic` function:

```
panic!("throwing some error");
```

We can also check for an error using `is_err`:

```
result.is_err()
```

This returns a `bool` value. As we can see, Rust supports a range of error handling. It is advised to keep these as simple as possible. For most processes in a simple web app, unwrapping straight away and throwing the error as soon as possible will manage most situations.

Now that we can utilize basic data structures while navigating Rust's quirks, we have to address problems around controlling the ownership of these data structures.

Controlling variable ownership

As Rust does not have a garbage collector, it maintains memory safety by enforcing strict rules around variable ownership that are enforced when compiling. These rules can initially bite developers from dynamic languages and lead to frustration, giving Rust its false *steep learning curve* reputation. However, if these rules are understood early, the helpful compiler makes it straightforward to adhere to them. Rust's compile-time checking is done to protect against the following memory errors:

- **Use after frees**: This is where memory is accessed once it has been freed, which can cause crashes. It can also allow hackers to execute code via this memory address.

- **Dangling pointers**: This is where a reference points to a memory address that no longer houses the data that the pointer was referencing. Essentially, this pointer now points to null or random data.

- **Double frees**: This is where allocated memory is freed, and then freed again. This can cause the program to crash and increases the risk of sensitive data being revealed. This also enables a hacker to execute arbitrary code.

- **Segmentation faults**: This is where the program tries to access the memory it's not allowed to access.

- **Buffer overrun**: An example of this is reading off the end of an array. This can cause the program to crash.

Protection is achieved by Rust following ownership rules. These ownership rules flag code that can lead to the memory errors we just mentioned (given as follows). If they are broken, they are flagged up as compile-time errors. These are defined here:

- Values are owned by the variables assigned to them.

- As soon as the variable goes out of scope, it is deallocated from the memory it is occupying.

- Values can be used by other variables, as long as we adhere to the following rules:

- **Copy**: This is where the value is copied. Once it has been copied, the new variable owns the value, and the existing variable also owns its own value.

- **Move**: This is where the value is moved from one variable to another. However, unlike clone, the original variable no longer owns the value.

- **Immutable borrow**: This is where another variable can reference the value of another variable. If the variable that is borrowing the value falls out of scope, the value is not deallocated from memory as the variable borrowing the value does not have ownership.

- **Mutable borrow**: This is where another variable can reference and write the value of another variable. If the variable that is borrowing the value falls out of scope, the value is not deallocated from memory as the variable borrowing the value does not have ownership.

Considering that scopes play a big role in the ownership rules, we'll explore them in more detail in the next section.

Scopes

The key rule to remember when it comes to ownership in Rust is that when let is used to create a variable, that variable is the only one that owns the resource. Therefore, if the resource is moved or reassigned, then the initial variable no longer owns the resource.

Once the scope has ended, then the variable and the resource are deleted. A good way to demonstrate this is through scopes. Scopes in Rust are defined by curly brackets. The classic way of demonstrating this is through the following example:

```
fn main() {
    let one: String = String::from("one");
    {

        println!("{}", one);
        let two: String = String::from("two");
    }
    println!("{}", one);
    println!("{}", two);
}
```

Commenting out the last print statement will enable the code to run. Keeping it will cause the code to crash due to the fact that two is created inside a different scope and then deleted when the inner scope ends. We can also see that one is available in the outer scope and the inside scope. However, it gets interesting when we pass the variable into another function:

```
fn print_number(number: String) {
    println!("{}", number);
}

fn main() {
    let one: String = String::from("one");
    print_number(one);
```

```
    println!("{}", one);
}
```

The error from the preceding code tells us a lot about what's going on:

```
6 |        let one: String = String::from("one");
  |            --- move occurs because `one` has type
  |            `std::string::String`, which does not implement the
  |            `Copy` trait
7 |        print_number(one);
  |                     --- value moved here
8 |        println!("{}", one);
  |                       ^^^ value borrowed here after move
```

The stem of the error has occurred because String does not implement a copy trait. This is not surprising as we know that String is a type of wrapper implemented as a vector of bytes. This vector holds a reference to str, the capacity of str in the heap memory, and the length of str, as denoted in the following diagram:

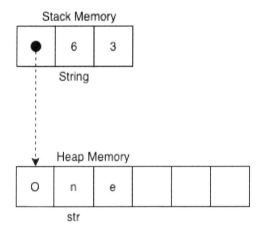

Figure 1.1 – String relationship to str

Having multiple references to the value breaks our rules. Passing one through our print function moves it into another scope, which is then destroyed. If we passed ownership to a function but still allowed references outside the function later on, these references will be pointing to freed memory, which is unsafe.

The compiler is very helpful in telling us that the variable has been moved, which is why it cannot print it. It also gives us another hint. Here, you can see that the built-in `print` method tries to borrow `String`. When you borrow a variable, you can access the data, but for only as long as you need it. Borrowing can be done by using the & operator. Therefore, we can get around this issue with the following code:

```
fn alter_number(number: &mut String) {
    number.push("!".chars().next().unwrap());
}

fn print_number(number: &String) {
    println!("{}", number);
}

fn main() {
    let mut one: String = String::from("one");
    print_number(&one);
    alter_number(&mut one);
    println!("{}", one);
}
```

In the preceding code, we borrowed the string to print it. In the second function, we did a mutable borrow, meaning that we can alter the value. We then defined a string literal, converted it into an array of chars, called the next function since it is a generator, and then unwrapped it and appended it to the string. We can see by the final `print` statement that the `one` variable has been changed.

If we were to try and change the value in the `print_number` function, we would get an error because it's not a mutable borrow, despite `one` being mutable. When it comes to immutable borrows, we can make as many as we like. For instance, if we are borrowing for a function, the function does not need to own the variable. If there is a mutable borrow, then only one mutable borrow can exist at one time, and during that lifetime, no immutable borrows can be made. This is to avoid data races.

With integers, this is easier as they implement the copy trait. This means that we don't have to borrow when passing the copy trait into a function. It's copied for us. The following code prints an integer and increases it by one:

```
fn alter_number(number: &mut i8) {
    *number += 1
}

fn print_number(number: i8) {
    println!("{}", number);
}

fn main() {
    let mut one: i8 = 1;
    print_number(one);
    alter_number(&mut one);
    println!("{}", one);
}
```

Here, we can see that the integer isn't moved into `print_number`; it's copied. However, we still have to pass a mutable reference if we want to alter the number. We can also see that we've added a * operator to the number when altering it. This is a dereference. By performing this, we have access to the integer value that we're referencing. Remember that we can directly pass the integer into the `print_number` function because we know the maximum size of all i8 integers.

Running through lifetimes

Now that we have borrowing and referencing figured out, we can look into lifetimes. Remember that a borrow is not sole ownership. Because of this, there is a risk that we could reference a variable that's deleted. This can be demonstrated in the following classic demonstration of a lifetime:

```
fn main() {
    let one;
    {
        let two: i8 = 2;
        one = &two;
    } // ----------------------> two lifetime stops here
```

```
println!("r: {}", one);
}
```

This gives us the following error:

```
|            one = &two;
|                  ^^^^ borrowed value does not live long enough
|        }
|        - `two` dropped here while still borrowed
|
|        println!("r: {}", one);
|                          --- borrow later used here
```

Since the reference is defined in the inner scope, it's deleted at the end of the inner scope, meaning that the end of its lifetime is at the end of the inner scope. However, the lifetime of the one variable carries on to the end of the scope of the main function. Therefore, the lifetimes are not equal.

While it is great that this is flagged when compiling, Rust does not stop here. This concept also translates functions. Let's say that we build a function that references two integers, compares them, and returns the highest integer reference. The function is an isolated piece of code. In this function, we can denote the lifetimes of the two integers. This is done by using the ' prefix, which is a lifetime notation. The names of the notations can be anything you wish, but it's a general convention to use a, b, c, and so on. Let's look at an example:

```
fn get_highest<'a>(first_number: &'a i8, second_number: &'a
    i8) -> &'a i8 {
    if first_number > second_number {
        first_number
    } else {
        second_number
    }
}


fn main() {
    let one: i8 = 1;
    {
        let two: i8 = 2;
        let outcome: &i8 = get_highest(&one, &two);
```

```
        println!("{}", outcome);
    }
}
```

As we can see, the first and second lifetimes have the same notation of a. They will both have to be present for the duration of the function. We also have to note that the function returns an i8 integer with the lifetime of a. Therefore, the compiler knows that we cannot rely on the outcome outside the inner scope. However, we may want to just use the two variable that is defined in the inner scope for reference in the function, but not for the result.

This might be a little convoluted, so to demonstrate this, let's develop a function that checks the one variable against the two variable. If one is lower than two, then we return zero; otherwise, we return the value of one:

```
fn filter<'a, 'b>(first_number: &'a i8, second_number: &'b
    i8) -> &'a i8 {
    if first_number < second_number {
        &0
    } else {
        first_number
    }
}


fn main() {
    let one: i8 = 1;
    let outcome: &i8;
    {
        let two: i8 = 2;
        outcome = filter(&one, &two);
    }
    println!("{}", outcome);
}
```

Here, we assigned the lifetime of 'a to `first_number`, and the lifetime of 'b to `second_number`. Using 'a and 'b, we are telling the compiler that the lifetimes are different. We then tell the compiler in the return typing of the function that the function returns an i8 integer with the lifetime of 'a. Therefore, we can rely on the result of the `filter` function, even if the lifetime of `second_number` finishes.

If we switch the `second_number` lifetime type of 'a, we get the following expected error:

```
|            outcome = filter(&one, &two);
|                                   ^^^^ borrowed value
                                does not live long enough
|    }
|    - `two` dropped here while still borrowed
|    println!("{}", outcome);
|                   ------- borrow later used here
```

Even though we're still just returning `first_number` that is available in the outer scope, we're telling the compiler that we're returning a variable with the 'a lifetime, which is assigned to `first_number` and `second_number`. The compiler is going to side with the shortest lifetime to be safe when both lifetimes are denoted to be the same in the function.

Now that we understand the quirks behind data types, borrowing, and lifetimes, we're ready to build our own structs that have the functionality to create a hash map that accepts a range of data types.

Building structs

In dynamic languages, classes have been the bedrock of developing data structures with custom functionality. In terms of Rust, structs enable us to define data structures with functionality. To mimic a class, we can define a Human struct:

```
struct Human {
    name: String,
    age: i8,
    current_thought: String
}


impl Human {
    fn new(input_name: &str, input_age: i8) -> Human {
```

```
            return Human {
                name: input_name.to_string(),
                age: input_age,
                current_thought: String::from("nothing")
            }
        }
        fn with_thought(mut self, thought: &str ) -> Human {
            self.current_thought = thought;
            return self
        }

        fn speak(&self) -> () {
            println!("Hello my name is {} and I'm {} years
                old.", &self.name, &self.age);
        }
    }


fn main() {
    let developer = Human::new("Maxwell Flitton", 31);
    developer.speak();
    println!("currently I'm thinking {}",
            developer.current_thought);

    let new_developer = Human::new("Grace", 30).with_thought(
        String::from("I'm Hungry"));
    new_developer.speak();
    println!("currently I'm thinking {}",
            new_developer.current_thought);

}
```

This looks very familiar. Here, we have a Human struct that has name and age attributes.
The impl block is associated with the Human struct. The new function inside the impl
block is essentially a constructor for the Human struct. The constructor states that
current_thought is a string that's been initialized with *nothing* because we want it to
be an optional field.

We can define the optional `current_thought` field by calling the `with_thought` function directly after calling the `new` function, which we can see in action when we define `new_developer`. `Self` is much like `self` in Python, and also like `this` in JavaScript as it's a reference to the `Human` struct.

Now that we understand structs and their functionality, we can revisit hash maps to make them more functional. Here, we will exploit `enums` to allow the hash map to accept an integer or a string:

```rust
use std::collections::HashMap;


enum AllowedData {
        S(String),
        I(i8)
}


struct CustomMap {
        body: HashMap<String, AllowedData>
}
```

Now that the hash map has been hosted as a `body` attribute, we can define our own constructor, `get`, `insert`, and `display` functions:

```rust
impl CustomMap {


        fn new() -> CustomMap {
                return CustomMap{body: HashMap::new()}
    }


    fn get(&self, key: &str) -> &AllowedData {
            return self.body.get(key).unwrap()
    }


    fn insert(&mut self, key: &str, value: AllowedData) -> ()
{
            self.body.insert(key.to_string(), value);
    }


    fn display(&self, key: &str) -> () {
```

```
                match self.get(key) {
                    AllowedData::I(value) => println!("{}",
                        value),
                    AllowedData::S(value) => println!("{}",
                        value)
                }
            }
        }
    }

fn main() {
    // defining a new hash map
    let mut map = CustomMap::new();

    // inserting two different types of data
    map.insert("test", AllowedData::I(8));
    map.insert("testing", AllowedData::S(
        "test value".to_string()));

    // displaying the data
    map.display("test");
    map.display("testing");
}
```

Now that we can build structs and exploit enums to handle multiple data types, we can tackle more complex problems in Rust. However, as the problem's complexity increases, the chance of repeating code also increases. This is where traits come in.

Verifying with traits

As we can see, enums can empower our structs so that they can handle multiple types. This can also be translated for any type of function or data structure. However, this can lead to a lot of repetition. Take, for instance, a User Struct. Users have a core set of values, such as a username and password. However, they could also have extra functionality based on roles. With users, we have to check roles before firing certain processes.

We also want to add the same functionality to a number of different user types. We can do this with traits. In this sense, we're going to use traits like a *mixin*. Here, we will create three traits for a user struct: a trait for editing data, another for creating data, and a final one for deleting data:

```rust
trait CanEdit {
    fn edit(&self) {
        println!("user is editing");
    }
}

trait CanCreate {
    fn create(&self) {
        println!("user is creating");
    }
}

trait CanDelete {
    fn delete(&self) {
        println!("user is deleting");
    }
}
```

Here, if a struct implements a trait, then it can use and overwrite the functions defined in the `trait` block. Next, we can define an admin user struct that implements all three traits:

```rust
struct AdminUser {
    name: String,
    password: String,
}

impl CanDelete for AdminUser {}
impl CanCreate for AdminUser {}
impl CanEdit for AdminUser {}
```

Now that our user struct has implemented all three traits, we can create a function that only allows users inside that have the `CanDelete` trait implemented:

```rust
fn delete<T: CanDelete>(user: T) -> () {
    user.delete();
}
```

Similar to the lifetime annotation, we use angle brackets before the input definitions to define T as a CanDelete trait. If we create a general user struct and we don't implement the CanDelete trait for it, Rust will fail to compile if we try to pass the general user through the delete function; it will complain, stating that it does not implement the CanDelete trait.

Now, with what we know, we can develop a user struct that inherits from a base user struct and has traits that can allow us to use the user struct in different functions. Rust does not directly support inheritance. However, we can combine structs with basic composition:

```rust
struct BaseUser {
    name: String,
    password: String
}

struct GeneralUser {
    super_struct: BaseUser,
    team: String
}

impl GeneralUser {

    fn new(name: String, password: String, team: String) ->
    GeneralUser {
        return GeneralUser{super_struct: BaseUser{name,
            password}, team: team}
    }
}

impl CanEdit for GeneralUser {}

impl CanCreate for GeneralUser {
    fn create(&self) -> () {
        println!("{} is creating under a {} team",
            self.super_struct.name, self.team);
    }
}
```

Here, we defined what attributes are needed by a user in the base user struct. We then housed that under the `super_struct` attribute for the general user struct. Once we did this, we performed the composition in the constructor function, which is defined as new, and then we implemented two traits for this general user. In the `CanCreate` trait, we overwrote the `create` function and utilized the `team` attribute that was given to the general user.

As we can see, building structs that inherit from base structs is fairly straightforward. These traits enable us to slot in functionality such as mixins, and they go one step further by enabling typing of the struct in functions. Traits get even more powerful than this, and it's advised that you read more about them to enhance your ability to solve problems in Rust.

With what we know about traits, we can reduce code complexity and repetition when solving problems. However, a deeper dive into traits at this point will have diminishing returns when it comes to developing web apps. Another widely used method for structs and processes is macros.

Metaprogramming with macros

Metaprogramming can generally be described as a way in which the program can manipulate itself based on certain instructions. Considering the strong typing Rust has, one of the simplest ways in which we can meta program is by using generics. A classic example of demonstrating generics is through coordinates:

```
struct Coordinate <T> {
    x: T,
    y: T
}


fn main() {
    let one = Coordinate{x: 50, y: 50};
    let two = Coordinate{x: 500, y: 500};
    let three = Coordinate{x: 5.6, y: 5.6};
}
```

Here, the compiler is looking for all the times where the coordinate struct is called and creates structs with the types that were used when compiling. The main mechanism of metaprogramming in Rust is done with macros. Macros enable us to abstract code. We've already been using macros in our `print` functions. The `!` notation at the end of the function denotes that this is a macro that's being called. Defining our own macros is a blend of defining a function and using a lifetime notation within a `match` statement in the function. In order to demonstrate this, we will define a macro that capitalizes a string:

```
macro_rules! capitalize {
    ($a: expr) => {
        let mut v: Vec<char> = $a.chars().collect();
        v[0] = v[0].to_uppercase().nth(0).unwrap();
        $a = v.into_iter().collect();
    }
}


fn main() {
    let mut x = String::from("test");
    capitalize!(x);
    println!("{}", x);
}
```

Instead of using the term `fn`, we use the `macro_rules!` definition. We then say that `$a` is the expression that's passed into the macro. We get the expression, convert it into a vector of chars, uppercase the first char, and then convert it back into a string.

Note that we don't return anything in the capitalize macro and that when we call the macro, we don't assign a variable to it. However, when we print the x variable at the end, we can see that it is capitalized. This does not behave like an ordinary function. We also have to note that we didn't define a type. Instead, we just said it was an expression; the macro still does checks via traits. Passing an integer into the macro results in the following error:

```
|        capitalize!(32);
|        --------------- in this macro invocation
|
= help: the trait `std::iter::FromIterator<char>` is not
implemented for `{integer}`
```

Lifetimes, blocks, literals, paths, meta, and more can also be passed instead of an expression. While it's important to have a brief understanding of what's under the hood of a basic macro for debugging and further reading, diving more into developing complex macros will not help us when it comes to developing web apps.

We must remember that macros are a last resort and should be used sparingly. Errors that are thrown in macros can be hard to debug. In web development, a lot of the macros are already defined in third-party packages. Because of this, we do not need to write macros ourselves to get a web app up and running. Instead, we will mainly be using derive macros out of the box.

Derive macros can be analogous to decorators in JavaScript and Python. They sit on top of a function or struct and change its functionality. A good way to demonstrate this in action is by revisiting our coordinate struct. Here, we will put it through a `print` function we define, and then try and print it again with the built-in print macro:

```
struct Coordinate {
    x: i8,
    y: i8
}

fn print(point: Coordinate) {
    println!("{} {}", point.x, point.y);
}

fn main() {
    let test = Coordinate{x: 1, y:2};
    print(test);
    println!("{}", test.x)
}
```

Unsurprisingly, we get the following error when compiling:

```
|       let test = Coordinate{x: 1, y:2};
|           ---- move occurs because `test` has type
|           `Coordinate`, which does not implement the `Copy`
|           trait
|       print(test);
|           ---- value moved here
```

```
|          println!("{}", test.x)
|                       ^^^^^^ value borrowed here after move
```

Here, we can see that we're getting the error that the coordinate was moved into our function and was then borrowed later. We can solve this with the & notation. However, it's also worth noting the second line in the error, stating that our struct does not have a copy trait. Instead of trying to build a copy trait ourselves, we can use a derive macro to give our struct a copy trait:

```
#[derive(Clone, Copy)]
struct Coordinate {
    x: i8,
    y: i8
}
```

Now, the code will run. The copy trait is fired when we move the coordinate into our print function. We can stack these traits. By merely adding the debug trait to the derive macro, we can print out the whole struct using the :? operator in the print macro:

```
#[derive(Debug, Clone, Copy)]
struct Coordinate {
    x: i8,
    y: i8
}

fn main() {
    let test = Coordinate{x: 1, y:2};
    println!("{:?}", test)
}
```

This gives us a lot of powerful functionality in web development. For instance, we will be using them in JSON serialization using the serde crate:

```
use serde::{Serialize, Deserialize};

#[derive(Serialize, Deserialize)]
struct Coordinate {
```

```
    x: i8,
    y: i8
}
```

With this, we can pass the coordinate into the crate's functions to serialize into JSON, and then deserialize. We can create our own derive macros, but the code behind our own derive macros has to be packaged in its own crate. While we will go over cargo and file structure in the next chapter, we will not be building our own derive macros.

Summary

When it comes to Rust, we saw that there are some traps if you're coming from a dynamic programming language. However, with a little bit of knowledge of referencing and basic memory management, we can avoid common pitfalls and write safe, performant code in a quick fashion that can handle errors. By utilizing structs, composition, and traits, we can build objects that are analogous to classes in standard dynamic programming languages. On top of this, these traits enabled us to build mixin-like functionality that not only enables us to slot in functionality when it's useful to us, but also perform checks on the structs through typing. This ensures that the container or function is processing structs with certain attributes belonging to the trait that we can utilize in the code.

With our fully functioning structs, we bolted on even more functionality with macros and looked under the hood of basic macros by building our own capitalize function, giving us guidance for further reading and debugging. We also got to see a brief demonstration of how powerful macros, when combined with structs, can be in web development with JSON serialization.

With this brief introduction to Rust, we can now move on to the next chapter and look into setting up a Rust environment on our own computers. This will allow us to structure files and code so that we can build programs that can solve real-world problems.

Questions

1. What is the difference between `str` and `String`?

2. Why can't string literals be passed through a function (string literal meaning `str` as opposed to `&str`)?

3. How do we access the data belonging to a key in a hash map?

4. When a function results in an error, can we handle other processes or will the error crash the program instantly?

5. When borrowing, how does Rust ensure that there's no data race?

6. When would we need to define two different lifetimes in a function?

7. How can structs utilize inheritance?

8. How can we slot in extra functionality and freedom into a struct?

9. How do we allow a container or function to accept different data structures?

10. What's the quickest way to add a trait, such as `copy`, to a struct?

Further reading

- *Hands-On Functional Programming in Rust* (2018) by Andrew Johnson, Packt Publishing

- *Mastering Rust* (2019) by Rahul Sharma and Vesa Kaihlavirta, Packt Publishing

- *The Rust Programming Language* (2018): `https://doc.rust-lang.org/stable/book/`

2
Designing Your Web Application in Rust

We previously explored the syntax of Rust, enabling ourselves to tackle memory management quirks and build data structures. However, as any experienced engineer will tell you, structuring code across multiple files and directories is an important aspect of building software.

In this chapter, we will build a basic command line to do program managing dependencies with **Rust's Cargo**. Our program will be structured in a scalable way where we build and manage our own modules, which will be imported into other areas of the program and utilized.

In this chapter, we will cover the following topics:

- Building and managing a software project with Cargo and crates
- Documenting code with Cargo's auto-documentation
- Building structs that inherit other structs and utilizing them in a program spanning multiple files
- Building module interfaces and factories
- Reading and writing JSON data to a file

Technical requirements

As we move towards building web apps in Rust, we are going to have to start relying on third-party packages to do some of the heavy lifting for us. Rust manages dependencies through a package manager called **Cargo**. In order to use Cargo, we are going to have to install Rust on our computer from the URL `https://www.rust-lang.org/tools/install`.

This installation delivers the programming language Rust and Cargo.

You can find all the code files on GitHub: `https://github.com/PacktPublishing/Rust-Web-Programming/tree/master/Chapter02`.

The CiA video for this book can be viewed at: `http://bit.ly/3jULCrw`

Managing Cargo

Before we start structuring our program with Cargo, we should compile a basic Rust script and run it. In order to do this, make a file called `hello_world.rs` with a `main` function housing the `println!` function with a string. Once this is done, we can navigate to the file and run the `rustc` command:

```
rustc hello_world.rs
```

This command compiles the file into a binary to be run. If we compile it on **Windows**, we can run the binary with the following command:

```
.\hello_world.exe
```

If we compile it on **Linux** or **macOS**, we can run it with the following command:

```
./hello_world
```

The console should then print out the string. While this can come in useful when building a standalone script, it is not recommended for managing programs spanning multiple files. It is not even recommended when relying on dependencies. This is where Cargo comes in. Cargo manages everything – the running, testing, documentation, building, and dependency – out of the box with a few simple commands.

Building with Cargo

Building with Cargo is fairly straightforward. All we have to do is navigate to a directory where we want to build our project, and run the following command:

```
cargo new web_app
```

This builds a basic structure for our app with the following directory:

```
└── web_app
    ├── Cargo.toml
    └── src
        └── main.rs
```

The `src` directory is where we will house our code for the program. The `Cargo.toml` file is where metadata around the program is defined, and the entry point for the program is in the `main.rs` file. Inside the `main.rs` file, we have a `main` function housing a `print` statement. Now, in development, we want to run the program multiple times with incremental changes. In order to do this, we move into the `web_app` directory and run the following command:

```
cargo run
```

This compiles code in an unoptimized manner with debug information in the newly created `./target/debug/` directory under the binary `web_app`. Once the compilation process has been completed, it runs in the console directly.

If we want to build a release, we simply run the following command:

```
cargo build --release
```

This compiles an optimized version of our app in the `./target/release/` directory under the binary `web_app`. It has to be noted that if we want to push to a **Git** repository, it is a good idea to include the target directory in the `.gitignore` file to avoid us from uploading the metadata and binaries on the build. Now that we've installed Rust and built the basic structure for a coding project, we can start using its power to import third-party libraries with crates.

Shipping crates with Cargo

Third-party libraries are referred to as crates. Adding them and managing them with Cargo is straightforward. In this section, we will explore this process by utilizing the `rand` crate, available at `https://rust-random.github.io/rand/rand/index.html`.

It has to be noted that the documentation for this crate is pretty clear and well-structured with links to structs, traits, and modules. This is not a reflection on the rand crate itself. This is standard documentation for Rust that we will cover in the next section. To use this crate in our project, we open the Cargo.toml file and add the rand create under the [dependencies] section:

```
[dependencies]
rand = "0.7.3"
```

Now that we've defined our dependency, we can use the rand crate to build a random number generator:

```
use rand::prelude::*;

fn generate_float(generator: &mut ThreadRng) -> f64 {
    let placeholder: f64 = generator.gen();
    return placeholder * 10.0
}

fn main() {
    let mut rng: ThreadRng = rand::thread_rng();

    let random_number = generate_float(&mut rng);
    println!("{}", random_number);
}
```

Here, we have defined a function called generate_float, which uses the crate to generate and return a float between 0 and 10. Once we've done this, we print the number. The implementation of the rand crate is handled by the rand documentation. Our use statement is importing the rand crate. Here, the documentation tells us to import (*) from the rand::prelude module, which simplifies the importing of common items as shown in the crate documentation at https://rust-random.github.io/rand/rand/prelude/index.html.

The ThreadRng struct is a random number generator that generates an f64 value between 0 and 1, which is elaborated on in the rand crate documentation at https://rust-random.github.io/rand/rand/rngs/struct.ThreadRng.html.

Here, we get to see the power of the documentation. With a few clicks on the introduction page of the rand documentation, we can dig into the declarations of the structs and functions used in the demonstration. Now our code is built, we can run our program with the `cargo run` command. While Cargo is compiling, it pulls code from the `rand` crate and compiles that into the binary.

We can also note that there is now a `cargo.lock` file. As we know that `cargo.toml` is for us to describe our own dependencies, `cargo.lock` is generated by Cargo and we should not edit it ourselves as it contains exact information about our dependencies.

This seamless functionality combined with the easy-to-use documentation shows how Rust improves the development process through marginal gains via the development ecosystem as well as the quality of the language. However, all these gains from the documentation are not purely dependent on the third-party libraries; we can also autogenerate our own documentation.

Documenting with Cargo

Speed and safety are not the only benefits of picking a new language such as Rust to develop in. Over the years, the software engineering community keeps learning and growing. Simple things such as good documentation can make or break a project. In order to demonstrate this, we can define markdown language within the Rust file with the following:

```
/// This function generates a float number using a number
/// generator passed into the function.
///
/// # Arguments
/// * generator (&mut ThreadRng): the random number
/// generator to generate the random number
///
/// # Returns
/// (f64): random number between 0 -> 10
fn generate_float(generator: &mut ThreadRng) -> f64 {
    let placeholder: f64 = generator.gen();
    return placeholder * 10.0
}
```

Here, we've denoted the markdown with the /// markers. This does two things: it tells other developers who look at the code what the function does, and it also renders markdown in our autogeneration.

Before we run the document command, we can define and document a basic user struct and a basic user trait to also show how these are documented:

```rust
/// This trait defines the struct to be a user.
trait IsUser {

    /// This function proclaims that the struct is a user.
    ///
    /// # Arguments
    /// None
    ///
    /// # Returns
    /// (bool) true if user, false if not
    fn is_user() -> bool {
        return true
    }
}
/// This struct defines a user
///
/// # Attributes
/// * name (String): the name of the user
/// * age (i8): the age of the user
struct User {
    name: String,
    age: i8
}
```

Now that we have documented a range of different structures, we can run the auto-documentation process with the following command:

```
cargo doc
```

After the process has finished, we can open the documentation with the following command:

```
cargo doc --open
```

Here, we can see that the documentation is rendered in the same way as the **rand** crate:

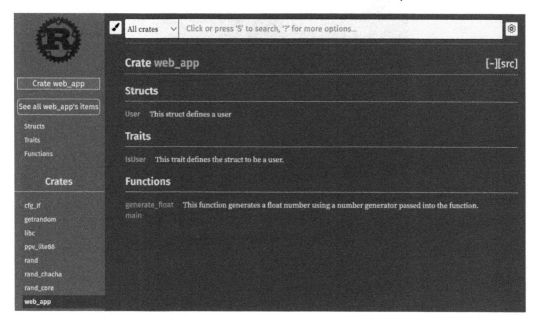

Figure 2.1 – Documentation view of web app

Here, we can see that our **web_app** is actually a crate. We can also see that the documentation of the **rand** crate is also involved. If we click on the **User** struct, we can see the declaration of the struct, the markdown that we wrote for the attributes, and the trait implications as shown:

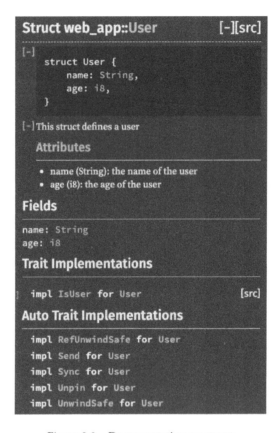

Figure 2.2 – Documentation on struct

It has to be noted that in future sections of the book, we will not include markdown in the code snippets to maintain readability. However, markdown-documented code is provided in the book's GitHub repo.

Now that we have a well-documented, running Cargo project, we need to be able to pass parameters into it in order to enable different configurations to run depending on the context.

Interacting with Cargo

In order to enable our program to have some flexibility depending on the context, we need to be able to pass parameters into our program and also keep track of the parameters in which the program is running. We can do this using the `std` (standard library) keyword:

```
use std::env;
let args: Vec<String> = env::args().collect();
println!("{:?}", args);
```

What happens here is that we collect the arguments from the environment and print them utilizing the debug operator. Let's run Cargo with the following command:

```
cargo run some_variable another_variable
```

This gives us the following output for the variables:

```
["target/debug/web_app", "some_variable", "another_variable"]
```

Here, we see our variables in an array. This is not surprising; many other languages accept variables after the `run` command. However, we also notice that the path to the binary being run is the first item in the `args` vector. Cargo is running the unoptimized debug version. We can run the release version with the following command:

```
cargo run --release some_variable
```

This gives us the following outcome:

```
["target/release/web_app", "some_variable"]
```

In the future, we may want to change the way that the program runs based on the type of binary being run. For instance, we can make the assumption that we will be running the debug binary when developing, and we will be running the release binary in production. We can do a simple check of the binary based on the following:

```
let args: Vec<String> = env::args().collect();
let path: &str = &args[0];

if path.contains("/debug/") {
    println!("The development app is running");
}
else if path.contains("/release/") {
    println!("The production server is running");
```

```
}
else {
    panic!("The setting is neither debug or release");
}
```

Here, we access the path of the binary. We then determine which binary is running via checking which substring the path contains. If neither binary is being run, we then throw an error.

In a dynamic programming language, it is custom to merely pass in a config file based on the parameter passed into the program. For instance, running a Flask app in Python with a config file requires the following command:

```
python app.py ./path/to/config.json
```

The benefit of our approach is that it reduces the risk of us passing the wrong configuration file. Now that we have managed to pass in parameters and partition logic based on the type of binary being run, we are ready to start building a more comprehensive program. In order to do this, we are going to have to explore structuring our code over multiple files.

Structuring code

Structuring code is an important part of developing any web app. Because of this, we have to get comfortable breaking down a problem into components that Rust can manage and execute. For our exercise, we will create a simple to-do program where we can create, update, and delete to-do items via a command line. This is a simple app. The process here is to explore how to build well-structured code that is scalable without getting into the weeds of the complexity of the logic of the app. In order to build this well in Rust, we are going to have to break the processes down into chunks:

1. Build structs for pending and done to-do items.

2. Build a factory that enables the structs to be built in the to_do module.

3. Build traits that enable a struct to delete, create, edit, and get the to-do items. These are then imported into the factory so that the pending and done structs can implement them.

4. Build a read and write to file module to be utilized by other modules.

5. Build a config module that can alter the behavior of the app based on the environment.

Before we start tackling these points, let's get our app running. Navigate to the desired directory and start a new Cargo project called `todo_app`. Once this is done, we are going to put our logic that is concerned with to-do items into a `to_do` module. This can be achieved by creating a `to_do` directory and putting a `mod.rs` file at the base of it:

```
├── main.rs
└── to_do
    ├── mod.rs
```

With this, we are ready to start building our to-do structs so we can import them and use them in the `main` function. Do not worry about the `mod.rs` file at the moment, we will cover that in the next section.

Building to-do structs

Right now, we have two different types of to-do items: a pending item and a done item. Both of these will have the same attributes, title, and status. However, as we remember with traits, it would be advantageous for us to have two different structs as we want maximum flexibility in defining the functionality for each item type.

We also might want to add a different to-do item type in the future. Because of this, it is logical to have a base struct that holds the common attributes, and then two structs inheriting the base struct: one for the pending to-do item, and another for the finished to-do item. In order to achieve this, we need the following directory structure in our module:

```
├── main.rs
└── to_do
    ├── mod.rs
    ├── structs
    │   ├── base.rs
    │   ├── done.rs
    │   ├── mod.rs
    │   └── pending.rs
```

We can see that we have created another directory, `structs`, and we have housed all our structs in there. In `base.rs`, we define the base struct:

```
pub struct Base {
    pub title: String,
    pub status: String
```

```
}


impl Base {


    pub fn new(input_title: &str, input_status: &str) -> Base {
        return Base {title: input_title.to_string(),
                     status: input_status.to_string()}
    }
}
```

Here, we have a standard struct with a constructor. We also have to note that there is a `pub` keyword before the function, struct, and attribute definitions. This is because we aim to use this struct outside of the file. If we did not declare them as public, then the compiler would refuse to compile if we did use them externally.

Now that we have defined it as public, we have to declare it in our `to_do/structs/mod.rs` file:

mod base;

This enables other files within the module to access the base file. However, because we only want our base struct to be used within the module, we do not make it public.

We want to use our base struct within the module but not externally. Now that we have made our `base` class accessible to the rest of the module, we can define our done to-do item in the `done.rs` file:

```
use super::base::Base;


pub struct Done {
    pub super_struct: Base
}


impl Done {


    pub fn new(input_title: &str) -> Done {
        let base: Base = Base::new(input_title,
                                    "done");
        return Done{super_struct: base}
    }
}
```

Here, we access the base struct through the to_do/structs/mod.rs file using super in the import line at the top of the file. We also lock down the status in the constructor (the new function) and build our base struct with this. We do this in order to ensure that a Done struct does not define another status apart from *done*.

We do the same for our pending to-do item in our pending.rs file:

```
use super::base::Base;


pub struct Pending {
    pub super_struct: Base
}


impl Pending {

    pub fn new(input_title: &str) -> Pending {
        let base: Base = Base::new(input_title,
                            "pending");
        return Pending{super_struct: base}
    }
}
```

Now that we have the structs we need, we can define them in our to_do/structs/ mod.rs file publicly to allow the main file to use them:

```
mod base;
pub mod done;
pub mod pending;
```

Now that our structs are ready, we can make the structs available by publicly defining them in the to_do/mod.rs file:

```
pub mod structs;
```

Now our module is ready for use in the main function with the following:

```
mod to_do;


use to_do::structs::done::Done;
use to_do::structs::pending::Pending;
```

```rust
fn main() {
    let done: Done = Done::new("shopping");
    println!("{}", done.super_struct.title);
    println!("{}", done.super_struct.status);

    let pending: Pending = Pending::new("laundry");
    println!("{}", pending.super_struct.title);
    println!("{}", pending.super_struct.status);
}
```

Here, we can see that we defined our module, and then imported the two structs that we want to use. We then define them and then print them.

This is useful, however, as the program grows, we could end up with long import lists as we import every public struct that the module houses. This is also not scalable. If we needed to use our module in another module, we would also have to rewrite a lot of imports. Other developers might also implement our module incorrectly. In order to prevent these problems from happening, we can build an interface. Let's discuss this more in the next section.

Managing structs with factories

We can build our interface with the **factory pattern**. This is where we select the right struct based on the input, build it, and return it. This can be done in the to_do/mod.rs file:

```rust
pub mod structs;

use structs::done::Done;
use structs::pending::Pending;

pub enum ItemTypes {
    Pending(Pending),
    Done(Done)
}

pub fn to_do_factory(item_type: &str, item_title: &str) ->
        Result<ItemTypes, &'static str> {
    if item_type == "pending" {
```

```
        let pending_item = Pending::new(item_title);
        Ok(ItemTypes::Pending(pending_item))
    }
    else if item_type == "done" {
        let done_item = Done::new(item_title);
        Ok(ItemTypes::Done(done_item))
    }
    else {
        Err("this is not accepted")
    }
}
```

Here, we lock down the structs by removing the pub definition as we will only allow it to be used via the interface, which is the to_do_factory function. In this function, we check the input type and build the struct depending on that type. We also package an error if we pass in a type that we do not have. We can also see that we have used an enum to enable the return of the two types of items.

At this point, there is a refactoring opportunity. It could be argued that we only needed one struct, and that the type could be handled in the factory, reducing the need for multiple structs. This is a true observation. However, we do plan to start adding traits to our structs. Right now, the multiple structs might seem a little excessive, but we have to maintain flexibility in our code.

Now that our interface is defined, we can utilize this in the main function by calling the factory with some parameters and using a match statement:

```
mod to_do;

use to_do::ItemTypes;
use to_do::to_do_factory;

fn main() {
    let to_do_item: Result<ItemTypes, &'static str> =
        to_do_factory(
            "pending", "make");

    match to_do_item.unwrap() {
```

```
        ItemTypes::Pending(item) => println!(
            "it's a pending item with the title: {}",
            item.super_struct.title),


        ItemTypes::Done(item) => println!(
            "it's a done item with the title: {}",
            item.super_struct.title)
    }
}
```

This may seem excessive for now – the simple parameter checking and the getting of the struct could have been done in the `main` function. However, as the complexity grows, `main` will become unmanageable. It is best to keep the logic surrounding the definition and construction of to-do items in its own module.

Right now, our to-do items do not do anything. They house different attributes, but they cannot delete, save, update, or get. All they can do is house attributes. In order to define functionality, we need to give our structs some traits.

Defining functionality with traits

Now that we have our traits, it is time for them to have some functionality. We are going to do this with traits. For scalability and flexibility, we will keep our traits as simplistic and isolated as possible. Defining a trait for each type of process gives us the ability to fine-tune the functionality for each type.

In order to achieve this, we have to add the directory `traits` inside the `structs` directory. Inside the `traits` directory, we have a file for each process and a `mod.rs` file to declare them:

```
├── mod.rs
└── structs
    ├── base.rs
    ├── done.rs
    ├── mod.rs
    ├── pending.rs
    └── traits
        ├── create.rs
        ├── delete.rs
        ├── edit.rs
```

```
├── get.rs
└── mod.rs
```

First, let's define functions that print the process. We will interact with the environment of reading and writing to a file in the next section. We can deduce that the create, delete, edit, and get trait functions will all require a title. Therefore, in the get file, we can define the following trait:

```
pub trait Get {
    fn get(&self, title: &str) {
        println!("{} is being fetched", title);
    }
}
```

Here, we bind the get function with the &self parameter, which enables the struct calling the function directly like some_struct. get(&String::from("something")). We also take the title. Again, for now, we will just print a statement to ensure that the mapping of traits across multiple files works.

With the edit process, we can have multiple functions for different processes. Right now, all we need is a function to set an item to done, and another function to set an item to pending. We can define these in the edit.rs file:

```
pub trait Edit {
    fn set_to_done(&self, title: &str) {
        println!("{} is being set to done", title);
    }
    fn set_to_pending(&self, title: &str) {
        println!("{} is being set to pending", title);
    }
}
```

In terms of Create, there is only one function that we need, which is create. This can be defined in the create.rs file:

```
pub trait Create {
    fn create(&self, title: &str) {
        println!("{} is being created", title);
    }
}
```

Similar to this, all we need is a single `delete` function in the `Delete` trait in the `delete.rs` file:

```
pub trait Delete {
    fn delete(&self, title: &str) {
        println!("{} is being deleted", title);
    }
}
```

Now we have all our traits, we have to publicly define them in the `mod` file of the traits directory so they can be accessed from outside:

```
pub mod create;
pub mod delete;
pub mod edit;
pub mod get;
```

Now that they are accessible, we have to make them accessible to the structs by publicly defining them in the `mod.rs` file in the structs directory:

```
pub mod traits;
mod base;
pub mod done;
pub mod pending;
```

This enables our structs to use `super` to access the traits. For the Done struct, we should allow the program to get, edit, and delete by implementing these traits in the Done struct:

```
use super::base::Base;
use super::traits::get::Get;
use super::traits::delete::Delete;
use super::traits::edit::Edit;


pub struct Done {
    pub super_struct: Base
}
```

```
impl Done {

    pub fn new(input_title: &str) -> Done {
        let input_status: String = String::from("done");
        let base: Base = Base::new(input_title, "done");
        return Done{super_struct: base}
    }
}
impl Get for Done {}
impl Delete for Done {}
impl Edit for Done {}
```

For the `Pending` struct, we are going to enable it to create, edit, get, and delete:

```
use super::base::Base;
use super::traits::create::Create;
use super::traits::edit::Edit;
use super::traits::get::Get;
use super::traits::delete::Delete;

pub struct Pending {
    pub super_struct: Base
}
impl Pending {
    pub fn new(input_title: &str) -> Pending {
        let base: Base = Base::new(input_title, "pending");
        return Pending{super_struct: base}
    }
}
impl Create for Pending {}
impl Edit for Pending {}
impl Get for Pending {}
impl Delete for Pending {}
```

Now the structs are enhanced with our traits, we can see how scalable this is. If we add another to-do item struct, we can slot in a range of traits to instantly give it the functionality we need. We can also remove/add traits from/to our existing structs with ease. This demonstrates the power that structs give us. Now that we have our traits, we can demonstrate how they can be used in main with the following:

```
mod to_do;

use to_do::ItemTypes;
use to_do::to_do_factory;
use to_do::structs::traits::create::Create;

fn main() {
    let to_do_item: Result<ItemTypes, &'static str> =
        to_do_factory(
            pending", "washing");
    match to_do_item.unwrap() {
        ItemTypes::Pending(item) => item.create(
        &item.super_struct.title),
        ItemTypes::Done(item) => println!(
        "it's a done item with the title: {}",
        item.super_struct.title)
    }
}
```

It has to be noted that we imported the Create trait into main. Even though the Create trait is implemented for the Pending struct, it will not be able to get fired if it is not imported because it will not be found by the compiler.

What we have done here is build our own module, which contains an entry point. We've then imported it into the main function and ran it. Now the basic structure is built and working, we need to get the module to interact with the environment passing variables in and writing to a file to become useful.

Interacting with the environment

In order to interact with the environment, we have to manage two things. First, we need to load, save, and edit the state of to-do items. Second, we also have to accept user input to edit and display data. Our program can achieve this by running the following steps for each process:

1. Collect arguments from the user.

2. Define a command (`get`, `edit`, `delete`, and `create`) and define a to-do title from commandments.

3. Load a JSON file that stores the to-do items from previous runs of the program.

4. Run a `get`, `edit`, `delete`, or `create` function based on the command passed into the program, saving the result of the state in a JSON file at the end.

We can start making this four-step process possible by initially loading our state with the `serde` crate.

Reading and writing JSON files

To install the `serde` crate, we define the dependency in the `Cargo.toml` file under the `[dependencies]` section:

```
[dependencies]
serde_json = {version = "1.0",
              default-features = false,
              features = ["alloc"]}
```

To manage the read and write to the JSON file, it makes sense to build our own module as there will be a number of places where we write data to the file. However, the module itself will be fairly small, consisting of just `read` and `write` functions. It would not be practical to dedicate an entire directory to it. We can create our own module with just one file in the same directory of the main file. In our `src/state.rs` file, we define the `read` and `write` methods:

```
use std::fs::File;
use std::fs;
use std::io::Read;

use serde_json::Map;
use serde_json::value::Value;
```

```
use serde_json::json;


pub fn read_file(file_name: &str) -> Map<String, Value> {
    let mut file = File::open(
        file_name.to_string()).unwrap();
    let mut data = String::new();
    file.read_to_string(&mut data).unwrap();
    let json: Value = serde_json::from_str(&data).unwrap();
    let state: Map<String, Value> =
        json.as_object().unwrap().clone();
    return state
}
```

In the read function, we take the file path as a string and use the standard library to open it. We directly unwrap it. If there is an error here, then there is no point in continuing the program. We then define a mutable string under the name of data and read the file to that string (remember strings are references to string literals).

We then use serde to convert that string into a JSON value and then define that value as an object and clone it to get a serde JSON map. If we do not clone it, we will merely be returning a reference. We go through the trouble of converting it to a map to get the extra functionality.

Further down the src/state.rs file, we define the write file:

```
pub fn write_to_file(file_name: &str,
                     state: &mut Map<String, Value>) {
    let new_data = json!(state);
    fs::write(file_name.to_string(),
        new_data.to_string()).expect("Unable to write file");
}
```

Here, we accept the file path and the map, convert the map back to JSON using the macro, and then convert it to a string to write to the file.

In order to check to see if this works, we need to import it into `main`, read a JSON file, get some parameters from the user, and write a new input into the file:

```
mod state;

use std::env;
use state::{write_to_file, read_file};
use serde_json::value::Value;
use serde_json::{Map, json};

fn main() {
    let args: Vec<String> = env::args().collect();
    let status: &String = &args[1];
    let title: &String = &args[2];

    let mut state: Map<String, Value> =
        read_file(String::from("./state.json"));
    println!("{:?}", state);

    state.insert(title.to_string(), json!(status));
    write_to_file("./state.json", &mut state);
}
```

Here, we collect the environment arguments passed by the user and collect it to a vector of strings. We then define the commands from the `args` vector. Once we've done that, we load the data from the JSON file and print it using the debug notation. An example outcome (depending on the content of the JSON file) from this `print` statement is the following:

```
{"shopping": String("pending"), "washing": String("done")}
```

We then insert the new entry and then write to a file. Our root path is going to be where the `Cargo.toml` file is, so we define an empty JSON file called `state.json` next to the `Cargo.toml` file. To allow our to-do items to interact with the state, we need to enable our to-do item traits to manipulate the state.

Revisiting traits

Considering that the state has been defined, we now have a better idea of what our `trait` functions actually need. We can initially start with our simplest trait, which is get. Here, we have to get a to-do item by the title from the state and print it. If it is not there, we print out that the title was not in the map:

```
use serde_json::Map;
use serde_json::value::Value;


pub trait Get {
    fn get(&self, title: &String, state: &Map<String, Value>) {
        let item: Option<&Value> = state.get(title);
        match item {
            Some(result) => {
                println!("\n\nItem: {}", title);
                println!("Status: {}\n\n", result);
            },
            None => println!("item: {} was not found", title)
        }
    }
}
```

Here, we take the state, call the `get` function for the map, and then manage that with a `match` statement and print the outcome.

The trait we can tackle is the `Create` trait. In this trait, we need to insert our new entry into the state, and then use our `write_to_file` function to write the updated state to the JSON file we are using to store our to-do items:

```
use serde_json::Map;
use serde_json::value::Value;
use serde_json::json;


use crate::state::write_to_file;


pub trait Create {
    fn create(&self, title: &String, status: &String,
            state: &mut Map<String, Value>) {
        state.insert(title.to_string(), json!(status));
```

```
            write_to_file("./state.json", state);
            println!("\n\n{} is being created\n\n", title);
        }
    }
```

Here, we can see that we use the `state` module defined in `main` with the `use crate` command. The `delete` trait has the same approach but with the `remove` function is called on the map:

```
use serde_json::Map;
use serde_json::value::Value;

use crate::state::write_to_file;

pub trait Delete {
    fn delete(&self, title: &String,
                state: &mut Map<String, Value>) {
        state.remove(title);
        write_to_file("./state.json", state);
        println!("\n\n{} is being deleted\n\n", title);
    }
}
```

For the `Edit` trait, we need two functions – one to set a to-do item to pending, and another to set a to-do item to done in the state, as shown:

```
use serde_json::Map;
use serde_json::value::Value;
use serde_json::json;

use crate::state::write_to_file;

pub trait Edit {
    fn set_to_done(&self, title: &String,
                state: &mut Map<String, Value>) {
        state.insert(title.to_string(),
                    json!(String::from("done")));
        write_to_file("./state.json", state);
        println!("\n\n{} is being set to done\n\n", title);
```

```
        }
    fn set_to_pending(&self, title: &String,
                        state: &mut Map<String, Value>) {
        state.insert(title.to_string(),
                        json!(String::from("pending")));
        write_to_file("./state.json", state);
        println!("\n\n{} is being set to pending\n\n", title);
    }
}
```

Our traits can now interact with the JSON file and do the processes that they are intended to do. However, simply directly interacting with the traits in the main file is not scalable. As the program grows, we may need to use these traits somewhere else. In order to protect against this, we can make our own interface for managing the use of these traits by creating our own process module.

Processing traits and structs

Like our state module, the process module is only going to need a few functions. Therefore, we can define the module in a src/processes.rs file. The purpose of this module is to direct the flow of the commands. We need an entry point to process the input and direct it to the right function to process the item. First of all, let's import all the structs and traits we need:

```
use serde_json::Map;
use serde_json::value::Value;


use super::to_do::ItemTypes;
use super::to_do::structs::done::Done;
use super::to_do::structs::pending::Pending;
use super::to_do::structs::traits::get::Get;
use super::to_do::structs::traits::create::Create;
use super::to_do::structs::traits::delete::Delete;
use super::to_do::structs::traits::edit::Edit;
```

We then define the functions that enable us to process Done and Pending structs:

```
fn process_pending(item: Pending,
                command: String, state: &Map<String, Value>) {
    let mut state = state.clone();
    match command.as_str() {
        "get" => item.get(&item.super_struct.title, &state),
        "create" => item.create(&item.super_struct.title,
                    &item.super_struct.status, &mut state),
        "delete" => item.delete(&item.super_struct.title,
                                &mut state),
        "edit" => item.set_to_done(&item.super_struct.title,
                                &mut state),
        _ => println!("command: {} not supported", command)
    }
}
fn process_done(item: Done,
                command: String, state: &Map<String, Value>) {
    let mut state = state.clone();
    match command.as_str() {
        "get" => item.get(&item.super_struct.title, &state),
        "delete" => item.delete(&item.super_struct.title,
                                &mut state),
        "edit" => item.set_to_pending(&item.super_struct.title,
                                    &mut state),
        _ => println!("command: {} not supported", command)
    }
}
```

Now that we have defined functions that process our to-do structs, we can build an entry point that takes a struct, memory state, and command so we can funnel the struct into the right function:

```
pub fn process_input(item: ItemTypes, command: String,
                     state: &Map<String, Value>) {
    match item {
        ItemTypes::Pending(item) => process_pending(item,
            command, state),
        ItemTypes::Done(item) => process_done(item,
            command, state)
    }
}
```

What we have here is essentially a match statement mapping to other match statements. This gives us a lot of flexibility. If we are to add a type, all we have to do is add a line in the match statement of the process_input function (our entry point). We can also add extra conditional statements in the functions. We can quickly delete and add commands because anything added that does not match is caught by the _ operator.

It has to be noted that we have to import the traits into the file. Even though the traits have been implemented by the structs in the to-do module, the file calling the trait bound to the struct has to still be imported to be recognized. This interface can be passed around the program and utilized anywhere. If another developer needs another entry point where a to-do item is processed, then we know they will process the to-do items in a standardized way.

Now that all the modules are fully functional and working with each other, we can implement them in the main function:

```
mod state;
mod to_do;
mod processes;

use std::env;
use state::read_file;
use serde_json::value::Value;
use serde_json::Map;
use to_do::to_do_factory;
use processes::process_input;
```

```
fn main() {
    let args: Vec<String> = env::args().collect();

    let command: &String = &args[1];
    let title: &String = &args[2];

    let state: Map<String, Value> =
        read_file("./state.json");

    let status: String;
    match &state.get(*&title) {
        Some(result) => {
            status = result.to_string().replace('\"', "");
        }
        None=> {
            status = "pending";
        }
    }
    let item = to_do_factory(&status,
                              title).expect(&status);
    process_input(item, command.to_string(), &state);
}
```

Here, everything that we have learned is on display. We get the args from the
environment, define the commands, and read the data from the JSON file to get the state
of the to-do list. We then utilize what we know about scopes, defining the status as
a string outside the match block so we can rely on the status outside of the match block.
In the match block, we make an assumption. If the item does not exist in the state, then
we define the status as pending. It would not make sense to create a new done item. We
then pass the status to the interface or our to-do module. We finally pass our item struct,
command, and state to the entry point of our process module.

Now we have built our app, we can fully test it via the following procedure:

```
cargo run
```

Our program crashes because the index is out of bounds. This is because we did not put in any commands. If we run the following:

```
cargo run create washing
```

We get a message that the washing is being created and our empty JSON file now looks like this:

```
{"washing":"pending"}
```

Running the get command (`cargo run get washing`) gives us the following printout:

```
Item: washing
Status: "pending"
```

Running the edit command (`cargo run edit washing`), we get a printout telling us that the washing has been set to done, and our JSON file looks like this:

```
{"washing":"done"}
```

Running the delete command (`cargo run delete washing`) deletes the washing item in the JSON file.

Summary

What we have essentially done here is build a program that accepts some command-line inputs, interacts with a file, and edits it depending on the command and data from that file. The data is fairly simple: a title and a status.

We could have done this all in the main function with multiple match statements and if, else if, and else blocks. However, this is not scalable. Instead, we built structs that inherited other structs, which then implemented traits. We then packaged the construction of these structs into a factory enabling other files to use all that functionality in a single line of code.

We then built a processing interface so the command input, state, and struct could be processed, enabling us to stack on extra functionality and change the flow of the process with a few lines of code. Our main function only has to focus on collecting the command-line arguments and coordinating when to call the module interfaces. We have now explored and utilized how Rust manages modules, giving us the building blocks to build real-world programs that can solve problems and add features without being hurt by tech debt and a ballooning main function. Now that we can do this, we are ready to start building scalable web apps that can grow.

In the next chapter, we will learn about the **Actix web framework** to get a basic web server up and running.

Questions

1. What does the −release argument in Cargo do when added to build and run?

2. How do we enable a file to be accessible within and outside a module?

3. What are the advantages of having traits with a single scope?

4. What steps would we have to take to add an on hold to-do item that will only allow get and edit functionality?

5. What are the benefits of the factory?

6. How do we effectively map a range of processes based on some parameters?

Section 2: Processing Data and Managing Displays

Although Rust is still a fairly new language compared to more traditional languages such as Python, JavaScript, and PHP, this does not mean that the tools for building web servers are not available in Rust. In fact, processing HTTP requests, processing the data on the server, and displaying the content can be done with fairly minimal boiler plate code safely in Rust. While the tools are maturing, you will notice that processing data through web requests can be achieved through fairly minimal code. In fact, the code is so minimal, you will struggle to see the difference between other frameworks apart from the syntax.

This section covers the Actix Web framework to host routes. We'll then use the serde crate to serialize data in order to pass it to and from the web server. We'll then display content via HTML with JavaScript, enabling the page to interact with the web app API.

This section comprises the following chapters:

- *Chapter 03, Handling HTTP Requests*
- *Chapter 04, Processing HTTP Requests*
- *Chapter 05, Displaying Content in the Browser*

3
Handling HTTP Requests

Solving problems with well-structured code can only get us so far. To enable our solution to reach multiple people quickly without the need to install **Rust**, we are going to need to serve our to-do application on a web server. Fortunately, Rust has a range of web frameworks. In this chapter, we will build a basic web app that handles views using the **Actix Web** framework in a scalable way.

In order to achieve this, we will be building server views in a modular fashion. We will also cover the basics of *asynchronous programming* in order to briefly look under the hood of how the Actix Web framework works.

In this chapter, we will cover the following topics:

- Building a basic server using the Actix Web framework
- Exploring and understanding closures in order to refine the building of that server
- Exploring and understanding the basics of threads in Rust using asynchronous programming

- Exploring and understanding the basics of futures with `async` and `await` notation to confidently code solutions in the Actix Web framework

- Practicing the structuring of modules in order to chain factories together to enable factory functions to orchestrate factories for other modules

- Configuring a server in a module to manage views in a scalable manner

Technical requirements

The code files for this chapter can be found on GitHub at `https://github.com/PacktPublishing/Rust-Web-Programming/tree/master/Chapter03`.

In order to complete this chapter, we have to ensure that the setup from the previous chapter is complete.

The CiA video for this book can be viewed at: `http://bit.ly/3jULCrw`

Introducing the Actix Web framework

At the time of writing this book, the Actix Web framework is the most popular Rust web framework due to the number of forks, watches, and contributors. It has an active community, good feature support, and impressive benchmark scores. The framework **Rocket** is not far behind in terms of popularity; however, it uses **Rust nightly** to run, which is less stable. For the rest of the book, we will be building our to-do app in Actix. However, introductions to the Rocket and **Warp** web frameworks will be covered in their own chapters at the end of the book.

The power of Rust is that it enables users to rapidly develop with high-level, memory-safe structs with low memory consumption and fast execution times. However, it also allows fine-grain control if needed. If a developer really wants to, they can deactivate the memory safety in Rust and continue to develop and run Rust programs (though it is not recommended). Rust's crates are no exception to this. The Actix Web framework exposes us to some underlying web server concepts, inviting us to safely alter them if needed. Launching a basic web server using the Actix Web framework will introduce some new concepts that we must tackle before we start developing our features on top of it.

Launching a basic Actix Web server

To support an Actix Web server, we need to make a new Cargo project. In order to enable an Actix server to run, we need to define the following dependencies in the `Cargo.toml` file:

```
[dependencies]
actix-web = "2"
actix-rt = "1.0"
```

`actix-web` is the main framework housing the structs that define the routes and server. `actix-rt` enables us to run everything on the current thread.

The following code is the standard example implementation that gets a server up and running quickly while showing us the features of the framework concisely:

```rust
use actix_web::{web, App, HttpRequest, HttpServer, Responder};

async fn greet(req: HttpRequest) -> impl Responder {
    let name = req.match_info().get("name").unwrap_or("World");
    format!("Hello {}!", name)
}

#[actix_rt::main]
async fn main() -> std::io::Result<()> {
    HttpServer::new(|| {
        App::new()
            .route("/", web::get().to(greet))
            .route("/{name}", web::get().to(greet))
    })
        .bind("127.0.0.1:8000")?
        .run()
        .await
}
```

Here, we use the Actix Web structs to define a view that extracts data from the request. We then redefine our `main` function as an `async` function by utilizing the macro from the `actix-rt` crate. Without this macro, the program would fail to compile as `main` functions are not allowed to be asynchronous. We then build a new server and define the routes mapping them to the function we want. We then bind to an address, run, and then await the result.

While the `async` functionality is new, we will focus on this later on in the chapter. For now, should turn our attention to the closure that is passed into the new function of the `HttpServer` struct.

Understanding closures

Closures are essentially functions; however, they have a few differences. It has to be noted that functions can be defined on the fly via | | brackets as opposed to () brackets. A simple example of this is printing a parameter:

```
let test_function: fn(String) = |string_input: &str| {
    println!("{}", string_input);
};


test_function("test");
```

What happens here is that we assign the `test_function` variable to our function that prints out the input. The type is an `fn` type. There are some advantages to this. Because it's a variable that is assigned, we can exploit scopes.

Normal functions defined by themselves are available through the file/module that they are imported or defined in. However, there will be times in web development where we want the availability of the function to be restricted to a certain lifetime. Shifting the closure into an inner scope can easily achieve this:

```
{
    let test_function: fn(String) = |string_input: &str| {
        println!("{}", string_input);
    };
}
test_function("test");
```

Here, the call of our function is outside the scope, which will result in a `function not found in this scope` error.

Closure definitions have a similar syntax. However, they can input parameters and interact with outside variables in their scope:

```
let test = String::from("test");

let test_function = || {
    println!("{}", test);
};

test_function();
```

Note that we have not defined a type for the `test_function` variable. This is because a closure is a unique anonymous type that cannot be written out. The closest analogy to a closure is a struct that houses captured variables.

Closures can also have return values that can be interacted with like a normal function:

```
let test = String::from("test");

let test_function = || {
    println!("{}", test);
    return test + &String::from(" case")
};

let outcome: String = test_function();
```

Here, `outcome` will denote the string returned from the closure under the `test_function` variable.

Now that we have more of an understanding of closures, we can look back at our `main` function with confidence. We know that a closure is being called in the `HttpServer::new` function. Seeing as the `App` struct is the final line in the closure, the app has to be returned from the closure in order for the `bind` and `run` functions to be enacted. With this insight into closures, we can be a bit more confident with our HTTP server creation:

```
#[actix_rt::main]
async fn main() -> std::io::Result<()> {
    HttpServer::new(|| {
        println!("function is firing");
        let app = App::new()
```

```
            .route("/", web::get().to(greet))
            .route("/{name}", web::get().to(greet));
        return app
    })
        .bind("127.0.0.1:8000")?
        .workers(3)
        .run()
        .await
}
```

Here, we define the app and return it, and chuck in a `print` statement. We can do whatever we want in the closure as long as we return a constructed App struct. We also added a `workers` function with the parameter 3. When we run this, we can see that we get the following output:

```
Finished dev [unoptimized + debuginfo] target(s) in 16.46s
Running `target/debug/basic_setup`
function is firing
function is firing
function is firing
```

This tells us that the closure was fired three times. Altering the number of workers shows us that there is a direct relationship between this and the number of times the closure is fired. If the `workers` function is left out, then the closure is fired in relation to the number of cores your system has.

Now that we understand the nuances around the building of the App struct, it is time to look at the main change in the structure of the program, **asynchronous programming**.

Understanding asynchronous programming

Up until this chapter, we have been writing code in a sequential manner. This is good enough for standard scripts. However, in web development, asynchronous programming is important, as there are multiple requests to servers and API calls introduce idle time. In some other languages, such as **Python**, we can build web servers without touching any asynchronous concepts. While asynchronous concepts are utilized in these web frameworks, the implementation is defined under the hood. This is also true for the Rust framework Rocket. However, as we have seen, it is directly implemented in Actix Web.

When it comes to utilizing asynchronous code, there are two main concepts we have to understand:

- **Processes**: A process is a program that is being executed. It has its own memory stack, registers for variables, and code.

- **Threads**: A thread is a lightweight process that is managed independently by a scheduler. However, it does share data with other threads and the main program.

In this section, we will be looking at threads in order to see the effect that threads have on our code. One of the best ways to explore threads in any programming language is to code a brief pause in each thread, and time to process the program overall. We can time our Rust program with the following code:

```rust
use std::{thread, time};

fn do_something(number: i8) -> i8 {
    println!("number {} is running", number);
    let two_seconds = time::Duration::new(2, 0);
    thread::sleep(two_seconds);
    return 2
}
fn main() {
    let now = time::Instant::now();
    let one: i8 = do_something(1);
    let two: i8 = do_something(2);
    let three: i8 = do_something(3);

    println!("time elapsed {:?}", now.elapsed());
    println!("result {}", one + two + three);
}
```

Here, we define a standard function that sleeps. It has to be noted that although we are calling the sleep function from the standard library thread module, there is nothing in this code that spins off a thread yet. In the main function, we start the timer, set off three functions, then stop the timer, printing the sum of the outcomes afterward. With this, we get the following output:

```
number 1 is running
number 2 is running
```

```
number 3 is running
time elapsed 6.007948964s
result 6
```

This is not surprising. We have the functions running sequentially. Each function sleeps for 2 seconds, and the total time elapsed at the end of the whole process is just over 6 seconds.

Now we are going to spin off a thread for each function:

```
use std::{thread, time};
use std::thread::JoinHandle;

fn do_something(number: i8) -> i8 {
    println!("number {} is running", number);
    let two_seconds = time::Duration::new(2, 0);
    thread::sleep(two_seconds);
    return 2
}
fn main() {
    let now = time::Instant::now();
    let thread_one: JoinHandle<i8> = thread::spawn(
        || do_something(1));
    let thread_two: JoinHandle<i8> = thread::spawn(
        || do_something(2));
    let thread_three: JoinHandle<i8> = thread::spawn(
        || do_something(3));

    let result_one = thread_one.join();
    let result_two = thread_two.join();
    let result_three = thread_three.join();
    println!("time elapsed {:?}", now.elapsed());
    println!("result {}", result_one.unwrap() +
                          result_two.unwrap() +
                          result_three.unwrap());

}
```

Here, you can see that we pass a closure through each thread. If we try and just pass the do_something function through the thread, we get an error complaining that the compiler expected an FnOnce<()> closure and found an i8 instead. This is because a standard closure implements the FnOnce<()> public trait, whereas our do_something function simply returns i8.

When FnOnce<()> is implemented, the closure can only be called once. This means that when we create a thread, we can ensure that the closure can only be called once, and then when it returns, the thread ends. As our do_something function is the final line of the closure, i8 is returned. However, it has to be noted that just because the FnOnce<()> trait is implemented, it does not mean that we cannot call it multiple times. This trait only gets called if the context requires it. This means that if we were to call the closure outside of the thread context, we could call it multiple times.

Once we have spun off the three threads, we get a JoinHandle struct from the spawn functions of each thread we created. We call the join function for each of them. The join function waits for the associated thread to finish. We then print the time elapsed. The join functions return a Result struct, therefore they have to be unwrapped to access the return value of the closure passed into the thread. We then sum these results together to print the end result. If we do not call the join function, then the main process will run and finish before the threads have finished. This threading code gives the following output:

```
number 1 is running
number 3 is running
number 2 is running
time elapsed 2.000784532s
result 6
```

As we can see, the whole process took just over 2 seconds to run. This is because all three threads are running concurrently. We can also notice that thread three is fired before thread two. Do not worry if you get a sequence of 1, 2, 3. Threads finish in an indeterminate order. The scheduling is deterministic, however, there are thousands of events happening under the hood that require the CPU to do something. As a result, the exact time slices that each thread gets is never the same. These tiny changes add up. Because of this, we cannot guarantee that the threads will finish in a determinate order.

Spawning threads gives us a hands-on understanding of asynchronous programming. However, we remember that the Actix Web server does not use this syntax; it defines functions with an async and await syntax. In order to feel more comfortable with the web framework, we need to look into this syntax.

Understanding async and await

The `async` and `await` syntax manages the same concepts covered in the previous section, however, there are some nuances. Instead of simply spawning off threads, we create futures and then manipulate them as and when needed.

In computer science, a future is an unprocessed computation. This is where the result is not yet available, but when we call or wait, the future will be populated with the result of the computation. Futures can also be referred to as promises, delays, or deferred. In order to explore futures, we will create a new Cargo project, and utilize the futures created in the `Cargo.toml` file:

```
[dependencies]
futures = "0.3.5"
```

Now we have our futures, we can define our own `async` function in the `main.rs` file:

```
async fn do_something(number: i8) -> i8 {
    println!("number {} is running", number);
    let two_seconds = time::Duration::new(2, 0);
    thread::sleep(two_seconds);
    return 2
}
```

This is the standard `thread` function that we defined earlier on to signpost that the thread is running and returning a value from the thread. The only difference is that we have an `async` keyword before the `fn` definition. The simplest way to handle this function is to call it, and then block the program until the computation is finished:

```
use futures::executor::block_on;
use std::{thread, time};

fn main() {
    let now = time::Instant::now();
    let future_one = do_something(1);
    let outcome = block_on(future_one);
    println!("time elapsed {:?}", now.elapsed());
    println!("Here is the outcome: {}", outcome);
}
```

Here, the `future_one` variable is a `Future`. Running this gives us the following output:

```
number 1 is running
time elapsed 2.000179301s
Here is the outcome: 2
```

This is expected as it is the same as the thread output in the previous section. The result of the `async` function can also be extracted by using `await`. In order to do this, we need to have an `async` block:

```
let future_two = async {
    return do_something(2).await
};
let future_two = block_on(future_two);
println!("Here is the outcome: {:?}", future_two);
```

This seems a little verbose as it is doing the same as simply calling the `block_on` function on the future from the `do_something` function call. However, `await` can be called within another `async` function. We can also be more flexible within the `async` block. For instance, we can package two futures and return them:

```
let future_two = async {
    let outcome_two = do_something(2).await;
    let outcome_three = do_something(3).await;
    return [outcome_two, outcome_three]
};
let future_two = block_on(future_two);
println!("Here is the outcome: {:?}", future_two);
```

This gives the following output:

```
number 2 is running
number 3 is running
Here is the outcome: [2, 2]
```

However, if we time it, we can see that the functions are fired in a sequential fashion that takes just over 4 seconds. This is not very helpful as we might as well not bother with the `async` syntax if we are going to get the same timing results as normal sequential programming.

Joining seemed to work in the previous section. Seeing as futures also have a `join` function, it makes sense to utilize this to split the time taken in half by getting two futures to run at the same time:

```
use futures::join;


let second_outcome = async {
    let future_two = do_something(2);
    let future_three = do_something(3);
    return join!(future_two, future_three)
};


let now = time::Instant::now();
let result = block_on(second_outcome);
println!("time elapsed {:?}", now.elapsed());
println!("here is the result: {:?}", result);
```

However, this does not give us the result that we were expecting:

```
number 2 is running
number 3 is running
time elapsed 4.000327517s
here is the result: (2, 2)
```

The futures are being run sequentially. The only difference is that we return the result of the futures in a tuple. Despite the `futures::join` function being counter-intuitive, we can use another crate to create our own asynchronous `join` function by using the `async_std` crate. Before we do this, we can define the crate in the `Cargo.toml` file dependencies section:

```
async-std = "1.6.3"
```

With this crate, we can now run our futures asynchronously:

```
use std::vec::Vec;
use async_std;
use futures::future::join_all


let third_outcome = async {
    let mut futures_vec = Vec::new();
```

```
    let future_four = do_something(4);
    let future_five = do_something(5);
    futures_vec.push(future_four);
    futures_vec.push(future_five);

    let handles = futures_vec.into_iter().map(
        async_std::task::spawn).collect::<Vec<_>>();
    let results = join_all(handles).await;
    return results
};

let now = time::Instant::now();
let result = block_on(third_outcome);
println!("time elapsed for join vec {:?}", now.elapsed());
println!("Here is the result: {:?}", result);
```

Here, what we have done is to define our futures in an `async` block, and then append them to a vector denoted as `futures_vec`. We then get our futures-populated vector and call the `into_iter` function on it. This returns an iterator, which we can use to loop through the futures.

We can also return an iterator by simply calling the `iter` function. However, calling this will yield `&T`. Merely referencing a future is not a future. We need the future directory if we are going to apply the `spawn` function to it. Our `into_iter` function enables us to yield `T`, `&T`, or `&mut T`, depending on the context and needs.

We then apply the `async_std::task::spawn` function to each future in the vector using the map function. The `async_std::task::spawn` function seems familiar to the `thread::spawn` function we used earlier on so, again, *why bother with all this extra headache?* We could just loop through the vector and spawn a thread for each task. The difference here is that the `async_std::task::spawn` function is spinning off an async task in the same thread. *Therefore, we are concurrently running both futures in the same thread!*

We then use the `collect` function to collect the results of this mapping into a vector called `handles`. Once this is done, we pass this vector into the `join_all` function to join all the async tasks and wait for them to be completed using `await`. With this, we get the following output:

```
number 4 is running
number 5 is running
```

```
time elapsed for join vec 2.004575514s
Here is the result: [2, 2]
```

It's working! We have managed to get two `async` tasks running at the same time in the same thread, resulting in both futures being executed in just over 2 seconds!

As we can see, spawning threads and async tasks in Rust is fairly straightforward. However, we have to note that passing variables into threads and async tasks is not straightforward. Rust's borrowing mechanism ensures memory safety. We have to go through extra steps when passing data into a thread. Further discussion on the general concepts behind sharing data between threads is not conducive to our web project. However, we can briefly signpost what types allow this:

- `std::sync::Arc`: This type enables threads to reference outside data:

```
use std::sync::Arc;
use std::thread;

let names = Arc::new(vec!["dave", "chloe", "simon"]);
let reference_data = Arc::clone(&names);

let new_thread = thread::spawn(move || {
    println!("{}", reference_data[1]);
});
```

- `std::sync::Mutex`: This type enables threads to mutate outside data:

```
use std::sync::Mutex;
use std::thread;

let count = Mutex::new(0);

let new_thread = thread::spawn(move || {
    *count.lock().unwrap() += 1;
});
```

Inside the thread here, we dereference the result of the lock, unwrap it, and mutate it. It has to be noted that the shared state can only be accessed once the lock is held.

Looking back at the basic web server that we built in the previous section, we have explored nearly all of the new concepts that were introduced. The last concept that has to be understood is the definition of the `main` function. We can see that the `main` function is an `async` function. However, if we simply try and define the `main` function as an `async` function, it will return a `future` as opposed to running the program.

This is made possible by the `#[actix_rt::main]` macro provided by the `atix-rt` crate. This is a runtime implementation and enables everything to be run on the current thread. The `#[actix_rt::main]` macro marks the `async` function (which in this case, is the `main` function), to be executed by the Actix system.

At the risk of getting into the weeds here, the Actix crate runs concurrent computation based on the actor model. This is where an actor is a computation. Actors can send and receive messages to each other. Actors can alter their own state, but they can only affect other actors through messages, which removes the need for lock-based synchronization (the mutex we covered is lock-based). Further exploration of this model will not help us in developing web apps. However, the Actix crate does have good documentation on coding concurrent systems with Actix at `https://actix.rs/book/actix/sec-0-quick-start.html`.

We've covered a lot here. Do not feel stressed if you do not feel like you have retained all of it. We've briefly covered a range of topics around asynchronous programming. We do not need to understand it inside out to start building applications based on the Actix Web framework.

However, this whistle-stop tour is invaluable when it comes to debugging and designing applications. For an example in the wild, we can look at this smart **Stack Overflow** solution to running multiple servers in one file: `https://stackoverflow.com/questions/59642576/run-multiple-actix-app-on-different-ports`.

Basic views are defined for each server. As we can see, even if they are two different servers, there is no extra notation needed:

```
use actix_web::{web, App, HttpServer, Responder};
use futures::future;


async fn utils_one() -> impl Responder {
    "Utils one reached\n"
}
```

```
async fn health() -> impl Responder {
    "All good\n"
}
```

Once the views are defined, the two servers are defined in the main function:

```
#[actix_rt::main]
async fn main() -> std::io::Result<()> {
    let s1 = HttpServer::new(move || {
            App::new().service(web::scope("/utils").route(
                "/one", web::get().to(utils_one)))
        })
        .bind("0.0.0.0:3006")?
        .run();
    let s2 = HttpServer::new(move || {
            App::new().service(web::resource(
                "/health").route(web::get().to(health)))
        })
        .bind("0.0.0.0:8080")?
        .run();
    future::try_join(s1, s2).await?;

    Ok(())
}
```

We can confidently deduce that s1 and s2 are futures that the run function returns. We then join these two futures together and wait for them to finish. With this real-life example, we can see that our understanding of async programming enables us to break down what is happening when building and running multiple servers.

With our newfound confidence in async programming, there is nothing stopping us from creating 20 futures and stuffing them into a try_join! macro to run 20 servers, though this is not advised, as increasing the number of servers will increase the use of resources with diminishing returns on performance.

Now that we are truly comfortable with the Actix Web framework, we can practically look at building a scalable app with it. We will start by managing the views for our app.

Managing views using the Actix Web framework

In the *Launching a basic Actix Web server* section, we defined our views in the `main.rs` file. However, this is not scalable. If we continue to define all our routes in `main`, we will end up with a lot of imports and route definitions in one file. This makes it hard to navigate and manage. If we want to change a URL prefix for a block of views, the editing in this context is error-prone. The same goes for disabling a block of views.

In order to manage our views, we need to create our own modules for each set of views. To manage our views, we create a new Cargo project called `managing_views`. We then define the following project structure:

```
├── main.rs
└── views
    ├── auth
    │   ├── login.rs
    │   ├── logout.rs
    │   └── mod.rs
    ├── mod.rs
    └── path.rs
```

The `main.rs` file is to house our definition of the server. We then define a URL path helper struct for all our views in the `path.rs` file. We define our login and logout views in the `login.rs` and `logout.rs` files. We then build the routes via a `factory` function in the `views/auth/mod.rs` file. We then orchestrate the firing of the factory in a `factory` function in the `views/mod.rs` file.

Now that our structure has been defined, we can build our `main.rs` file:

```rust
use actix_web::{App, HttpServer};
mod views;


#[actix_rt::main]
async fn main() -> std::io::Result<()> {
    HttpServer::new(|| {
        let app = App::new();
        return app
    })
        .bind("127.0.0.1:8000")?
```

```
    .run()
    .await
}
```

Here, we import our empty `views` module, define our app in the closure, and run it. Running it right now will give us a server with no views, so we can start working on the `views` module.

The first file we can work on is the `views/path.rs` file, which houses a struct that defines a path. We start here because this struct does not have any dependencies. This struct is going to be used to define a standard prefix for a URL, which is fused with a string passed into the `define` function to build a URL string:

```
pub struct Path {
    pub prefix: String
}

impl Path {
    pub fn define(&self, following_path: String) -> String {
        return self.prefix.to_owned() + &following_path
    }
}
```

In our `define` function, we take the reference of the struct as a `&self` parameter so the same struct instance can be used multiple times to define multiple URLs with the same prefix. It has to be noted that the functions with such signatures have a resemblance to methods, meaning that they are used as methods. It also has to be noted that we use a `to_owned` function on the reference to the struct instance's prefix. The `to_owned` function creates owned data from borrowed data by cloning. We want our `define` function to return a string URL that can be passed into other functions, however, we also want our `Path` struct to retain the `prefix` attribute so it can be used again for other views.

Now that we have defined our path, we can move on to our basic login and logout views. We are approaching this next because the views also have no dependencies. Considering that this chapter is focused on managing views as opposed to logging in and out, these views will simply return a string. Processing data in views is covered in the next chapter. Authentication is covered in *Chapter 7, Managing User Sessions*.

In our `views/auth/login.rs` file, we define the following login view:

```
pub async fn login() -> String {
    format!("Login view")
}
```

Here, we have a standard `async` function that returns a string. We can also define our logout view in the `views/auth/logout.rs` file in the same fashion:

```
pub async fn logout() -> String {
    format!("Logout view")
}
```

Now that we have defined our views, we need to build them in a `factory` function in the `views/auth/mod.rs` file:

```
use actix_web::web;
mod login;
mod logout;
use super::path::Path;


pub fn auth_factory(app: &mut web::ServiceConfig) {
    let base_path: Path = Path{prefix: String::from("/auth")};

    app.route(&base_path.define(String::from("/login")),
            web::get().to(login::login))
        .route(&base_path.define(String::from("/logout")),
            web::get().to(logout::logout));
}
```

On the imports, we can note that we get the `Path` struct from the parent directory of the `auth` directory by using `super`. Before, we have been using `super` to get us into the `mod.rs` file in the same directory. However, if we use `super` in a `mod.rs` file, then we import files in the parent directory `mod.rs` file. If we wanted to, we could import the `Path` struct into the `views/auth/login.rs` file by using `use super::super::path;`.

We can also see that once we have imported all the things we need, we define a `factory` function that does not return anything and takes in the app to define routes on it. However, instead of passing in `actix_web::App`, we pass in an `actix_web::web::ServiceConfig` struct. Even if we try to pass in the `actix_web::App` struct, `actix_web` will not allow us.

One of the structs needed to define the type for the function to pass the app in is private. The `actix_web::web::ServiceConfig` struct enables us to configure the app further. We use this to define routes, however, we can set application data, register an HTTP service, or register an external resource for URL generation resources using this struct.

Once we've passed in the `config` struct, we define the routes as we would if we were defining a route in the `main.rs` file where the server definition is. We can also see how the `Path` struct is used. There is a slight advantage to using the `Path` struct. The URL prefix is defined once, reducing the chance of the odd typo happening in the prefix if we are defining many routes. It also makes maintenance easier. If we are to change a prefix for a set of views, we only have to change it once in the `Path` struct construction in the factory.

Now that we have our `views/auth` module fully operational, we can merely pass in the `config` struct through the factory to build all the routes for the auth. In the future, we will also build other modules for views. Because of this, we need another factory that can orchestrate the multiple view factories. This can be defined in the `views/mod.rs` file:

```
use actix_web::web;
mod path;
mod auth;


pub fn views_factory(app: &mut web::ServiceConfig) {
    auth::auth_factory(app);
};
```

As we can see, we import the `auth` module and use it to build our views in the factory. We note that we pass the `config` struct into the factory, and then pass it into `auth_factory`. The app parameter can be passed into multiple factories after each other as it is a reference and the factories are called in sequential order. We also imported the `path` file. While this is not used in the file, we need it for the super call in the auth factory. This is why we don't get a warning when running the code.

Now we have a scalable, well-structured way of managing our views, all we have to do is import this views factory and call it in the `main.rs` file:

```
use actix_web::{App, HttpServer};
mod views;


#[actix_rt::main]
async fn main() -> std::io::Result<()> {
    HttpServer::new(|| {
        let app = App::new().configure(views::views_factory);
        return app
    })
        .bind("127.0.0.1:8000")?
        .run()
        .await
}
```

As we can see, this is pretty much the same. All we have to do is call the `configure` function on the `App` struct. We then pass the views factory into the `configure` function, which will pass the `config` struct into our `factory` function for us. As the `configure` function returns `Self`, meaning the `App` struct, we can return the result at the end of the closure.

Now we have a functioning server that builds views in a scalable way! We can simply cut off all our `auth` views by merely commenting out the following line in the `views/mod.rs` file:

```
auth::auth_factory(app);
```

This also gives us a lot of flexibility. By defining our own factories for each views module, there is nothing stopping us from adding extra parameters to individual factories to customize the build. For instance, if for some reason, we want to disable the `logout` function based on an environment or config variable, we can merely add a conditional in our factory in the `views/auth/mod.rs` file:

```
use actix_web::web;
mod login;
mod logout;
use super::path::Path;
```

```
pub fn auth_factory(app: &mut web::ServiceConfig, logout: bool)
{
    let base_path: Path = Path{prefix: String::from("/auth")};
    let app = app.route(&base_path.define(String::from("/
        login")),
                            web::get().to(login::login));

    if logout {
        app.route(&base_path.define(String::from("/logout")),
                web::get().to(logout::logout));
    }
}
```

All we have to add is a `logout` parameter. We then assign the result of the `route` function to the `app` variable. We then call the `route` function on that variable if the `logout` variable is true. Remember, we don't have to return anything; we just need to call the functions.

It is important to keep logic isolated. The logic for building the views for the `auth` module stays in the auth factory. However, the collection of the variables around the configuration should be defined in `views/mod.rs`:

```
use actix_web::web;
mod path;
mod auth;
use std::env;


pub fn views_factory(app: &mut web::ServiceConfig) {
    let args: Vec<String> = env::args().collect();
    let param: &String = &args[args.len() - 1];
    if param.as_str() == "cancel_logout" {
        println!("logout view isn't being configured");
        auth::auth_factory(app, false);
    } else {
        println!("logout view is being configured");
        auth::auth_factory(app, true);
    }
}
```

Here, we collect the parameters from the environment. If it is `cancel_logout`, the logout view will not be configured. Keeping the logic of parameters in the `views/mod.rs` factory increases the flexibility by enabling us to configure multiple factories with one parameter. We can also revisit the `Path` struct and the advantage it offers here. If we were to change the prefix of a set of views on the fly, we would only need one conditional or match statement for the `Path` struct at the beginning of the `factory` function as opposed to every route definition function.

Our objective was to build a basic app that serves and manages views in a scalable way. Here, we have an app that serves views. These views can slot in and out and be defined in their own modules. To run without the logout view, we use the following command line:

```
cargo run cancel_logout
```

If not, then we just run `cargo run`. If we run our app with the logout view being configured, we have the following URLs and outputs:

```
http://127.0.0.1:8000/auth/login
```

This gives the following string:

```
Login view
```

It also gives this:

```
http://127.0.0.1:8000/auth/logout
```

We get the following string:

```
Logout view
```

We'll now move on to the next section, where we will put it all together.

Putting it together

We have covered a lot in order to get some basic views up and running on an Actix Web server. We could have done this all on one page:

```
use actix_web::{web, App, HttpRequest, HttpServer, Responder};
pub async fn logout() -> String {
    format!("Logout view")}
pub async fn login() -> String {
    format!("Login view")}
```

```
#[actix_rt::main]
async fn main() -> std::io::Result<()> {
    HttpServer::new(|| {
        let app = App::new()
            .route("/auth/login", web::get().to(login))
            .route("/auth/logout", web::get().to(logout));
        return app
    })
        .bind("127.0.0.1:8000")?
        .run()
        .await
}
```

However, if we did this instead, we would be running before we could walk. Instead, we took the time to understand the mechanisms underpinning the server's running.

Summary

In this chapter, we covered the basics of threading, futures, and async functions. As a result, we were able to look at a multi-server solution in the wild and understand confidently what was going on. With this, we built on the concepts we learned in the previous chapter to build modules that define views. In addition, we chained factories to enable our views to be constructed on the fly and added to the server. With this chained factory mechanism, we can slot entire view modules in and out of the configuration when the server is being built.

We also built a utility struct that defines a path, standardizing the definition of a URL for a set of views. In future chapters, we will use this approach to build authentication, JSON serialization, and frontend modules. With what we've covered, we'll be able to build views that extract and return data from the user in a range of different ways in the next chapter. With this modular understanding, we have a strong foundation that enables us to build real-world web projects in Rust where logic is isolated, can be configured, and where code can be added in a manageable way.

In the next chapter, we will work with processing requests and responses. We will learn how to pass params, bodies, headers, and forms to views and process them, returning JSON. We will be using these new methods with the to-do module we built in the previous chapter to enable our interaction with to-do items to achieve through server views.

Questions

1. What parameter is passed into the `HttpServer::new` function and what does the parameter return?

2. How is a closure different from a function?

3. What is the difference between a process and a thread?

4. What is the difference between an `async` function and a normal one?

5. What is the difference between `await` and `join`?

6. What is the advantage of chaining factories?

7. What is the advantage of having a utility struct such as the `Path` struct?

4

Processing HTTP Requests

Up to this point, we have utilized the **Actix web framework** to serve basic views. However, this can only get us so far when it comes to extracting data from the request and passing data back to the user.

In this chapter, we will fuse code from *Chapter 2, Designing Your Web Application in Rust*, and *Chapter 3, Handling HTTP Requests*, in order to build server views that process to do items. We will then explore **JSON serialization** for extracting data and returning it to make our views more user-friendly. We also extract data from the header with middleware before it hits the view.

In this chapter, we will cover the following topics:

- Extracting and passing parameters to `Actix-web` views
- Utilizing the `serde` crate to serialize structs to and from JSON
- Utilizing `Actix-web` to build responses with JSON bodies, headers, and response codes
- Building middleware logic that intercepts the request before it hits the view
- Extracting data from headers

Let's get started!

Technical requirements

For this chapter, we need to download and install **Postman**. We will need Postman to make API requests to our server. You can download it from `https://www.postman.com/downloads/`.

We will also be building on the server code we created in the previous chapter, which can be found at `https://github.com/PacktPublishing/Rust-Web-Programming/tree/master/Chapter03/managing_views`.

You can find the full source code that will be used in this chapter here: `https://github.com/PacktPublishing/Rust-Web-Programming/tree/master/Chapter04`.

The managing views code will be the basis of this chapter, and we will add features to this code base. We will be fusing this with the to do module we wrote in *Chapter 2, Designing Your Web Application in Rust*, which can be found at `https://github.com/PacktPublishing/Rust-Web-Programming/tree/master/Chapter02/processing_structs_and_traits`.

The CiA videos for this book can be viewed at: `http://bit.ly/3jULCrw`.

Getting to know the initial setup

In this section, we will cover the initial setup of two fusing pieces of code we built in *Chapter 2, Designing Your Web Application in Rust*, with the code that we built in *Chapter 3, Handling HTTP Requests*. This fusion will give us the following structure:

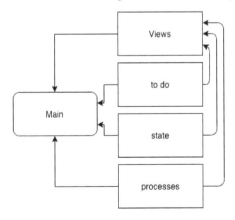

Figure 4.1 – Structure of our app and its modules

Here, we will register all the modules in the `main` file, and then pull all these modules into the views to be used. We are essentially swapping the command-line interface from *Chapter 2, Designing Your Web Application in Rust*, with web views. Combining these modules gives us the following files in the code base:

```
├── main.rs
├── processes.rs
├── state.rs
```

Our `to_do` module that we will be bolting on has the following structure:

```
├── to_do
│   ├── mod.rs
│   └── structs
│       ├── base.rs
│       ├── done.rs
│       ├── mod.rs
│       ├── pending.rs
│       └── traits
│           ├── create.rs
│           ├── delete.rs
│           ├── edit.rs
│           ├── get.rs
│           └── mod.rs
```

Our bolt-on `views` module from *Chapter 3, Handling HTTP Requests*, contains the following code:

```
└── views
    ├── auth
    │   ├── login.rs
    │   ├── logout.rs
    │   └── mod.rs
    ├── mod.rs
    ├── path.rs
```

The full structure containing all the necessary code can be found at the following GitHub repository: `https://github.com/PacktPublishing/Rust-Web-Programming/tree/master/Chapter04/basic_setup`.

Note that although we are bolting on modules from previous chapters, there is one file that is going to be new to us, and this is `main.rs`. Here, we have some crossover code from the two chapters that we are splicing:

```
use actix_web::{App, HttpServer};
mod state;
mod to_do;
mod views;
mod processes;

#[actix_rt::main]
async fn main() -> std::io::Result<()> {
    HttpServer::new(|| {
        let app = App::new().configure(
            views::views_factory);
        return app})
        .bind("127.0.0.1:8000")?
        .run()
        .await
}
```

Here, we define the modules, and then we define our server. Because the server is utilizing `views_factory`, we will not have to alter this file for the rest of this chapter. Instead, we will chain the factory functions that will be called in the `views_factory` function.

At this point, we can sit back and appreciate the dividends from all the hard work that we did in the previous chapters. The isolation of principles and well-defined modules enabled us to slot our logic from our command-line program into our server interface with minimal effort. Now, all we have to do is connect it to our `views` module, and then pass parameters into those views.

Passing parameters

In *Chapter 3, Handling HTTP Requests*, we built a couple of basic views. However, our views were just serving a couple of basic GET views that just display a string. Now that we are familiar with basic views, we are going to pass parameters and data into the view. Our `to do` views module will take the following structure:

```
├── auth
│   ├── login.rs
```

```
|    ├── logout.rs
|    └── mod.rs
├── mod.rs
├── path.rs
└── to_do
     ├── create.rs
     └── mod.rs
```

To demonstrate this, we are going to build a basic view that takes a parameter from the URL and creates a to do item. To do this, we will have to do the following:

1. Load the current state of the to do item list.

2. Get the title of the new to do item from the URL.

3. Pass the title and the pending string through to_do_factory.

4. Pass the result of the previous step, along with the create string and the state, into the process module interface.

5. Return a string to the user to signal that the process has finished.

Because the preceding process mainly consists of interacting with neatly packaged module interfaces, this can all be achieved with this simple function, which can be found in the views/to_do/create.rs file:

```
use serde_json::value::Value;
use serde_json::Map;
use actix_web::HttpRequest;


use crate::to_do;
use crate::state::read_file;
use crate::processes::process_input;


pub async fn create(req: HttpRequest) -> String {
    let state: Map<String, Value> = read_file(String::from(
        "./state.json")); // 1


    let title: String = req.match_info().get("title"
    ).unwrap().to_string();
```

```
let title_reference: String = title.clone(); // 2

let item = to_do::to_do_factory(&String::from("pending"),
           title).expect("create "); // 3
process_input(item, "create".to_string(), &state); // 4
return format!("{} created", title_reference) // 5
}
```

This code demonstrates that the logic inside our future views will mainly consist of rearranging these interfaces in an order that makes sense to the purpose of the view. To make this view available to the server, we are going to have to package it as a straightforward factory function in the `views/to_do/mod.rs` file:

```
use actix_web::web;
mod create;
use super::path::Path;


pub fn item_factory(app: &mut web::ServiceConfig) {
    let base_path: Path = Path{prefix: String::from("/item")};
    app.route(&base_path.define(
        String::from("/create/{title}")),
            web::get().to(create::create));
}
```

Here, we can see that our factory takes the same approach at the auth views factory, by utilizing the `Path` and `ServiceConfig` structs. We can also see that our title parameter is defined with curly brackets, `{title}`, which is extracted via the `HttpRequest` struct in our create view by using the `match_info().get("title")` function. Now, in our `src/views/mod.rs` file, we need to clean up some of the previous logic and introduce our `item_factory`:

```
use actix_web::web;
mod path;
mod auth;
mod to_do;


pub fn views_factory(app: &mut web::ServiceConfig) {
```

```
    auth::auth_factory(app);
    to_do::item_factory(app);
}
```

We have also removed the `define logout` parameter in order for this to compile. We will also have to clean up our `auth_factory` in the `views/auth/mod.rs` file:

```
use actix_web::web;
mod login;
mod logout;
use super::path::Path;


pub fn auth_factory(app: &mut web::ServiceConfig) {
    let base_path: Path = Path{prefix: String::from("/auth")};

    let app = app.route(&base_path.define(
        String::from("/login")),
                        web::get().to(login::login))
    .route(&base_path.define(String::from("/logout")),
            web::get().to(logout::logout));
}
```

Now, our app is fully functional, and we can interact with it by using the `cargo run` command. `http://127.0.0.1:8000/item/create/code%20in%20rust` gives us the following output in a web browser window:

```
code in rust created
```

On top of this, our `state.json` file contains the following content:

```
{"code in rust":"pending"}
```

It worked! We now have a server that accepts a GET request, extracts parameters from the URL, creates a new pending to do item, and then stores it in our JSON file. It has to be noted that while we are going to use a JSON file for data storage purposes, we will define a database for the app in *Chapter 6, Data Persistence with PostgreSQL*. Also, note that a `20` in the URL denotes a space.

The GET method works for us, but it is not the most appropriate method for creating a to-do item. GET methods can be cached, bookmarked, kept in the browser's history, and have restrictions in terms of their length. Bookmarking, storing them in browser history, or caching them doesn't just present security issues, it also increases the risk of the user accidentally making the same call again. Because of this, it is not a good idea to alter data with a GET request. To protect against this, we can use POST requests, which do not cache, end up in browser history, and cannot be bookmarked.

Our `create` function can be turned into a POST method by changing the `get` function to a `post` function in our `to do` views module in the `views/to_do/mod.rs` file:

```
pub fn item_factory(app: &mut web::ServiceConfig) {
    let base_path: Path = Path{prefix: String::from("/item")};
    app.route(&base_path.define(
        String::from("/create/{title}")),
            web::post().to(create::create));
}
```

The change is in the last line of the `item_factory` function. If we run this again, our URL that created a to do item no longer works in the browser. Instead, we get a **404 error** as the page cannot be found. This makes sense as the browser URL is a GET request. We can perform a POST function using Postman:

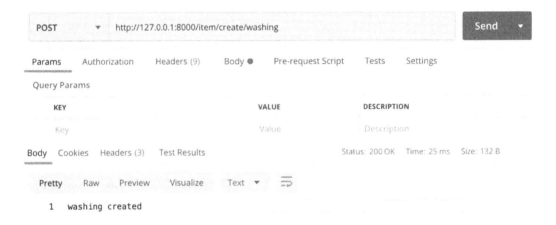

Figure 4.2 – Postman API call to our app

Here, we can see that we create a washing to do item with the same URL pattern. We can see that we get a **200** code, and then a **washing created** string in the body. Checking our JSON state file shows us that the system is still working as we have the code in rust and washing to do items, which are both pending. We can have the same URL pattern accept both POST and GET methods, by merely calling the route function twice in the to do views factory with the post and get functions:

```
pub fn item_factory(app: &mut web::ServiceConfig) {
    let base_path: Path = Path{prefix: String::from("/item")};

    app.route(&base_path.define(
        String::from("/create/{title}")),
            web::post().to(create::create));

    app.route(&base_path.define(String::from(
        "/create/{title}")),
            web::get().to(create::create));
}
```

Considering the differences we covered earlier between the GET and POST methods, it is sensible to just have a POST method for our create function.

Looking back at our Postman GUI, we have to think ahead. With our create function, one line of text is good enough to tell us that the item has been created. In fact, we do not even have to return anything in the body; the return status number is enough to tell us that the item has been created. However, when it comes to getting a list of to do items, we will need structured data. In order to achieve this, we will have to serialize JSON data and return it to us.

Using macros for JSON serialization

JSON serialization is directly supported via the Actix-web crate. We can demonstrate this by creating a GET view that returns all our to do items in the views/to_do/get. rs file:

```
use actix_web::{web, Responder};
use serde_json::value::Value;
use serde_json::Map;
```

```
use crate::state::read_file;


pub async fn get() -> impl Responder {
    let state: Map<String, Value> = read_file(String::from(
        "./state.json"));
    return web::Json(state);
}
```

Here, we simply read our JSON file and return it, we pass it into the web::Json struct, and then we return it. The web::Json struct implements the Responder trait. We have to define this new view by adding the module definition to the views/to_do/mod.rs file, and then add the route definition to the factory function:

```
Mod get
. . .
app.route(&base_path.define(String::from("/get")),
        web::get().to(get::get));
```

Running http://127.0.0.1:8000/item/get gives us the following JSON data in the response body:

```
{"code in rust":"pending","washing":"pending"}
```

While this does the job, it is not flexible. We might need two different lists – one for the done items and another for the pending ones. They also might want a count of the number of items and structured data. For instance, we may need to add a timestamp for when the item was created or done. Having a simple JSON body for the item as the title and having the status as the value does not enable us to scale the complexity when needed.

In order to have more control over the type of data that we are going to return to the user, we are going to have to build our own serialization structs. Our serialization struct is going to present two lists: one for completed items and another for pending items. These lists will be populated with objects consisting of a title and a status.

As you may recall from *Chapter 2, Designing Your Web Application in Rust*, our **pending** and **Done** item structs are inherited via composition from a **Base** struct. Therefore, we have to access the title and the status from the **Base** struct. However, our **Base** struct is not accessible to the public. We will have to make it accessible so that we can serialize the attributes for each to do item:

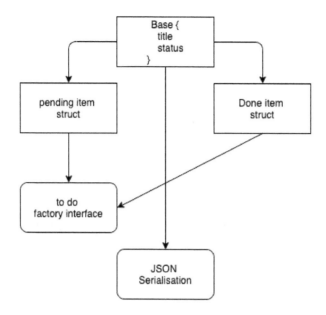

Figure 4.3 – Relationship that our to do structs have to our interfaces

This can be done by changing the declaration of the base module in the `to_do/`
`structs/mod.rs` file from `mod base;` to `pub mod base;`. Now that the
Base struct is directly available outside of the module, we can build our own
`json_serialization` module in the `src` directory with the following structure:

```
├── json_serialization
|   ├── mod.rs
|   └── to_do_items.rs
```

Our new module needs to have the following dependencies added to
the `Cargo.toml` file:

```
futures = "0.3.5"
serde = "1"
```

Now that we have everything, we can define a JSON schema in our `src/json_`
`serialization/to_do_items.rs` file and define the parameters and types for a
JSON body:

```
use serde::Serialize;
use crate::to_do::ItemTypes;
```

```
use crate::to_do::structs::base::Base;


#[derive(Serialize)]
pub struct ToDoItems {
    pub pending_items: Vec<Base>,
    pub done_items: Vec<Base>,
    pub pending_item_count: i8,
    pub done_item_count: i8
}
```

Here, all we have done is define a standard public struct with parameters. We then used the `derive` macro to implement the `Serialize` trait. This enables the struct attributes to be serialized to JSON with the name of the attribute as the key. For instance, if the `ToDoItems` struct had a `done_item_count` of one, then the JSON body would denote it as `"done_item_count": 1`.

Now that the serialization has been defined, we have to consider processing the data. It would not be scalable if we have to sort the data and count it before calling the struct. This would add unnecessary code to the view regarding processing data for serialization as opposed to the logic belonging to the view in question. It would also enable duplicate code. There is only going to be one way we sort, count, and serialize the data. If other views needed to return the list of items, then we would have to duplicate the code again.

Considering this, it makes sense to build a constructor for the struct, where we ingest a vector of to do items, sort them into the right attributes, and then count them:

```
impl ToDoItems {
    pub fn new(input_items: Vec<ItemTypes>) -> ToDoItems {
        let mut pending_array_buffer = Vec::new();
        let mut done_array_buffer = Vec::new();

        for item in input_items {
            match item {
                ItemTypes::Pending(packed) =>
                pending_array_buffer.push(
                    packed.super_struct),
                ItemTypes::Done(packed) =>
                done_array_buffer.push(
                    packed.super_struct)
            }
```

```
        }
        let done_count: i8 = done_array_buffer.len() as i8;
        let pending_count: i8 = pending_array_buffer.len()
            as i8;
        return ToDoItems{
            pending_items: pending_array_buffer,
                done_item_count: done_count,
            pending_item_count: pending_count,
                done_items: done_array_buffer
        }
    }
}
```

What we do here is accept a vector of ItemTypes. We then unpack them with a match statement and push (append) them into the right mutable vector. We then call the len function on each vector. The len function returns a usize, which is a pointer-sized unsigned integer type. Because of this, we cast it as an i8 and then redefine and return our struct, which is ready to be serialized into JSON.

In order to utilize our struct, we have to define it in our GET view, in our views/to_do/get.rs file, and then return it:

```
use actix_web::{web, Responder};
use serde_json::value::Value;
use serde_json::Map;
use crate::state::read_file;
use crate::to_do::{ItemTypes, to_do_factory};
use crate::json_serialization::to_do_items::ToDoItems;


pub async fn get() -> impl Responder {
    let state: Map<String, Value> = read_file(String::from(
        "./state.json"));
```

```
    let mut array_buffer = Vec::new();

    for (key, value) in state {
        let item_type: String = String::from(
                        value.as_str().unwrap());
        let item: ItemTypes = to_do_factory(
                        &item_type, key).unwrap();
        array_buffer.push(item);
    }
    let return_package: ToDoItems =
        ToDoItems::new(array_buffer);
    return web::Json(return_package);
}
```

Here is another moment where everything clicks together: we use our `read_file` interface to get the state from the JSON file. We then loop through the map, converting the item type into a string and feeding it into our `to_do_factory` interface. Once we have the constructed item from the factory, we append it to a vector and feed that vector into our JSON serialization struct.

In order for our `json_serialization` module to function in our application, we have to declare it in our `main.rs` file with the `mod json_serialization;` line of code. We also have to derive serialization on the base struct in our `to_do` module by adding the macro we defined in our `src/to_do/structs/base.rs` file, as follows:

```
use serde::Serialize;

#[derive(Serialize)]
pub struct Base {
    pub title: String,
    pub status: String
}
```

Now, our GET function returns the following JSON:

```
{
    "pending_items": [
        {
            "title": "code in rust",
            "status": "pending"
```

```
        },
        {
            "title": "washing",
            "status": "pending"
        }
    ],
    "done_items": [],
    "pending_item_count": 2,
    "done_item_count": 0
}
```

This is a clean, well-structured response that can be expanded and edited if we need to do so as our app develops. We can stop here, but note that our GET view returned an implementation of the `Responder` trait. This means that if our `ToDoItems` struct also implements this, it can be directly returned in a view. We can do this in our `json_serialization/to_do_items.rs` file with the following `impl` block:

```
impl Responder for ToDoItems {
    type Error = Error;
    type Future = Ready<Result<HttpResponse, Error>>;

    fn respond_to(self, _req: &HttpRequest) -> Self::Future {
        let body = serde_json::to_string(&self).unwrap();
        ready(Ok(HttpResponse::Ok()
            .content_type("application/json")
            .body(body)))
    }
}
```

The `respond_to` function is fired when the `view` function is returned. Here, we return a type that we define ourselves called `Future`. This is comprised of a `Ready` struct from the `futures` crate, which denotes that the future is immediately ready with a value. Inside this is a `Result` struct, which can either be an error or an `HttpRequest`.

We serialize the `own` struct using `&self` and attach that to the body. Now, merely returning our struct without doing any other processing in our GET function can be done by creating a new to-do item and simply returning it. This is demonstrated in the following code block:

```
let return_package: ToDoItems = ToDoItems::new(array_buffer);
return return_package
```

This gives us the same response we received previously! Now, we are at the point where we can refactor. It is reasonable to assume that all our to do views will require an updated list of to do items once the operation is over. This refactoring can be done by lifting all the code from the GET function into a function called `return_state` in a `utils` file in the `views/to_do/utils.rs` directory (remember to define the file in `mod.rs`). The `return_state` function returns the `ToDoItems` struct. This then shortens our GET view to the following:

```
use actix_web::Responder;
use super::utils::return_state;

pub async fn get() -> impl Responder {
    return return_state()
}
```

Now, our JSON serialization process for returning data is fully locked down. We can now move on to extracting data from request bodies in order to edit and delete to do items.

Extracting data

Extracting data from the request body is fairly straightforward. All we have to do is define a struct with the attributes we want, and then pass that through as a parameter in the `view` function. Then, the data from the request body will be serialized to that schema. We can do this by defining the following struct in our `json_serialization/to_do_item.rs` file:

```
use serde::Deserialize;

#[derive(Deserialize)]
pub struct ToDoItem {
```

```
        pub title: String,
        pub status: String
}
```

Here, we have used the `Deserialize` macro. Now that we have this, we can start building our edit view in the `views/to_do/edit.rs` file. Because the view requires a lot of code, we will be breaking it down into sections. First, we need to import all of the crates that we are going to use:

```
use actix_web::{web, HttpResponse};
use serde_json::value::Value;
use serde_json::Map;

use super::utils::return_state;
use crate::state::read_file;

use crate::to_do::to_do_factory;
use crate::json_serialization::to_do_item::ToDoItem;
use crate::processes::process_input;
```

Here, we can see that we are using the standard structs for loading the state. We also have our utility function for returning the current state of our to do items for the user. We will also use our processes to process the edit, and `ToDoItem`, which we just defined, for the serialization. We have also imported a `HttpResponse` struct to improve the response we will give to our users. Now that we have all the structs that we need, we can define, view, and gather all the data needed for our edit process:

```
pub async fn edit(to_do_item: web::Json<ToDoItem>) ->
        HttpResponse {
    let state: Map<String, Value> = read_file(String::from(
                                      "./state.json"));
    let title_reference: &String = &to_do_item.title.clone();
    let title: String = to_do_item.title.clone();
```

Here, we can see that we wrap our `ToDoItem` struct in a `Json` struct. Our `to_do_item` parameter is then our `ToDoItem` struct, once it's been deserialized. We then load our state and build a couple of references for the title of the item to be used later. After that, we must check our state to see if the to do item actually exists. If it does not, then we cannot edit it, so we can return a not found (404 code) with a message stating that the title cannot be found:

```
let status: String;
match &state.get(title_reference) {
    Some(result) => {
        status = result.to_string().replace('\"', "");
    }
    None=> {
        return HttpResponse::NotFound().json(
            format!("{} not in state", title_reference))
    }
}
```

Remember, the `get` function from the state returns `Option`, which is either some or none. Here, the `HttpResponse` struct with the `NotFound` constructor gives us a response struct that has a 404 code. The `.json` file then attaches our message. If the state does contain, then we assign the `status` variable to the status from the state.

Now that we have this, we need to see if the status is the same as the status that was passed into the view. If it is the same, then there is no point running the edit process as we will be wanting to edit the to do item to the status that it already is. Therefore, we might as well just return the current state to the user:

```
if &status == &to_do_item.status {
    return HttpResponse::Ok().json(return_state())
}
```

Here, we can see that we can pass our JSON structs into the json function and they will be serialized and returned with the response. If the status is different, we then have to edit the item and return the state:

```
match to_do_factory(&status, title) {
    Err(_item) => return HttpResponse::BadRequest().json(
        format!("{} not accepted", status)),
    Ok(item) => process_input(item, String::from("edit"),
        &state)
}
return HttpResponse::Ok().json(return_state())
```

We know that our to_do_factory only accepts pending and done statuses for now. If another type of status is passed, then to_do_factory will throw an error. If there is an error, we must return a bad request, along with a message stating that the status that was passed in is not supported. If the status is correct, then the item that was created in to_do_factory is edited with the state in the process_input function. Once this is done, we return a 200 status, with the state in the body. We must then remember to define this in the views/to_do/mod.rs file:

```
mod edit; // add at the top of the file


// add inside the item_factory function
app.route(&base_path.define(String::from("/edit")),
        web::put().to(edit::edit));
```

With this, we have added an edit view to our app. Now, we can expect the following Postman call:

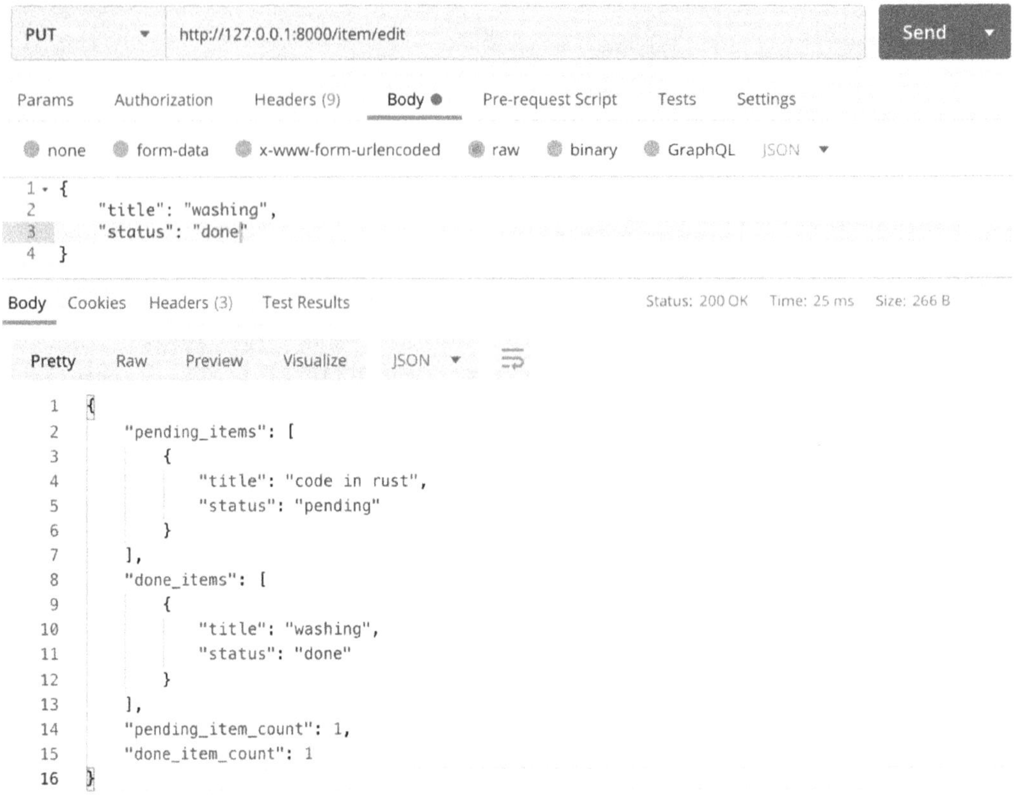

Figure 4.4 – API call to edit view

Here, we can see that the done items list is now populated, and that the counts have been altered. If we continue to make the same call, we will get the same response as we will be editing the **washing** item to `done` when it already has a `done` status. We will have to switch it back to `pending` or change the title in our call to get a different updated state. If we do not include **title** and **status** in the body of our call, then we will get a bad request response instantly, because the `ToDoItem` struct is expecting those two fields.

Now that we have locked down the process of receiving and returning JSON data in the URL parameters and body, we are nearly done. However, we have one more method to cover that's used for data extraction that is important, and this is the header. Headers are used to store meta information such as security credentials.

For instance, if we needed to authorize a range of requests, it would not be scalable to put them in all our JSON structs. We also have to acknowledge that the request body could be large, especially if the requester is being malicious. Therefore, it makes sense to access the security credentials before passing the request through to the view. This can be done by intercepting the request through what is commonly known as **middleware**. Once we've intercepted the request, we can access the security credentials, check them, and then process the view.

In order to achieve this, first of all, we have to develop a procedure for processing a security JSON web token. We will not focus on the security aspects here; instead, we will just be printing stuff out to the console as this chapter is about extracting, processing, and returning data. In *Chapter 7, Managing User Sessions*, we will explore the security nuances of checking and managing these tokens. For now, we can build the process by chaining three functions together, all of which return `Result` structs. In the `views/token.rs` file, we can start by importing the crates that we need:

```
use actix_web::dev::ServiceRequest;
```

This file has the following dependency that needs to be added to the `Cargo.toml` file. This can be done with the following dependency definition:

```
actix-service = "1.0.6"
```

We need this because we are going to be passing the service request directly into our entry point function. Our first function is the simplest for now. Now, we are going to check the password:

```
fn check_password(password: String) -> Result<String,
        &'static str> {
    if password == "token" {
        return Ok(password)
    }
    return Err("token not authorised")
}
```

Here, we merely take in a string, check to see if the string is what we want, and then return a result based on this. Again, a more legitimate way of checking passwords will be covered in *Chapter 7, Managing User Sessions*.

Now that we have our password checking function, we need to pass a password into the function. Previously, we noted that we are passing the `ServiceRequest` struct into the entry point function. Therefore, we are going to have to extract the password from the header with our extract token from the `header` function:

```
fn extract_header_token(request: &ServiceRequest) ->
        Result<String, &'static str> {
    match request.headers().get("user-token") {
        Some(token) => {
            match token.to_str() {
                Ok(processed_password) => Ok(
                    String::from(processed_password)),
                Err(_processed_password) => Err(
                    "there was an error processing token")
            }
        },
        None => Err("there is no token")
    }
}
```

Here, we get the token under the `user-token` key. If this key does not exist, then we return an error stating that is does not exist. If the token does exist, then we try and convert it into a string. If that fails, we then return an error pointing out that there was an error in processing the token; otherwise, we return the token as a string.

Now that we have password checking and password extraction functions, we just need a public function to act as an entry point to this process and orchestrate these functions:

```
pub fn process_token(request: &ServiceRequest) -> Result<
        String, &'static str> {
    match extract_header_token(request) {
        Ok(token) => check_password(token),
        Err(message) => Err(message)
    }
}
```

Here, we are matching the result of the extraction of the password, and then matching the password check. The benefit of this approach is that if we want to add extra functionality, we can slot it in and out of the process.

Now, we have to remember to define our entry point in our `views/mod.rs` file with `pub mod token;`. We can use this process in our middleware approach in the `main.rs` file. Here, we need to import the service:

```
use actix_service::Service;
```

Our main server has the same setup. However, we have inserted a `wrap_fn` function. This configures the middleware for the server via a closure:

```
#[actix_rt::main]
async fn main() -> std::io::Result<()> {
    HttpServer::new(|| {
        let app = App::new()
            .wrap_fn(|req, srv| {
                if *&req.path().contains("/item/") {
                    match views::token::process_token(&req) {
                        Ok(_token) => println!(
                            "the token is passable"),
                        Err(message) => println!(
                            "token error: {}", message)
                    }
                }
                let fut = srv.call(req);
                async {
                    let result = fut.await?;
                    Ok(result)
                }
            }).configure(views::views_factory);
        return app
    })
        .bind("127.0.0.1:8000")?
        .run()
        .await
}
```

In the closure, we pass in the service request and the routing. We then check to see if the item is in the path, checking the password and printing the outcome if this is the case. We then create a future with the `call` function belonging to the routing, and then await for this to complete and return the result.

Making a call to an item view with no `user-token` in the header gives us `token error: there is no token` in the console's output. Adding a token with an incorrect value (not "token") gives us `token error: token not authorised`, while adding the correct value give us `the token is passable`.

With all this, we have reached this chapter's objectives of building a range of request handlers that extract and return data using a range of processes.

Summary

Here, we have put all of what we have learned in the previous chapters to good use. We fused the logic from the to do item factory, loaded and saved it from a JSON file, and looked at the to do item process logic by using the basic views from `Actix-web`. With this, we have been able to see how the isolated modules click together. We will keep reaping the benefits of this approach in the next few chapters as we rip out the JSON file that loads and saves a database.

We also managed to utilize the `serde` crate to serialize complex data structures. This allows our users to get the full state update returned to them when they make an edit. We also built on our knowledge of futures, async blocks, and closures to intercept requests before they reach the view. Now, we can see that the power of Rust is enabling us to do some highly customizable things to our server, without us having to dig deep into the framework.

With this, it is clear that Rust has a strong future in web development. Despite its infancy, we can get things up and running with little to no code. With a few more lines of code and a closure, we are building our own middleware. Our JSON serialization structs were made possible with just one line of code, and the traits provided by `Actix` enabled us to merely define the parameter in the `view` function, thus enabling the view to automatically extract the data from the body and serialize it into the struct. This scalable, powerful, and standardized way of passing data is more concise than many high-level languages.

Now that we are processing and returning well-structured data to the user, we can start displaying it in an interactive way for our user to point and click when editing, creating, and deleting to do items. In the next chapter, we will be serving HTML with Rust. We will then insert CSS and JavaScript into the view to enable dynamic functionality.

In the next chapter, we will be serving **HTML**, **CSS**, and **JavaScript** from the `Actix-web` server. This will enable us to see and interact with to-do items via a graphical user interface, with the JavaScript making API calls to the endpoints we defined in this chapter.

Questions

1. What is the difference between a GET request and POST request?

2. Why would we have middleware when we check credentials?

3. How do you enable a custom struct to be directly returned in a view?

4. How do you enact middleware for the server?

5. How do you enable a custom struct to serialize data into the view?

5
Displaying Content in the Browser

While it is useful in some situations to just have the to do item API endpoints that we defined in the previous chapter, it is not useful for a user if this is all we have. While we can utilize frontend frameworks such as **React**, **Vue**, and **Angular**, these can be overkill for simple applications. With our app, we can directly serve **HTML**, **JavaScript**, and **CSS** from our server to the user.

In this chapter, we will cover the following topics:

- Serving HTML data using Rust
- Serving HTML files using Rust
- Injecting JavaScript files into views
- Injecting CSS files into views
- Creating a base CSS that can be inherited by multiple views
- Creating frontend components that can be injected into multiple views

By the end of this chapter, we will have created a single page that will render our to-do items. These items will have their own edit and delete buttons that will utilize JavaScript to make API calls to our server, which will then update the to-do item's state. Finally, we will create our own frontend components that can be utilized in different views.

Technical requirements

We will be building on the server code we created in the previous chapter, which can be found at `https://github.com/PacktPublishing/Rust-Web-Programming/tree/master/Chapter04/extracting_data`.

You can find the full source code that will be used in this chapter here: `https://github.com/PacktPublishing/Rust-Web-Programming/tree/master/Chapter05`.

The CiA videos for this book can be viewed at: `http://bit.ly/3jULCrw`.

Displaying HTML in the browser from a server

So far, we have been processing data and returning it in JSON format. This is great, and we will be continuing to use this JSON format throughout the rest of this book. However, it is not very useful for a standard user. We need the data to be displayed when the user visits the URL. This view utilizes buttons and forms, enabling the user to interact with the API endpoints. Before this, we had to use **Postman** to interact with those APIs.

There are a couple of crates that enable developers to render HTML for users in Rust. In order to do this, we will need to structure our own app views module, which takes the following structure:

```
└── views
├── app
│   ├── items.rs
│   └── mod.rs
```

In our `items.rs` file, we will be defining the main view that displays the to-do items. However, before we do that, we should explore the simplest way in which we can return HTML in the `items.rs` file:

```
use actix_web::HttpResponse;

pub async fn items() -> HttpResponse {
    HttpResponse::Ok()
        .content_type("text/html; charset=utf-8")
        .body("<h1>Items</h1>")
}
```

Here, we simply return a `HttpResponse` struct that has a HTML content type and a body of `<h1>Items</h1>`. In order to plumb this into the app, we have to define our factory in the `app/views/mod.rs` file, as follows:

```
use actix_web::web;
mod items;
use super::path::Path;

pub fn app_factory(app: &mut web::ServiceConfig) {
    let base_path: Path = Path{prefix: String::from("/")};
    app.route(&base_path.define(String::from("")),
            web::get().to(items::items));
}
```

We should be fairly familiar with the development of view factories by now. In this factory, we do not have any URL prefix because this is our main URL get functions for the user. Once we have defined our `app_factory`, we can call it in our `views/mod.rs` file. First, we have to define the app module at the top of the `views/mod.rs` file:

```
mod app;
```

Once we have defined the `views/mod.rs` file, we can call the app factory in the `views_factory` factory function within the same file:

```
app::app_factory(app);
```

Now that our HTML serving view is part of our app, we can run it. Calling the home URL in our browser giving us the following output:

Figure 5.1 – First rendered HTML view

Here, we can see that the header tag is being rendered. From this, we can see that the browser can render the HTML string in the response body. Considering this, there is nothing stopping us from reading an HTML file to a string, and then passing it to the body to be returned. In order to achieve this, we can build our own content loader.

To build a basic content loader, we will start by building a HTML file reading function in the `views/app/content_loader.rs` file:

```rust
use std::fs;


pub fn read_file(file_path: &str) -> String {
    let data: String = fs::read_to_string(
        file_path).expect("Unable to read file");
    return data
}
```

All we have to do here is return a string because this is all we need for the response body. We can then define the loader in the `views/app/mod.rs` file with the `mod content_loader;` line at the top of the file.

Now that we have a loading function, we need an HTML directory. This can be defined alongside the `src` directory, and is called `templates`. Inside the `templates` directory, we can add an HTML file called `templates/main.html` with the following content:

```html
<!DOCTYPE html>
<html lang="en">
    <head>
        <meta charSet="UTF-8"/>
        <meta name="viewport" content="width=device-width,
            initial-scale=1.0"/>
        <meta httpEquiv="X-UA-Compatible" content="ie=edge"/>
        <meta name="description" content="This is a simple
            to do app"/>
        <title>To Do App</title>
    </head>
    <body>
        <h1>To Do Items</h1>
    </body>
</html>
```

With the `meta` tags, we can define our `viewport`. This tells the browser how to handle the dimensions and scaling of the page content as there are different devices with different screen sizes. With `viewport`, we set the width of the page to the same width of the device screen.

We must then set the initial zoom of the page to `1`. With the `httpEquiv` tag, we will define it as `X-UA-Compatible`, which means we support older browsers. The final tag is simply a description of the page that can be used by search engines and more. Our `title` tag ensures that `to do app` is displayed on the browser tag. We then have our standard header title in our body.

With this, we can load this HTML file into our items view and then pass it into the response body, as shown here:

```
use actix_web::HttpResponse;
use super::content_loader::read_file;


pub async fn items() -> HttpResponse {
    let html_data = read_file(
        "./templates/main.html");
    HttpResponse::Ok()
        .content_type("text/html; charset=utf-8")
        .body(html_data)
}
```

With this, we can run the app and hit the main URL. Moreover, we can see that the tab has the desired label and content:

To Do Items

Figure 5.2 – View after loading the HTML page

At this point, we have to take stock of what is happening here. The app is loading the HTML file and passing the data from the HTML file as a string into the response body. The body of the HTML data is not the only thing that is being rendered by the browser.

The meta data that was defined in the head is also being rendered. Therefore, there is nothing stopping us from taking full advantage of building our frontend in these HTML files. We also have to note that the HTML files are not being compiled with the Rust app. Therefore, we can edit the HTML files and refresh the browser. Our changes will be shown instantly, without us having to recompile. With this in mind, we can add some input and functionality to our view:

```
<body>
    <h1>To Do Items</h1>
    <input type="text" id="name" placeholder="create to do
        item">
    <button id="create-button" value="Send">Create</button>
</body>
<script>
    let createButton = document.getElementById(
        "create-button");
    createButton.addEventListener("click", postAlert);

    function postAlert() {
        let titleInput = document.getElementById("name");
        alert(titleInput.value);
        titleInput.value = null;
    }
</script>
```

Here, we have a text input field and a **Create** button under the title. We can now bind the **Create** button to the `postAlert` function by creating an event listener. In the `postAlert` function, we get the value of the text input, print it out in an alert box, and then set the value to `null`.

Saving the HTML file and refreshing the URL gives us the following output:

To Do Items

create to do item　Create

Figure 5.3 – Interactive view from loading the HTML page

Filling in the text box and clicking the **Create** button gives us an alert stating the value that was entered into the text field. After this, the text field is then cleared, so the whole process can be done again.

Here, we can see that our string in the body of the response also returns JavaScript, and that this is also processed correctly by the browser. However, putting all our JavaScript into the HTML file has some limitations. We might want to use the same JavaScript code in different HTML views. We also do not want our HTML files to balloon into a massive mixture of JavaScript, CSS, and HTML in one file. Because of this, we should really manage our JavaScript in different files.

Here, we have managed to define HTML files and serve them to the browser without the need to add any additional third-party crates. In the next section, we will utilize some JavaScript files to give our HTML more functionality.

Injecting JavaScript into HTML

Once we have finished this section, we will have a not so pretty but fully functional main view where we can add, edit, and delete to do items using JavaScript to make calls to our Rust server. However, as you may recall, we did not add a `delete` API endpoint. In order to inject JavaScript into our HTML, we will have to carry out the following steps:

1. Create a `delete` item API endpoint.

2. Add a `JavaScript loading` function and replace the JavaScript tag in the HTML data with the loaded JavaScript data in the main item Rust view.

3. Add a JavaScript tag in the HTML file and add IDs to the HTML components so that we can reference the components in our JavaScript.

4. Build a `rendering` function for our to-do items in JavaScript and bind it to our HTML via IDs.

5. Build a `button rendering` function in JavaScript based off item data for the ID.

6. Build an `API call` function in JavaScript to talk to the backend.

7. Build the `get`, `delete`, `edit`, and `create` functions in JavaScript for our buttons to use.

Let's go over this in more detail:

1. Adding the `delete` API endpoint should be fairly straightforward now. If you want to, you can try and implement this view by yourself as you should be comfortable with the process now.

    If you are struggling, we can achieve this by importing the following dependencies into the `views/to_do/delete.rs` file:

    ```rust
    use actix_web::{web, HttpResponse};
    use serde_json::value::Value;
    use serde_json::Map;

    use super::utils::return_state;
    use crate::state::read_file;

    use crate::to_do::to_do_factory;
    use crate::json_serialization::to_do_item::ToDoItem;
    use crate::processes::process_input;
    ```

2. Once this is done, we can define the `delete` view function by using the following code:

    ```rust
    pub async fn delete(to_do_item: web::Json<ToDoItem>) ->
            HttpResponse {
        let state: Map<String, Value> =
            read_file("./state.json");
        let title: String = to_do_item.title.clone();
        let status: String = to_do_item.status.clone();

        match to_do_factory(&status, title) {
            Err(_item) => return
            HttpResponse::BadRequest().json(
                format!("{} not accepted", status)),
            Ok(item) => process_input(item,
                String::from("delete"), &state)
        }
        return HttpResponse::Ok().json(return_state())
    }
    ```

    Here, we load the state with the `read_file` function. We then extract the title and the status from Json<ToDoItem>. After that, we create a to do item struct by passing title and status through to_do_factory and then process it with a delete command. We then return our updated items by using the return_state function in the JSON body of the response.

After that, we must register our delete view by importing it at the top of the views/to_do/mods.rs file with mod delete. Then, we must define our view as a post method in our factory:

```
app.route(&base_path.define(String::from("/delete")),
          web::post().to(delete::delete));
```

3. Now that we have all our endpoints ready, we have to revisit our main app view. We established in the previous section that the JavaScript in the <script> section works even though this is just all part of one big string.

    To put our JavaScript into a separate file, our view must load the HTML file as a string that has a {{JAVASCRIPT}} tag in the <script> section of the HTML file. We can then load the JavaScript file as a string and replace the {{JAVASCRIPT}} tag with the string from the JavaScript file. After that, we need to return the full string in the body of the views/app/items.rs file:

```
pub async fn items() -> HttpResponse {
    let mut html_data = read_file(
        "./templates/main.html");
    let javascript_data = read_file(
        "./javascript/main.js");

    html_data = html_data.replace("{{JAVASCRIPT}}",
        &javascript_data);
    HttpResponse::Ok()
        .content_type("text/html; charset=utf-8")
        .body(html_data)
}
```

4. From this, we can see that we need to build a new directory in the root called
    `JavaScript`. We will create a file in it called `main.js`. By making this change to
    the app view, we are also going to have to change the `templates/main.html` file
    with the following code:

```
<body>
    <h1>Done Items</h1>
    <div id="doneItems"></div>
    <h1>To Do Items</h1>
    <div id="pendingItems"></div>
    <input type="text" id="name" placeholder="create
        to do item">
    <button id="create-button"
        value="Send">Create</button>
</body>
<script>
    {{JAVASCRIPT}}
</script>
```

Remember that our endpoints return pending items and completed items. Because
of this, we have defined both lists with their own titles. Our `div` with an ID of
`"doneItems"` is where we will insert the done to do items from an API call.

We can then insert our pending items from an API call into our `div` with an ID of
`"pendingItems"`. Once we've done that, we can define an input with text and a
button. This will be for our user to create a new item.

5. Now that our HTML has been defined, we are going to define the logic in our
    `javascript/main.js` file. First of all, we have to define the function that
    renders the items from an API call:

```
function renderItems(items, processType,
                     elementId, processFunction) {
    let placeholder = "<div>";
    let itemsMeta = [];
    for (i = 0; i < items.length; i++) {
        let title = items[i]["title"];
        let placeholderId = processType +
```

```
            "-" + title.replaceAll(" ", "-");

        placeholder += "<div>" + title +
            "<button " + 'id="' + placeholderId + '">'
            + processType +
            '</button>' + "</div>";
        itemsMeta.push({"id": placeholderId, "title":
            title});
    }
    placeholder += "</div>"
    document.getElementById(elementId).innerHTML =
        placeholder;

    for (i = 0; i < itemsMeta.length; i++) {
        document.getElementById(
            itemsMeta[i]["id"]).addEventListener(
            "click", processFunction);
    }
}
```

Here, the function takes in a list of items to render. `processType` is a string that defines what type of process is going to be carried out. For our pending items, we will have a `"edit"` process to enable the user to set the item to completed. The completed list will have a `"delete"` process to delete the completed item. The function then takes the `elementId` parameter. This is the ID in the HTML of the section being rendered. The `processFunction` parameter is a function that will fire the right API call for the desired process.

6. Inside the `renderItems` function, we define the string containing the HTML being inserted under the `placeholder` variable. This gets added `later` on. We must also define an empty array called `itemsMeta`, where we can place titles in order to add even listeners later on:

```
    let placeholder = "<div>"
    let itemsMeta = [];
```

Now, we must loop through our items. Within this loop, we will extract the title of the item and create an ID of `processType`. The title will be filled in with the following:

```
for (i = 0; i < items.length; i++) {
    let title = items[i]["title"];
    let placeholderId = processType +
        "-" + title.replaceAll(" ", "-");
```

7. We will then add a `div` with the item title to the `placeholder` string, and then a button with the ID that we have formed to `placeholder`:

```
placeholder += "<div>" + title +
    "<button " + 'id="' + placeholderId + '">'
    + processType +
    '</button>' + "</div>";
itemsMeta.push({"id": placeholderId, "title":
    title});
}
```

We have also pushed a dictionary with the ID and title to the `itemsMeta` array. Once the loop has finished, we will have all the items defined with buttons and titles in the `placeholder` string. We can then add a `</div>` to the end of the `placeholder` string. At this point, we are at the section of HTML that contains an ID that is the same as `elementId`. Here, we must define `innerHTML` of that as the `placeholder` string:

```
placeholder += "</div>"
document.getElementById(elementId).innerHTML =
    placeholder;
```

We can then loop through the `itemsMeta` array to define event listeners for each ID that belongs to those individual buttons. We must create event listeners tied to that `id` based on a click. We will pass `processFunction` through `renderItems`, thus closing the `renderItems` function after this:

```
for (i = 0; i < itemsMeta.length; i++) {
    document.getElementById(
        itemsMeta[i]["id"]).addEventListener(
        "click", processFunction);
    }
}
```

Now, `processFunction` will fire if a button that we created next to a to do item is clicked.

8. Now that we have our render function, we can move to our API call function and define it in the `javascript/main.js` file as well. The function takes in a URL, which is the endpoint of the API call. It also takes in a method, which is string of either POST, GET, and PUT. Now, we can define our request object:

```
function apiCall(url, method) {
    let xhr = new XMLHttpRequest();
    xhr.withCredentials = true;
```

Then, we must define the event listener inside the `apiCall` function. This renders the to do items with the JSON returned once the call has finished:

```
xhr.addEventListener('readystatechange', function() {
    if (this.readyState === this.DONE) {
        renderItems(JSON.parse(
            this.responseText)["pending_items"],
            "edit", "pendingItems", editItem);
        renderItems(JSON.parse(
            this.responseText)["done_items"],
            "delete", "doneItems", deleteItem);
    }
});
```

Here, we can see that we are passing in the IDs that we defined in the `templates/main.html` file. We also passed in the response from the API call. We can also see that we passed in the `editItem` function, meaning that we are going to fire an `edit` function when a button alongside a pending item is clicked, turning the item into a done item. Considering this, if a button does belong to a done item, the `deleteItem` function is fired. For now, we will continue building the `apiCall` function. After this, we will build the `editItem` and `deleteItem` functions. We also know that every time the `apiCall` function is called, the items are rendered.

Now that we have defined the event listener, we will prep the API call object with the method and the URL, define the headers, and then return the request object so that we can send it whenever we need to:

```
xhr.open(method, url);
xhr.setRequestHeader('content-type',
    'application/json');
xhr.setRequestHeader('user-token', 'token');
```

```
                return xhr
    }
```

9. Note that the header is just hardcoding the accepted token that is hardcoded in the backend. We will cover how to properly define auth headers in *Chapter 7, Managing User Sessions*. Now that our API call function has been defined, we can move on to the edit Item function:

```
function editItem() {
    let title = this.id.replaceAll("-", "
        ").replace("edit ", "");
    let call = apiCall("/item/edit", "PUT");
    let json = {
        "title": title,
        "status": "done"
    };
    call.send(JSON.stringify(json));
}
```

Here, we can see that the HTML section that the event listener belongs to can be accessed via this. We know that if we remove the "edit" word and switch "-" with an empty space, this will convert the ID into the title of the to do item. We can then utilize the apiCall function to define our endpoint and method. Once this has been defined, we can pass the title into a dictionary with the status set to done. This is because we know that we are switching the pending item to done. Once we've done this, we can send the API call with the JSON body.

10. We can use the same approach for the deleteItem function:

```
function deleteItem() {
    let title = this.id.replaceAll("-", " ").replace(
        "delete ", "");
    let call = apiCall("/item/delete", "POST");
    let json = {
        "title": title,
        "status": "done"
    };
    call.send(JSON.stringify(json));
}
```

With that, our rendering process has been fully processed. We have defined the `edit` and `delete` functions, as well as a `render` function. Now, we have to load the items when the page has initially loaded without having to click any buttons. This can be done with a simple API call:

```
function getItems() {
    let call = apiCall("/item/get", 'GET');
    call.send()
}
getItems();
```

Here, we can see that we just get the API call and GET method and send them. Note that our `getItems` function is being called outside the function. This will be fired once, when the view is loaded.

This has been a long stint of coding; however, we are nearly there. We only have to define the functionality of the create text input and button. We can manage this with a simple event listener and API call for the create endpoint:

```
document.getElementById("create-button").
    addEventListener(
    "click", createItem);


function createItem() {
    let title = document.getElementById("name");
    let call = apiCall("/item/create/" + title.value,
        "POST");
    call.send();
    document.getElementById("name").value = null;
}
```

We also set the text input value to null. Hitting the main view for the app gives us the following output:

Done Items

washing

To Do Items

Figure 5.4 – Main page with rendered to do items

Now, to see if our frontend works the way we want it to, we can do the following:

1. Press the **delete** button next to the **washing** done item.

2. Type in eat cereal for breakfast and click **Create**.

3. Type in eat ramen for breakfast and click **Create**.

4. Click **edit** for the **eat ramen for breakfast** item.

These steps should yield the following result:

Figure 5.5 – Main page after completing the aforementioned steps

Here, we have a fully functioning web app. All the buttons work, and the lists are instantly updated. However, it does not look very pretty. There is no spacing, and everything is in black and white. To alter this, we need to integrate CSS into our HTML file.

Injecting CSS into HTML

Injecting CSS follows the same approach as injecting JavaScript. We will have a CSS tag in the HTML file that will be replaced with the CSS from the file. To achieve this, we must carry out the following steps:

1. Add CSS tags to our HTML file.
2. Create a base CSS file for the whole app.
3. Create a CSS file for our main view.
4. Update our Rust crate to serve the CSS and JavaScript.

Let us have a closer look at the preceding steps by initially adding CSS tags to our HTML files with the following sections.

Adding CSS tags to our HTML file

First of all, let's make some changes to our templates/main.html file:

```
<style>
    {{BASE_CSS}}
    {{CSS}}
</style>
<body>
    <div class="mainContainer">
        <h1>Done Items</h1>
        <div id="doneItems"></div>
        <h1>To Do Items</h1>
        <div id="pendingItems"></div>
        <div class="inputContainer">
            <input type="text"
                id="name" placeholder="create to do item">
            <div class="actionButton"
                id="create-button"
                value="Send">Create</div>
        </div>
    </div>
</body>
<script>
    {{JAVASCRIPT}}
```

```
</script>
```

Here, we can see that we have two CSS tags. The {{BASE_CSS}} tag is for base CSS and will be consistent in multiple different views, such as the background color and column ratios, depending on the screen size. The {{BASE_CSS}} tag is for managing CSS classes for this particular view. The css/base.css and css/main.css files have been made for our views. Note that we have put all the items in a div with a class called mainContainer.

This will enable us to center all the items on the screen. We also added some more classes so that the CSS can reference them, and then changed the button for Create to div. Now, we can define our base CSS in our css/base.css file.

Creating a base CSS file for the whole app

We will execute the following steps to create a base CSS file:

1. First, we must define the body background color and font. We must also ensure that the background color covers 100% of the window, even if the content does not cover all the window with the height tag. We can do this by defining the following code:

   ```css
   body {
       background-color: #92a8d1;
       font-family: Arial, Helvetica, sans-serif;
       height: 100vh;
   }
   ```

2. We must then define a media query for when the size of the window is the same as a smartphone. If a smartphone is accessing our app, we do not want multiple columns; we want it to span the entire width. We can define this using a CSS grid, as follows:

   ```css
   @media(max-width: 500px) {
       body {
           padding: 1px;
           display: grid;
           grid-template-columns: 1fr;
       }
   }
   ```

3. If our screen gets a little bigger, we can split our page into three different vertical columns. However, the middle column has a width ratio of 5:1 compared to the two other columns, which are either side. This is because our screen is still not very big, and we want our items to take up most of the screen. We can adjust this by adding another media query with different parameters:

```css
@media(min-width: 501px) and (max-width: 550px) {
    body {
        padding: 1px;
        display: grid;
        grid-template-columns: 1fr 5fr 1fr;
    }
    .mainContainer {grid-column-start: 2;}
}
```

4. If our screen gets larger, we want to adjust the ratios even more as we do not want the width of our items to get out of control. In order to achieve this, we must define a 3:1 ratio for the middle column versus the two side columns, and then a 1:1 ratio for anything more than that:

```css
@media(min-width: 551px) and (max-width: 1000px) {
    body {
        padding: 1px;
        display: grid;
        grid-template-columns: 1fr 3fr 1fr;
    }
    .mainContainer {grid-column-start: 2;}
}
@media(min-width: 1001px) {
    body {
        padding: 1px;
        display: grid;
        grid-template-columns: 1fr 1fr 1fr;
    }
    .mainContainer {grid-column-start: 2;}
}
```

Now that we have defined the general CSS for all our views, we can move on to the view-specific CSS in our css/main.css file.

Creating a CSS file for our main view

In order to create a CSS file for the main view, we'll have to carry out these steps:

1. Here, we have to break down our app components. We have a list of to do items. Each item in the list will be a div, which has a different background color:

    ```
    .itemContainer {
        background: #034f84;
        margin: 0.3rem;
    }
    ```

    Here, we can see that this class has a margin of 0.3. We are using rem because we want the margin to scale relatively to the font size of the root element. We also want our item to slightly change color if our curser hovers over it:

    ```
    .itemContainer:hover {
        background: #034f99;
    }
    ```

2. Inside an item container, the title of our item is denoted with a paragraph tag. We want to define the style of all the paragraphs in the item containers but not elsewhere. We can define the style of the paragraphs in the container by using the following code:

    ```
    .itemContainer p {
        color: white;
        display: inline-block;
        margin: 0.5rem;
        margin-right: 0.4rem;
        margin-left: 0.4rem;
    }
    ```

    inline-block allows the title to be displayed alongside div, which will be the acting as the button for the item. The margin definitions merely stop the title from being right up against the edge of the item container. We also ensure that the paragraph color is white.

3. With our item title styled, the only item styling left is the action button, which is either edit or delete. This action button is going to float to the right with a different background color so that we know where to click. To do this, we will define our button style with a class, as shown in the following code:

```
.actionButton {
    display: inline-block;
    float: right;
    background: #f7786b;
    border: none;
    padding: 0.5rem;
    padding-left: 2rem;
    padding-right: 2rem;
    color: white;
}
```

Now that we have defined our view specific CSS in our `css/main.css` file, we can update our Rust crate to define CSS and JavaScript.

Updating our Rust crate to serve our CSS and JavaScript

We'll be updating our Rust crate to include CSS, HTML, and JavaScript by executing the following steps:

1. Here, we've defined the display, made it float to the right, and defined the background color and padding. With this, we can ensure the color changes when we hover over the button by running the following code:

    ```
    .actionButton:hover {
        background: #f7686b;
        color: black;
    }
    ```

2. Now that we have covered all the concepts, we only have to define the styles for the input container. This can be done by running the following code:

    ```
    .inputContainer {
        background: #034f84;
        margin: 0.3rem;
        margin-top: 2rem;
    }


    .inputContainer input {
        display: inline-block;
    ```

```
        margin: 0.4rem;
    }
```

3. With that, we have defined all of the **CSS** that we need. However, our items will not utilize this unless we update our `renderItems` function with the following code:

```
function renderItems(items, processType,
                     elementId, processFunction) {
    let placeholder = "<div>"
    let itemsMeta = [];

    for (i = 0; i < items.length; i++) {
        let title = items[i]["title"];
        let placeholderId = processType +
            "-" + title.replaceAll(" ", "-");

        placeholder += '<div class="itemContainer">' +
            '<p>' + title + '</p>' +
            '<div class="actionButton" ' +
            'id="' + placeholderId + '">'
            + processType + '</div>' + "</div>";
        itemsMeta.push({"id": placeholderId, "title":
            title});
    }
    placeholder += "</div>"
    document.getElementById(elementId).innerHTML =
        placeholder;

    for (i = 0; i < itemsMeta.length; i++) {
        document.getElementById(
            itemsMeta[i]["id"]).addEventListener(
            "click", processFunction);
    }
}
```

Here, we can see that our title now has a paragraph tag, and that our button now utilizes the `actionButton` class.

4. We're done! We have defined all of the **CSS**, **JavaScript**, and **HTML** we'll need. Before we run the app, we need to load the data into the main view of the `views/app/items.rs` file. We can do this by reading the HTML, JavaScript, main CSS, and main CSS files. We must then replace our tags in the HTML data with the data from the other files:

```
pub async fn items() -> HttpResponse {
    let mut html_data = read_file(
        "./templates/main.html");
    let javascript_data: String = read_file(
        "./javascript/main.js");
    let css_data: String = read_file(
        "./css/main.css");
    let base_css_data: String = read_file(
        "./css/base.css");
    html_data = html_data.replace("{{JAVASCRIPT}}",
        &javascript_data);
    html_data = html_data.replace("{{CSS}}",
        &css_data);
    html_data = html_data.replace("{{BASE_CSS}}",
        &base_css_data);
    HttpResponse::Ok()
        .content_type("text/html; charset=utf-8")
        .body(html_data)
}
```

Now, when we spin up our server, we will have a fully running app with an intuitive frontend that will look as follows:

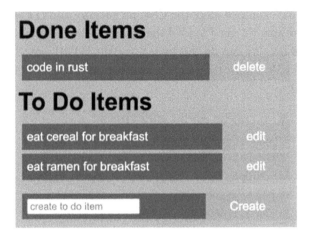

Figure 5.6 – Main page after CSS

Even though our app is functioning and we have configured the base CSS and HTML, we may want to have reusable standalone HTML structures that have their own CSS. These structures can be injected into views as and when needed. What this does is give us the ability to write a component once, and then import it into other HTML files. This, in turn, makes it easier to maintain, and ensures the component is consistent when it's used in multiple views. For instance, if we create an info bar at the top of the view, we will want it have the same styling as the other views. Therefore, it makes sense to create an info bar once as a component, and then insert it into other views.

Inheriting components

Sometimes, we will want to build a component that can be injected into views. To do this, we are going to have to load both the CSS and HTML, and then insert them into the correct parts of the HTML.

To do this, we must create a `add_component` function that takes the name of the component, creates tags from the component name, and loads the HTML and CSS based on the component's name. We will define this function in the `views/app/content_loader.rs` file:

```
pub fn add_component(component_tag: String,
                     html_data: String) -> String {
    let css_tag: String = component_tag.to_uppercase() +
                          &String::from("_CSS");
```

```
    let html_tag: String = component_tag.to_uppercase() +
                           &String::from("_HTML");
    let css_path = String::from("./templates/components/")
                   + &component_tag.to_lowercase() +
                   &String::from(".css");
    let css_loaded = read_file(&css_path);


    let html_path = String::from("./templates/components/")
                    + &component_tag.to_lowercase() +
                    &String::from(".html");
    let html_loaded = read_file(&html_path);


    let html_data = html_data.replace(html_tag.as_str(),
                                      &html_loaded);
    let html_data = html_data.replace(css_tag.as_str(),
                                      &css_loaded);
    return html_data
}
```

Here, we can see that we used the read_file function, which is defined in the same file. We then injected the component HTML and CSS into the view data. Note that we nested our components in a templates/components/ directory. For this instance, we are inserting a header component, so our add_component function will try and load the header.html and header.css files when we pass our header into the add_component function. In our templates/components/header.html file, we must define the following HTML:

```
<div class="header">
    <p>complete tasks: </p><p id="completeNum"></p>
    <p>pending tasks: </p><p id="pendingNum"></p>
</div>
```

Here, we are merely displaying the counts for the number of completed and pending to-do items. In our templates/components/header.css file, we must define the following CSS:

```
.header {
    background: #034f84;
    margin-bottom: 0.3rem;
}
```

```
.header p {
    color: white;
    display: inline-block;
    margin: 0.5rem;
    margin-right: 0.4rem;
    margin-left: 0.4rem;
}
```

For our `add_component` function to insert our CSS and HTML into the right place, we must insert the HEADER tag into the `<style>` section of the `templates/main.html` file:

```
. . .
    <style>
        {{BASE_CSS}}
        {{CSS}}
        HEADER_CSS
    </style>
    <body>
        <div class="mainContainer">
            HEADER_HTML
            <h1>Done Items</h1>
. . .
```

Now that all of our HTML and CSS has been defined, we need to import our `add_component` function into our `views/app/items.rs` file:

```
use super::content_loader::add_component;
```

In the same file, we have to add the header to the `items` view function. Use the following code to do so:

```
html_data = add_component(String::from("header"), html_data);
```

Now, we have to alter the apiCall function in our injecting_header/
javascript/main.js file to ensure that the header is updated with the to-do
item's counts:

```
document.getElementById("completeNum").innerHTML =
    JSON.parse(this.responseText)["done_item_count"];
document.getElementById("pendingNum").innerHTML = JSON.parse(
    this.responseText)["pending_item_count"];
```

Upon inserting our component, we get the following rendered view:

Figure 5.7 – Main page with header

As we can see, our header displays the data correctly. As long as we add the header tags to
the view HTML file and we call the add_component in our view, we will get that header.
With this, we have covered all this chapter's objectives.

Summary

In this chapter, we enabled our application so that it can be used by a casual user as opposed to having to rely on a third-party application such as Postman. We defined our own app views module that housed read file and insert functions. This resulted in us building a process that loaded an HTML file, inserted data from a JavaScript file and CSS file into the view data, and then served that data.

This gave us a dynamic view that automatically updated when we edited, deleted, or created a to-do item. We also explored some basics around CSS and JavaScript to make API calls from the frontend, as well as how to dynamically edit the HTML of certain sections of our view. We also styled the whole view based on the size of the window. Note we did not rely on external crates. This is because we want to be able to understand how we can process our own HTML data.

Also, we do not want to be dependent on the web framework that we are using. The external crates around HTML rendering are still fairly new, and there is a chance that breaking changes could be implemented. Unlike routing views on a server, loading and serving HTML, CSS, and JavaScript is fairly straightforward. Therefore, the trade-off of coding our own HTML serving mechanism to maintain stability is a sensible one.

While our app now works at face value, it is not scalable in terms of data storage. We do not have data filter processes. No checks are done on the data that we store, and we do not have multiple tables.

In the next chapter, we will build data models that interact with a **PostgreSQL** database that runs locally in Docker.

Questions

1. What is the simplest way to return HTML data to the user's browser?

2. What is the simplest (not scalable) way to return HTML, CSS, and JavaScript data to the user's browser?

3. How do you ensure that the background color and style standards of certain elements is consistent across all views of the app?

4. How do you update the HTML after an API call?

5. How do we enable a button to connect to our backend API?

Section 3: Data Persistence

Data persistence is essential for modern day web applications as the demand on web applications is increasing. Luckily Rust has tools that can enable data persistence on PostgreSQL and other databases. With these tools combined with JSON Web Tokens, we can manage the user sessions on our Rust application.

However, this is not the end of data persistence. Due to the increasing demand on web applications, we also have to optimize the persistence, reading, and writing of our data. This is where RESTful service concepts come in handy. Implementing these concepts will have us caching data in our frontend with JavaScript to prevent excessive strain on our Rust application and improve the user's experience. Logging processes in our server are also going to be a good way to determine where to optimize them.

This section focuses on persisting data through a PostgreSQL database and managing it through Docker and the Diesel crate. It also covers migrations, unique constraints, and API endpoints that create and delete users. It also covers the key concepts behind RESTful services and how to apply them to our Rust application. This also includes implementing RESTful concepts to our frontend JavaScript files.

This section comprises the following chapters:

- *Chapter 06, Data Persistence with PostgreSQL*
- *Chapter 07, Managing User Sessions*
- *Chapter 08, Building RESTful Services*

6
Data Persistence with PostgreSQL

The frontend has now been defined, and our app is working at face value. However, we know that our app is reading and writing from a **JSON** file.

In this chapter, we get rid of our JSON file and introduce a **PostgreSQL** database to store our data. We do this by setting up a database development environment using Docker. We also look into how to monitor the Docker database container. We then create migrations in order to build the schema for our database, and then build data models in **Rust** to interact with the database. We then refactor our app so that the create, edit, and delete endpoints interact with the database instead of the JSON file.

In this chapter, we will cover the following topics:

- Building our PostgreSQL database
- Connecting to PostgreSQL with Diesel
- Connecting our application to PostgreSQL
- Creating our data models and migrations
- Getting data from the database
- Inserting data into the database

- Editing the database
- Deleting data

By the end of the chapter, you will be able to manage an application that performs reading, writing, and deleting data in a PostgreSQL database with data models. If we make changes to the data models, we will be able to manage them with migrations.

Technical requirements

In this chapter, we will be using Docker to define and run a PostgreSQL database. This will enable our app to interact with a database on our local machine. Docker can be installed by following the instructions in the URL: `https://docs.docker.com/engine/install/`.

You can find the full source code used in this chapter here: `https://github.com/PacktPublishing/Rust-Web-Programming/tree/master/Chapter06`.

We will also be using `docker-compose` on top of Docker to orchestrate our Docker containers. This can be installed by following the instructions in the URL: `https://docs.docker.com/compose/install/`.

The CiA videos for this book can be viewed at: `http://bit.ly/3jULCrw`.

Building our PostgreSQL database

In this section, we will be able to monitor the state of Docker containers, and configure and run a PostgreSQL database Docker container. So far, we have been using a JSON file to store our to-do items. This has served us well so far. In fact, there is no reason why we cannot use a JSON file throughout the rest of the book. However, there are some downsides to this outside of the book.

If the reads and writes to our JSON file increase, then we can have some concurrency issues and data corruption. There is also no checking on the type of data. Therefore, another developer can write a function that writes different data to the JSON file, and nothing will stand in the way.

There is also an issue with migrations. If we want to add a timestamp to the to-do items, this will only affect new to-do items that we insert into the JSON file. Therefore, some of our to-do items will have a timestamp, and others won't, which would introduce bugs into our app. Our JSON file also has limitations in terms of filtering.

Right now, all we do is read the whole data file, alter an item in the whole dataset, and write the whole dataset to the JSON file. This is not effective and will not scale well. It also inhibits us from linking these to-do items to another data model-like user. Plus, we can only search right now using the status. If we used a SQL database that has a user table that is linked to a to-do item database, we would be able to filter to-do items based on the user, status, or title. We can even use a combination thereof.

With all this in mind, it makes sense to go through the extra steps necessary to set up a SQL database and run it. In order to do this, we are going to use **Docker**. Docker enables us to build isolated containers that run applications in the same way as our PostgreSQL database. With Docker, we are able to spin up multiple databases and apps, and then shut them down as and when we need. First of all, we need to take stock of our containers by running the following command in the terminal:

```
docker container ls -a
```

If Docker is a fresh install, we get the following output:

```
CONTAINER ID   IMAGE   COMMAND   CREATED   STATUS   PORTS   NAMES
```

As we can see, we have no containers. We also need to take stock of our images. This can be done by running the following terminal command:

```
docker image ls
```

The preceding command gives the following output:

```
REPOSITORY   TAG   IMAGE ID   CREATED   SIZE
```

Again, if Docker is a fresh install, then there will be no containers.

There are other ways in which we can create a database in Docker. For instance, we can create our own **Dockerfile**, where we define our own **operating system (OS)**, and configurations. However, we have `docker-compose` installed. Using `docker-compose` will make the database definition fairly straightforward. It will also enable us to add more containers and services. To define our PostgreSQL database, we code the following **YAML** code in a `docker-compose.yml` file in the root directory:

```yaml
version: "3.7"

services:

  postgres:
```

```
container_name: 'to-do-postgres'
image: 'postgres:11.2'
restart: always
ports:
  - '5432:5432'
environment:
  - 'POSTGRES_USER=username'
  - 'POSTGRES_DB=to_do'
  - 'POSTGRES_PASSWORD=password'
```

As you can see, at the top of the file, we have defined the version. Older versions such as 2 or 1 have different styles in which the file is laid out. The different versions also support different arguments. At the time of writing this book, **version 3** is the latest version. The following URL covers the changes between each docker-compose version: https://docs.docker.com/compose/compose-file/compose-versioning/.

We then define our database service that is nested under the postgres tag. Tags such as postgres and services denote dictionaries, and lists are defined with - for each element. If we were to convert our docker-compose file to JSON, it would have the following structure:

```
{
    "version": "3.7",
    "services": {
        "postgres": {
            "container_name": "to-do-postgres",
            "image": "postgres:11.2",
            "restart": "always",
            "ports": [
                "5432:5432"
            ],
            "environment": [
                "POSTGRES_USER=username",
                "POSTGRES_DB=to_do",
                "POSTGRES_PASSWORD=password"
            ]
        }
```

```
    }
  }
```

We can see that our service is a dictionary of dictionaries, denoting each service. With this, we can deduce that we cannot have two tags with the same name as we cannot have two dictionary keys that are the same. It also tells us that we can keep stacking on service tags with their own parameters.

With our database service we have a name, so when we look at our containers, we know what the container is doing when we list the containers. In terms of configuring the database and building it, we luckily pull the official postgres image. That has everything configured for us, and Docker will pull it from the repository. The image is similar to a blueprint. We can spin up multiple containers with their own parameters from that one image that we pulled. We then define the start policy as always. This means that the container will always restart when the parameters are changed, even if there is a failure, and when the container is stopped. We can also define it to only restart if there is a failure or if the container stops.

It should be noted that Docker containers have their own ports that are not open to the machine. However, we can expose container ports and map the exposed port to an internal port inside the Docker container. Considering this, we define our ports.

Here we keep it simple. We state that we accept incoming traffic to the Docker container on port 5432 and route it through to the internal port 5432. We then define our environment variables, which are the username, the name of the database, and the password. While we are using generic, easy-to-remember passwords and usernames for this book, it is advised that you switch to more secure passwords and usernames if pushing to production. We can build a spin up for our system by navigating to the root directory where our docker-compose file is by running the following command:

```
docker-compose up
```

This will pull down the postgres image from the repository and start constructing the database. Following a flurry of log messages, the terminal should come to rest with the following output:

```
LOG:  listening on IPv4 address "0.0.0.0", port 5432
LOG:  listening on IPv6 address "::", port 5432
LOG:  listening on Unix socket "/var/run/
postgresql/.s.PGSQL.5432"
LOG:  database system was shut down at 2020-10-02 17:36:45 UTC
LOG:  database system is ready to accept connections
```

As you can see, the datetime will vary; however, what we are told here is that our database is ready to accept connections. Yes, it is really that easy. This is why Docker adoption is unstoppable. *Ctrl + C* will stop our `docker-compose` file, thus shutting down our `postgres` container.

We now list all our containers with the following command:

```
docker container ls -a
```

The preceding command gives us the following output:

CONTAINER ID	IMAGE	COMMAND
c99f3528690f	postgres:11.2	"docker-entrypoint.s…"

CREATED	STATUS	PORTS
4 hours ago	Exited (0) About a minute ago	

NAMES
to-do-postgres

We can see that all the parameters are there. The ports, however, are empty. This is because we stopped our service. If we were to start our service again, and list our containers in another terminal, the port 5432 would be under the PORTS tag. We have to keep note of CONTAINER ID as it's going to be unique and different/random for each container. We will need to reference these if we're accessing logs.

We can then list our containers with the following command:

```
docker image ls
```

The preceding command will now give us the following output:

REPOSITORY	TAG	IMAGE ID
postgres	11.2	3eda284d1840

CREATED	SIZE
17 months ago	312MB

We can see that our image has been pulled from the `postgres` repository. We also have a unique/random ID for the image, and we also have a date when that image was created.

Now that we have a basic understanding of how to get our database up and running, we can run our `docker-compose` file in the background with the following command:

```
docker-compose up -d
```

The preceding command just tells us which containers have been spun up with the following output:

```
Starting to-do-postgres ... done
```

We can see our status when we list our containers with the following output:

STATUS	PORTS	NAMES
Up About a minute	0.0.0.0:5432->5432/tcp	to-do-postgres

The other tags are the same, but we can also see that the STATUS tag tells us how long the container has been running, and which port it is occupying. While our `docker-compose` file is running in the background, it does not mean we cannot see what is going on. We can access the logs of the container at any time by calling the `logs` command and referencing the ID of the container by means of the following command:

```
docker logs c99f3528690f
```

This should give out the same output as our standard `docker-compose up` command. To stop our `docker-compose` file, we can run the `stop` command, shown as follows:

```
docker-compose stop
```

This will stop our containers in our `docker-compose` file. It has to be noted that this is different from the `down` command, shown as follows:

```
docker-compose down
```

The `down` command will also stop our containers. However, the `down` command will delete the container. If our database container is deleted, we will also lose all our data.

There is a configuration parameter called `volumes` that can prevent the deletion of our data when the container is removed; however, this is not essential for local development on our computers. In fact, you will be wanting to delete containers and images from your laptop regularly. *I once did a purge on my laptop of containers and images that I was no longer using, and this freed up 23 GB!*

Docker containers on our local development machines should be treated as temporary. While Docker containers are multiple, and more lightweight than standard virtual machines, they are not free. The idea behind Docker running on our local machines is that we can simulate what running our application would be like on a server. If it runs in Docker on our laptop, we can be certain that it will also run on our server, especially if the server is being managed by a production-ready Docker orchestration tool such as **Kubernetes**.

In this section, we set up our environment. We also understood the basics of Docker, enough to build, monitor, shut down, and delete our database with just a few simple commands. Now we can move on to the next section, where we'll be interacting with our database with Rust and the `diesel` crate.

Connecting to PostgreSQL with Diesel

Now that our database is running, in this section, we are going to build a connection to this database. We do this by performing the following steps:

1. First, we utilize the `diesel` crate. In order to do this, we can add the following dependencies to our `cargo.toml` file:

    ```
    diesel = { version = "1.4.4", features = ["postgres"].
    }
    dotenv = "0.15.0"
    ```

    In the preceding code, we have included a `postgres` feature in our `diesel` crate. We have also included the `dotenv` crate. This crate enables us to define variables in a `.env` file, which will then be passed through into our program. We will use this to pass it in the database credentials and then into processes.

2. Now that we have this defined, we also need to install the `diesel` client. This is because we will be running migrations to the database through our terminal as opposed to our app. We can do this with the following command:

    ```
    cargo install diesel_cli --no-default-features
    --features postgres
    ```

3. Now we have installed our client, we need to define the environment's DATABASE_
    URL URL. This will enable our client commands to connect to the database with the
    following command:

    ```
    echo DATABASE_URL=postgres://username:password@localhost/
    to_do > .env
    ```

    In this URL, our username is denoted as username, and our password is denoted
    as password. Our database is running on our own computer, which is denoted as
    localhost, and our database is called to_do. This creates a .env file in the root
    file outputting the following contents:

    ```
    DATABASE_URL=postgres://username:password@localhost/to_do
    ```

    It should be noted that database URLs usually include the port. However, port
    number 5432 is the default port for postgres, so it does not have to be defined in
    the URL we used.

4. Now that our variables are defined, we can start to set up our database.
    We need to *spin up* our database container with docker-compose with our
    docker-compose up command. We then set up our database with the
    following command:

    ```
    diesel setup
    ```

    The preceding command then creates a migrations directory in the root with the
    following structure:

    ```
    ── migrations
    │   └── 00000000000000_diesel_initial_setup
    │       ├── down.sql
    │       └── up.sql
    ```

    The up.sql file is fired when the migration is upgraded, and the down.sql file is
    fired when the migration is downgraded.

5. Now, we need to create our migration that will create our to-do items. This
    can be done by commanding our client to generate the migration with the
    following command:

    ```
    diesel migration generate create_to_do_items
    ```

The preceding command gives us the following file structure in our migrations:

```
├── migrations
│   ├── 00000000000000_diesel_initial_setup
│   │   ├── down.sql
│   │   └── up.sql
│   └── 2020-10-04-211444_create_to_do_items
│       ├── down.sql
│       └── up.sql
```

Unfortunately, with the diesel crate, we will have to create our own SQL files. However, this is not too much of a hassle. In our create to-do items migrations folder, we define our to_do table with the following SQL entries in our up.sql file:

```
CREATE TABLE to_do (
    id SERIAL PRIMARY KEY,
    title VARCHAR NOT NULL,
    status VARCHAR NOT NULL
)
```

In the preceding code, we have an ID of the item, which will be unique. We then have title and status, and these will be wrapped in a CREATE TABLE command. In our down.sql file, we need to drop the table if we are downgrading the migration with the following SQL command:

```
DROP TABLE to_do
```

6. Now that our migration is ready, we can run it with the following terminal command:

```
diesel migration run
```

The preceding command runs the migration creating the to_do table. Sometimes, we might introduce a different field type in the SQL. In order to rectify this, we can change SQL in our up.sql and down.sql files and run the following redo terminal command:

```
diesel migration redo
```

This will run the down.sql file and then run the up.sql file.

7. Now that we have run the migrations, we can run commands in our database Docker container to inspect that our database has the to_do table with the right fields that we defined. We can do this by running commands directly on our database container. We can enter the container under the username username, while pointing to the to_do database by using the following terminal command:

```
docker exec -it 5fdeda6cfe43 psql -U username to_do
```

It should be noted that, in this case, my container ID is 5fdeda6cfe43, but your container ID will be different. After running this command, we get a shell interface with the following prompt:

```
to_do=#
```

After this, when we type in \c, this will connect us to the database. This will usually be denoted with a statement saying that we are now connected to the database, to_do, and as user, username. Once this is done, typing in \d will list the relations, giving us the following table in the terminal:

Schema	Name	Type	Owner
public username	__diesel_schema_migrations	table	
public username	to_do	table	
public username	to_do_id_seq	sequence	

From the preceding table, we can see that there is a migrations table to keep track of what migration version the database is on.

8. We also have our to_do table and the sequence for the to_do item IDs. To inspect the schema, all we have to do is type in \d+ to_do, which gives us the following schema in the terminal:

Column	Type	Collation	Nullable
id	integer		not null
title	character varying		not null
status	character varying		not null

	Default	Storage

```
| nextval('to_do_id_seq'::regclass) | plain
|                                    | extended
|                                    | extended
```

We can see that our schema is exactly what we expected. Our migrations have worked. However, we may want to explore the state of our migrations further.

9. This is done by inspecting the migrations table where we will be able to see each version, and when the version was executed. In order to see this data, we directly run the following SQL command:

```
SELECT * FROM __diesel_schema_migrations;
```

This gives us the following table as output:

```
     version      |            run_on
------------------+----------------------------
 00000000000000   | 2020-10-04 20:26:04.263955
 20201004211444   | 2020-10-04 22:27:48.762202
```

As you can see, these migrations can be useful for debugging as sometimes we can forget to run a migration after updating a data model.

In this section, we have used the `diesel` client to connect to our database in a Docker container. We then defined the database URL in an environment file. We then initialized some migrations and created a table in our database. What is even better is that we directly connected with the Docker container where we could run a range of commands to explore our database. Now that our database is fully interactive via our client in the terminal, we can now start building our `to-do` item database models, so that our **Rust** app can interact with our database.

Connecting our application to PostgreSQL

In the previous section, we managed to connect to the PostgreSQL database using the terminal. However, we now need our app to manage the reading and writing to the database for our to-do items. In this section, we will connect our application to the database running in Docker. In order to connect, we have to build a function that establishes a connection, and then returns it. In the `src/database.rs` file, we define the function with the following code block:

```
use diesel::prelude::*;
use diesel::pg::PgConnection;
use dotenv::dotenv;
```

```
use std::env;

pub fn establish_connection() -> PgConnection {
    dotenv().ok();

    let database_url = env::var("DATABASE_URL")
        .expect("DATABASE_URL must be set");
    PgConnection::establish(&database_url)
        .unwrap_or_else(|_| panic!("Error connecting to {}",
            database_url))
}
```

First of all, you might notice the use diesel::prelude::*; import command.
This command imports a range of connection, expression, query, serialization, and result
structs. Once the required imports are done, we define the connection function. First
of all, we need to ensure that the program will not throw an error if we fail to load the
environment using the dotenv().ok(); command.

Once this is done, we get our database URL from the environment variables and establish
a connection using a reference to our database URL. We then unwrap the result, and we
might panic about displaying the database URL if we do not manage to do this, as we want
to ensure that we are using the correct URL, with the right parameters. As the connection
is the final statement in the function, this is what is returned.

Now that we have our own connection, we need to define the schema. This will map
the variables of the to-do items to the data types. We can define our schema in the
src/schema.rs file with the following code block:

```
table! {
    to_do (id) {
        id -> Int4,
        title -> Varchar,
        status -> Varchar,
    }
}
```

Here, we are using the diesel macro table!, which specifies that a table exists. This
map is fairly straightforward, and we will be using this schema in the future to reference
columns and the table in database queries and inserts.

Now that we have built our database connection and defined a schema, we have to declare them in our `src/main.rs` file with the following imports:

```
#[macro_use] extern crate diesel;
extern crate dotenv;

use actix_web::{App, HttpServer};
use actix_service::Service;

mod schema;
mod database;
mod processes;
mod models;
mod state;
mod to_do;
mod json_serialization;
mod views;
```

Our first import also enables procedural macros. If we do not use the `#[macro_use]` tag, then we will not be able to reference our schema in our other files. As regards to our schema definition, we also would not be able to use the table macro. We also import the `dotenv` crate. We retain our modules that we created previously in *Chapter 5*, *Displaying Content in the Browser*. We also define our schema and database modules. After doing this, we have everything we need to start building our data models.

Creating our data models and migrations

We will use our data models to define parameters and behavior around the data from the database in Rust. They essentially act as a bridge between the database and the Rust app.

In this section, we will be defining the data models for to-do items. However, we need to enable our app to add more data models if needed. In order to do this, we need to perform the following steps:

1. We define a new to-do item data model struct.

2. Then, we define a constructor function in the new to-do item struct.

3. And lastly, we define a to-do item data model struct.

Before we start writing any code, we define the following file structure in the
src directory:

```
├── models
│   ├── item
│   │   ├── item.rs
│   │   ├── mod.rs
│   │   └── new_item.rs
│   └── mod.rs
```

Each data model has a directory in the models directory. Inside that directory, we have
two files that define the model, one for a new insert, and another for managing the data in
the database. The new insert data model does not have an ID field.

This is because the database will assign an ID to the item; we do not define it beforehand.
However, when we interact with items in the database, we will get their ID, and we may
want to filter by ID. Therefore, the existing data item model houses an ID field. We can
define our new item data model in the new_item.rs file with the following code block:

```rust
use crate::schema::to_do;


#[derive(Insertable)]
#[table_name="to_do"]
pub struct NewItem {
    pub title: String,
    pub status: String,
}
impl NewItem {
    pub fn new(title: String) -> NewItem {
        return NewItem{title, status:
            String::from("pending") }
    }
}
```

As you can see, we import our table definition because we are going to reference it.
We then define our new item with title and status, which are to be strings. We then
use a diesel macro to define the table as belonging to this struct, at the "to_do" table.
Do not be fooled by the fact that this definition uses quotation marks.

If we do not import our schema, the app will not compile because it will not understand the reference. We also add another `diesel` macro, stating that we allow the data to be inserted into the database with the `Insertable` tag. As covered before, we are not going to add any further tags to this macro because we only want this struct to insert data.

We have also added a `new` function to enable us to define standard rules around creating a new struct. For instance, here, we are only going to be creating new items that are pending. This reduces the risk of a rogue status being created. If we want to expand later on, the `new` function could accept a `status` input and run it through a `match` statement, throwing an error if the status is not one of the statuses that we are willing to accept.

With this in mind, we can define our item data model in the `item.rs` file with the following code block:

```
use crate::schema::to_do;


#[derive(Queryable, Identifiable)]
#[table_name="to_do"]
pub struct Item {
    pub id: i32,
    pub title: String,
    pub status: String,
}
```

As you can see, the only difference is that we do not have a constructor function. We have swapped the `Insertable` tag for `Queryable` and `Identifiable`, and we have added an `id` field to the struct. In order to make these available to the rest of the application, we define them in the `models/item/mod.rs` file with the following code block:

```
pub mod new_item;
pub mod item;
```

And then we define them in the `models /mod.rs` file with the following line of code:

```
pub mod item;
```

With this, we define our model's module in the `src/main.rs` file with the following line of code:

```
mod models;
```

Now we are able to access our data models throughout the app. We have also locked down the behavior around reading and writing to the database. Now we can move onto importing these data models and using them in our app.

Getting data from the database

When interacting with a database, it can take some time to get used to the way in which we do this. Different ORMs and languages have different quirks, and it is really just getting to understand the way in which queries are built and executed. While the underlying principles are the same, the syntax for these ORMs can vary greatly. Therefore, just clocking hours in using an ORM will enable you to become more confident and solve more complex problems. For us, we can start off with the simplest mechanism, getting all of the data from a table.

In order to explore this, we can get all the items from the to_do table and return them at the end of each view. We defined this mechanism in *Chapter 4, Processing HTTP Requests*. There is an isolated function called return_state, which loads the data from the JSON file. It then loops through this data, passing it through the to_do_factory function to enable it to be serialized, and then returns the data, which is then returned via the view. The following diagram exemplifies this:

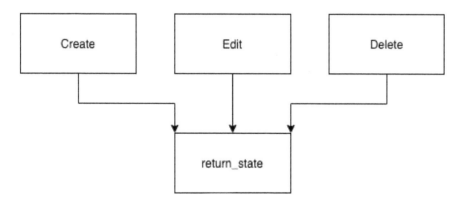

Figure 6.1 – Data flow from views

Because of this approach, all we have to do is switch the file reading code for a database call. Looping through the data and processing it via the to_do_factory function can still be utilized. We make our changes in the src/views/to_do/utils.rs file. First of all, we refactor the imports:

```
use crate::diesel;
use diesel::prelude::*;
```

```
use crate::to_do::to_do_factory;
use crate::json_serialization::to_do_items::ToDoItems;

use crate::database::establish_connection;
use crate::models::item::item::Item;
use crate::schema::to_do;
```

As you can see, we have imported the diesel crate and macros, which enable us to build database queries. We still use the vector from the standard library as we want to append our processed items in the vector to be returned. We then import our data processing factory and our serialization crates. This will enable us to package our items in order to be returned to the frontend. Finally, we import our database connection, our database model, and our table.

Now that we have everything we need, we refactor our function with the following code block:

```
pub fn return_state() -> ToDoItems {
    let connection = establish_connection();

    let items = to_do::table
        .order(to_do::columns::id.asc())
        .load::<Item>(&connection)
        .unwrap();

    let mut array_buffer = Vec::new();

    for item in items {
        let item = to_do_factory(&item.status,
            item.title).unwrap();
        array_buffer.push(item);
    }
    return ToDoItems::new(array_buffer);
}
```

First of all, we establish the connection. Once the database connection is established, we then get our table and build a database query from it. The first part of the query defines the order. As we can see, our table can also pass references to columns that also have their own functions.

We then define what struct is going to be used to load the data and pass in a reference to the connection. Because the macros define the struct in the load, if we passed the NewItem struct into the load function, we would get an error because the Queryable macro is not enabled for that struct.

We then unwrap it directly. With the data from the database, we loop through constructing our item structs and appending them to our buffer. Once this is done, we construct the JSON schema's ToDoItems from our buffer and return it. Now that we have enacted this change, all of our views will return data directly from the database. If we run this, there will be no items on the display. If we try and create any, they will not appear. However, although this is not being displayed, what we have done is get the data from the database and serialize it in a JSON structure that we want. This is the basis for returning data from a database and returning it to the requester in a standard way. This is the backbone of APIs built in Rust.

This is because we have not refactored any of the other endpoints. Therefore, the create endpoint is firing correctly; however, it is just creating items in the JSON state file that return_state no longer reads. In order for us to enable creation again, we have to refactor the create endpoint to insert a new item into the database.

Inserting data into the database

In this section, we build a view that creates a to-do item. If we remember the rules regarding us creating, we do not want to create duplicate to-do items. This can be done with a unique constraint. However, for now, it is good to keep things simple. Instead, we will make a database fail with a filter based on the title that is passed into the view. We then check, and if no results are returned, we insert a new to-do item into the database.

We do this by refactoring the code in the views/to_do/create.rs file. First of all, we reconfigure the imports, as seen in the following code block:

```
use crate::diesel;
use diesel::prelude::*;

use actix_web::HttpRequest;
use actix_web::Responder;

use crate::database::establish_connection;
use crate::models::item::new_item::NewItem;
use crate::models::item::item::Item;
```

```
use crate::schema::to_do;
use super::utils::return_state;
```

We import the necessary `diesel` imports to make a query as described in the previous section. We then import the `actix-web` structs needed for the view to process a request and define a result. We then import our database structs and functions to interact with the database. Now that we have everything, we can start working on our `create` view. Inside our `pub async fn create` function, we start by obtaining two references of the title of the `to-do` item from the request:

```
pub async fn create(req: HttpRequest) -> impl Responder {
    let title: String = req.match_info().get("title"
    ).unwrap().to_string();
    let title_ref: String = title.clone()
```

Once this is done, we establish a database connection and make a database call to our table using that connection, as seen in the following code block:

```
    let connection = establish_connection();
    let items = to_do::table
        .filter(to_do::columns::title.eq(
            title_ref.as_str()))
        .order(to_do::columns::id.asc())
        .load::<Item>(&connection)
        .unwrap();
```

As we can see, the query is pretty much the same as the query in the previous section. However, we have a `filter` section that refers to our title column that has to be equal to our title. If the item being created is truly new, no items will be created, and so the length of the result will be zero. Therefore, if the length is zero, we should create a `NewItem` data model, and then insert that into the database, in turn returning the state at the end of the function, as seen in the following code block:

```
    if items.len() == 0 {
        let new_post = NewItem::new(title);
        let _ = diesel::insert_into(
            to_do::table).values(&new_post)
            .execute(&connection);
    }
```

```
        return return_state()
}
```

We can see that diesel has an `insert` function, which we pass in the table, and the value, which is the reference to the data model we built. Now, using our app, we will be able to create to-do items, and then see these items pop up on the frontend of our application. Therefore, we can see that our `create` and `get state` functions are working and are engaging with our database. If you are having trouble, a common mistake is to forget to spin up our `docker-compose`.

Important Note:

Remember to do this, otherwise the app will not be able to connect to the database as it is not running.

However, we cannot edit our to-do items status to `Done`. In order to do this, we will have to edit our data in the database.

Editing the database

When we edit our data, we are going to get the data model from the database and then edit the entry with a database call function from diesel. In order to engage our `edit` function with the database, we can edit our view in the `views/to_do/edit.rs` file. We start by refactoring the imports, as can be seen in the following code block:

```
use crate::diesel;
use diesel::prelude::*;

use actix_web::{web, HttpResponse};

use super::utils::return_state;

use crate::database::establish_connection;
use crate::json_serialization::to_do_item::ToDoItem;
use crate::schema::to_do;
```

As we can see, there is a pattern happening. We have covered the imports and the meanings behind them previously. In our `edit` view, we only have to get one reference to the title this time, which is denoted in the following code block:

```
pub async fn edit(to_do_item: web::Json<ToDoItem>) ->
HttpResponse {
    let title_ref: String = to_do_item.title.clone();
```

We then establish a connection to the database and make a database call to get the item from the database. Right now, we should be comfortable with this. The code of how to connect to the database and get all the to-do items from the database that match the title is given as follows. However, it is advised to try and achieve this yourself before reading the following code block:

```
    let connection = establish_connection();
    let results = to_do::table.filter(to_do::columns::title
        .eq(title_ref));
```

Now that we have the result, we can make a `diesel` function that updates the database with a new attribute. This is done by means of the following command:

```
    let _ = diesel::update(results)
        .set(to_do::columns::status.eq("done"))
        .execute(&connection);

    return HttpResponse::Ok().json(return_state())
}
```

Here, we can see that we call the `update` function and fill it with the results that we obtained from the database. We then set the status column to `done`, and then execute using the reference to the connection. Now we can use this to edit our `to-do` items so that they can shift to the done list. However, we cannot delete them. In order to do this, we are going to have to refactor our final endpoint in order to completely refactor our app and be connected to a database.

Deleting data

As regards deleting data, we are going to take the same approach that we took with the previous section when editing. We are going to get an item from the database, pass it through the diesel `delete` function, and then return the state. Right now, we should be comfortable with this approach, so it is advised that you try and implement it by yourself in the `views/to_do/delete.rs` file. The code is given as follows for the imports:

```
use crate::diesel;
use diesel::prelude::*;

use actix_web::{web, HttpResponse};

use super::utils::return_state;

use crate::database::establish_connection;
use crate::json_serialization::to_do_item::ToDoItem;
use crate::models::item::item::Item;
use crate::schema::to_do;
```

From the preceding code, we are relying on the `diesel` crates and `prelude` so that we can use the `diesel` macros. Without `prelude`, we would not be able to use the schema. We then import the `actix` web structs that are needed to return data to the client. We then import the crates that we have built to manage our to-do item data. For the `delete` function, the code is as follows:

```
pub async fn delete(to_do_item: web::Json<ToDoItem>) ->
HttpResponse {
    let title_ref: String = to_do_item.title.clone();

    let connection = establish_connection();
    let items = to_do::table
        .filter(to_do::columns::title.eq(title_ref.as_str()))
        .order(to_do::columns::id.asc())
        .load::<Item>(&connection)
        .unwrap();
    let _ = diesel::delete(&items[0]).execute(&connection);
    return HttpResponse::Ok().json(return_state())
}
```

Here we have it. Our app should be working again, but with a connection to a database as opposed to our JSON file. In order to quality control this, let's perform the following steps:

1. Enter `buy canoe` in the text input and click the **Create** button.

2. Enter `go dragon boat racing` in the text input and click the **Create** button.

3. Click the **edit** button on the **buy canoe** item. After doing this, we should have the following output in the frontend:

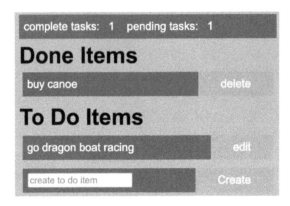

Figure 6.2 – Expected output

Here, we have brought our canoe, but we have not gone dragon boat racing yet. And here we have it. Our app is working seamlessly with our PostgreSQL database. We can create, edit, and delete our to-do items. Because of the structure that was defined in previous chapters, chopping out the JSON file mechanism for the database did not require a lot of work. The request for processing and returning data was already in place.

Summary

In this chapter, we constructed a development environment where our app could interact with the database using Docker. Once we did this, we explored the listing of containers and images to inspect how our system in general is going. We then created migrations using the diesel crate. After this, we installed the `diesel` client and defined the database URL as an environment variable, so that our Rust app and migrations could directly connect with the database container.

We then ran migrations and defined the SQL scripts that would fire when the migration ran, and ran these in turn. Once this was done, we inspected the database container again to see whether the migration had, in fact, been executed. We then defined the data models in Rust, and refactored our API endpoints, so that they could perform get, edit, create, and delete operations on the database in order keep track of the to-do items.

What we have done here is upgrade our database storage system. We are one step closer to having a production ready system as we are no longer relying on a JSON file to store our data. You now have the skills to perform database management tasks that enable you to manage changes, credentials/access, and schemas. We also performed all the basic operations on the database that are needed in order to run an app that creates, gets, updates, and deletes data. These stills are directly transferable to any other project you wish to undertake in Rust web projects.

In the next chapter, we will be building on these skills to build a user authentication system so that we can create users and check credentials when accessing the app. We will use a combination of a database, the extraction of data from headers, browser storage, and routing to ensure that the user has to be logged in to access the to-do items.

Questions

1. What are the advantages of having a database over a JSON file?

2. How do you create a migration?

3. How do we check the migration?

4. If we were to create a user data model in Rust with a name and an age, what should we do?

Further reading

- Diesel documentation: `http://diesel.rs/docs/`

7
Managing User Sessions

At this point, our app is manipulating data in a proper database by clicking buttons on the view. However, anyone who comes across our app can also edit the data. While our app is not the type of app that would require a lot of security, it is an important concept to understand and practice in general web development.

In this chapter, we will build a system that creates users. It will also manage user sessions by requiring the user to log in before they can alter any to-do items through the frontend app.

In this chapter, we will cover the following topics:

- Creating user data models with relationships with other tables with unique constraints of certain fields via database migrations
- Hashing and checking passwords, and **JSON Web Tokens (JWTs)**
- Logging users in and out of the app
- Storing auth credentials in the browser and passing them with every API call
- Managing user sessions

Let's get started!

Technical requirements

In this chapter, we will build on the code we built in the previous chapter. This can be found at `https://github.com/PacktPublishing/Rust-Web-Programming/tree/master/Chapter06/data_models`.

You can find the full source code for this chapter here: `https://github.com/PacktPublishing/Rust-Web-Programming/tree/master/Chapter07`.

The CiA videos for this book can be viewed at: `http://bit.ly/3jULCrw`

Creating our user model

Since we are managing user sessions in our app, we will need to store information about our users in order to check their credentials, before we allow our to-do items to be created, deleted, and edited. We will store our user data in our **PostgreSQL** database. While this is not essential, we will also link users in the database to to-do items. This will give us an understanding of how to alter an existing table and create links between tables. In order to create our user model, we are going to have to do the following:

1. Create a `user` data model.
2. Create a `NewUser` data model.
3. Alter the to-do item data model so that we can link it to a user model.
4. Update the schema file with the new table and altered fields.
5. Create and run migration scripts on the database.

In the following sections, we'll look at the preceding steps in detail.

Creating a user data model

Before we start, we will need to update the dependencies in the `Cargo.toml` file with the following dependencies:

```
[dependencies]
bcrypt = "0.8.2"
uuid = {version = "0.8", features = ["serde", "v4"]}
```

We will be using the `bcrypt` crate to hash and check passwords and the `uuid` crate to generate unique IDs for our user data models. As we covered in *Chapter 6, Data Persistence with PostgreSQL*, we will need to create two different structs for our user data model.

The new user will not have an `id` field yet because it does not exist in the database yet. This ID is created by the database when the new user is inserted into the table. We then have another struct that has all the same fields with the `id` field we added, since we might need to use this ID when we're interacting with existing users in the database. ID numbers can be useful for referencing other tables. They are short and we know that they are unique. We will be using a user ID to link the user to the to-do items. These data models can be housed in the following file structure in the `src/models` directory:

```
└── user
    ├── mod.rs
    ├── new_user.rs
    └── user.rs
```

We will define the data model in our `new_user.rs` file. First of all, we must define the imports, as shown here:

```
extern crate bcrypt;

use uuid::Uuid;
use diesel::Insertable;
use bcrypt::{DEFAULT_COST, hash};

use crate::schema::users;
```

Note that we have not defined the users in the schema yet. We will get around to this once we have finished coding all the data models.

Creating a NewUser data model

Now that the necessary imports have been made, we can define our `NewUser` data model with the following code:

```
#[derive(Insertable, Clone)]
#[table_name="users"]
pub struct NewUser {
    pub username: String,
    pub email: String,
    pub password: String,
    pub unique_id: String,
}
```

Here, we can see that we allowed our data model to be insertable. However, we are not allowing it to be queried. We want to ensure that when a user is retrieved from the database, their ID is present. We could move on to defining the general data model for users, but this is not secure. We need to ensure that our passwords are protected by hashing them.

You may have wondered why you cannot recover forgotten passwords; you can only reset them. This is because the password is **hashed**. Hashing passwords is a common practice when it comes to storing them. This is where we use an algorithm to obfuscate a password so that it cannot be read. Once this is done, it cannot be reversed.

The hashed password is then stored in a database. In order to check the password, the input password is hashed and compared to the hashed password in the database. This allows us to see if the input hashed password matches the hashed password stored in the database. This has a couple of advantages. First, it prevents employees who have access to your data from knowing your password. If there is a data leak, it also prevents the leaked data from directly exposing your password to whoever had the data.

Considering a lot of people use the same password for multiple things (even though they should not), you can only imagine the damage that may be caused to people using your app if you are not hashing passwords and there's a data breach. However, hashing gets more complicated than this. There is this concept called **salting**, which ensures that when you hash the same password, it does not result in the same hash. It does this by adding an extra bit of data to the password before it is hashed.

Explaining password security in more detail is beyond the scope of this book. However, it has to be stressed that password hashing is always a must when storing passwords. Luckily, there are a range of modules in all major languages that enable you to hash and check passwords with just a few lines of code. Rust is no different here.

To ensure that our passwords are hashed, follow these steps:

1. First, we will have to ensure that the input password is hashed in our `NewUser` constructor, which is defined as follows:

```
impl NewUser {
    pub fn new(username: String, email: String,
            password: String) -> NewUser {
        let hashed_password: String = hash(
            password.as_str(), DEFAULT_COST).unwrap();
        let uuid = Uuid::new_v4().to_string();
```

```
            return NewUser {username, email,
                            password: hashed_password,
                            unique_id: uuid}
    }
}
```

Here, we used the `hash` function from the `bcrypt` crate to hash our password. We also created a unique ID using the `Uuid` create and then constructed a new instance of the `NewUser` struct with those attributes. In our app, there is no real need for the unique ID. However, these can come in handy if you are communicating between multiple servers and databases.

2. Now that we have defined our `NewUser` data model, we can define our general user data model in the `user.rs` file with the following code. First of all, we must define the following imports:

```
extern crate bcrypt;

use diesel::{Queryable, Identifiable};
use bcrypt::verify;

use crate::schema::users;
```

Here, we can see that we are using the `verify` function, and that we are also allowing the general user data model struct to be queryable and identifiable.

3. With these imports, we can define the `User` struct with this code:

```
#[derive(Queryable, Clone, Identifiable)]
#[table_name="users"]
pub struct User {
    pub id: i32,
    pub username: String,
    pub email: String,
    pub password: String,
    pub unique_id: String
}
```

4. Now that our `User` struct has been defined, we can build a function that verifies if an input password matches the password belonging to the user with the following code:

```
impl User {
    pub fn verify(self, password: String) -> bool {
        return verify(password.as_str(),
                      &self.password).unwrap()
    }
}
```

5. Now that our models have been defined, we have to remember to register them in the `models/user/mod.rs` file with the following code:

```
pub mod new_user;
pub mod user;
```

Furthermore, we can make these modules accessible to the app by adding the following line to the `models/mod.rs` file:

```
pub mod item;
pub mod user;
```

With that, our data models for the users have been defined. However, we still need to link them to our to-do items.

Altering the to-do item data model

In order to link data models to our to-do items, we have to alter our to-do data models. This is fairly straightforward. All we have to do is add a field that links to the user, and then declare the link to the table with a macro. In the `models/item/item.rs` file, we can achieve this by adding the following code:

```
use crate::schema::to_do;
use super::super::user::user::User;


#[derive(Queryable, Identifiable, Associations)]
#[belongs_to(User)]
#[table_name="to_do"]
pub struct Item {
    pub id: i32,
```

```
    pub title: String,
    pub status: String,
    pub user_id: i32,
}
```

Here, we can see that we imported the user data model struct, defined it with a belongs_to macro, and added a user_id field in order to link the struct. Note that the belongs_to macro will not be callable if we do not include the Associations macro.

One last thing we need to do is add the user_id field to the fields and constructor in the models/item/new_item.rs file. We need to do this so that we can link the new to-do item to the user creating the item. This can be achieved by using the following code:

```
use crate::schema::to_do;

#[derive(Insertable)]
#[table_name="to_do"]
pub struct NewItem {
    pub title: String,
    pub status: String,
    pub user_id: i32,
}
impl NewItem {
    pub fn new(title: String, user_id: i32) -> NewItem {
        return NewItem{title, status: String::from("pending"),
            user_id
        }
    }
}
```

So, taking stock of what we have done, all our data model structs have been altered, and we are able to use them as and when we need them in the app when interacting with the database. However, we have not updated our database, and we have not updated the bridge connecting the app to the database. We will do this next.

Updating the schema file

To make sure that the mapping from the data model struct to the database is up to date, we have to update our schema with these changes. This means that we have to alter the existing schema for the to-do item table and add a user schema to the `src/schema.rs` file. This is denoted by the following code:

```
table! {
    to_do (id) {
        id -> Int4,
        title -> Varchar,
        status -> Varchar,
        user_id -> Int4,
    }
}
table! {
    users (id) {
        id -> Int4,
        username -> Varchar,
        email -> Varchar,
        password -> Varchar,
        unique_id -> Varchar,
    }
}
```

It has to be noted that our fields in the schema file are defined in the same order as the Rust data models. This is important because, if we do not do this, the fields will be mismatched when we're connecting to the database. We might also realize that our schema is merely just defining the fields and their type; it is not covering the relationship between the to-do table and the user table.

We do not have to worry about this because when we create and run our own migrations, this schema file will be updated with the relationship. This leads us on to creating our own migrations to complete this schema file.

Running migrations goes along the same lines as what we covered in *Chapter 6*, *Data Persistence with PostgreSQL*, which covered how to install the `diesel` client and connect to the database. First of all, we must run our database with the `docker-compose` command:

```
docker-compose up
```

We will need this running in the background when we actually run the migration. We can then create the migration scripts by running the following command:

```
diesel migration generate create_users
```

This creates a directory in the migrations, which includes `create_users` in the username of the directory. Inside this directory, we have two blank **SQL** files. Here, we will manually write our own SQL scripts for the migrations. Initially, this might make you complain as there are libraries in other languages that automatically generate these migrations, but there are some advantages to doing this.

First of all, it keeps our hand in SQL, which is another handy tool. This enables us to think about solutions that utilize SQL in the day-to-day problems that we are trying to solve. It also gives us more fine-grained control of how the migrations flow. For instance, in the migration that we are going to create, we are going to have to create the user table, and then create a base user, so that when we alter the column in the `to_do` table, we can fill it with the ID of the placeholder user row. We carry this out in our `up.sql` file with the following table definition:

```
CREATE TABLE users (
    id SERIAL PRIMARY KEY,
    username VARCHAR NOT NULL,
    email VARCHAR NOT NULL,
    password VARCHAR NOT NULL,
    unique_id VARCHAR NOT NULL,
    UNIQUE (email),
    UNIQUE (username)
);
```

This is fairly straightforward. Note that the `email` and `username` fields are unique. This is because we do not want users with duplicate usernames, passwords, and emails. It's good to put the constraint in at this level for a number of reasons. For instance, we could protect against this by doing a database call of the username and email, and refusing to insert a new user if this is the case.

However, there may be an error in the code, or someone might alter our code in the future. A new feature might be introduced that doesn't have this check, such as an edit feature. There might be a migration that alters rows or inserts new users. It is usually best practice to ensure that if you are used to writing your own SQL, that means that the operation has finished.

This SQL command is fired, and then the next command is fired afterward. Our next command in the up.sql file inserts a placeholder user row with the following command:

```
INSERT INTO users (username, email, password, unique_id)
VALUES ('placeholder', 'placeholder email',
'placeholder password', 'placeholder unique id');
```

Now that we have created our user, we then alter our to_do table. We can do this with the following command, in the same file under the previous command we just wrote:

```
ALTER TABLE to_do ADD user_id integer default 1
CONSTRAINT user_id REFERENCES users NOT NULL;
```

With that, our up.sql migration has been defined. Now, we have to define our down.sql migration. With the down migration, we basically have to reverse what we did in the up migrations. This means dropping the user_id column in the to_do table, and then dropping the user table entirely. This can be done with the following SQL code in the down.sql file:

```
ALTER TABLE to_do DROP COLUMN user_id;


DROP TABLE users
```

With this, our migrations are fully defined. We can run them with the following command:

```
diesel migration run
```

We have to keep in mind that the docker has to be running for the migration to have an effect on the database. Once this migration has been run, we will see that the following code has been added to the src/schema.rs file:

```
joinable!(to_do -> users (user_id));


allow_tables_to_appear_in_same_query!(
    to_do,
    users,
);
```

This enables our Rust data models to make queries with this relationship. With this migration finished, we can run our app again. However, before we do that, there is just one slight alteration that we have to make in the `src/views/to_do/create.rs` file, where the constructor of the new item in the create view function adds the default user ID with the following line of code:

```
let new_post = NewItem::new(title, 1);
```

Running our app now will result in the same behavior we described in *Chapter 6, Data Persistence with PostgreSQL*, in that our app is running with the migrations that we have made. However, we also need to see if our constructor for the new user works as we hash the password and generate the unique ID.

To do this, we need to build a create user endpoint. For this, we have to define the schema, and then a view that inserts that new user into the database. We can create our schema in the `src/json_serialization/new_user.rs` file with the following code:

```
use serde::Deserialize;
#[derive(Deserialize)]
pub struct NewUserSchema {
    pub name: String,
    pub email: String,
    pub password: String
}
```

After this, we can declare the new user schema in our `src/json_serialization/mod.rs` file with `pub mod new_user;`. Once our schema has been defined, we can create our own users' view module with the following file structure:

```
views
...
└── users
    ├── create.rs
    └── mod.rs
```

In our `create.rs` file, we need to build a create view function. First of all, import the following crates:

```
use crate::diesel;
use diesel::prelude::*;


use actix_web::{web, HttpResponse};


use crate::database::establish_connection;
use crate::json_serialization::new_user::NewUserSchema;
use crate::models::user::new_user::NewUser;
use crate::schema::users;
```

Since we have been building our views multiple times now, none of these imports should be surprising. Now that we've imported the correct crates, we must define the `create` view function with the following code:

```
pub async fn create(new_user: web::Json<NewUserSchema>) ->
        HttpResponse {
    let connection = establish_connection();

    let name: String = new_user.name.clone();
    let email: String = new_user.email.clone();
    let password: String = new_user.password.clone();

    let new_user = NewUser::new(name, email, password);

    let insert_result = diesel::insert_into(users::table)
        .values(&new_user)
        .execute(&connection);

    match insert_result {
        Ok(_) => HttpResponse::Created().await.unwrap(),
        Err(_) => HttpResponse::Conflict().await.unwrap()
} }
```

Here, we have established a database connection, extracted the fields from the JSON body, created a new `NewUser` struct, and then inserted it into the database. There is a slight difference here compared to the other views. In the return response, we are having to **await** and then **unwrap** it. This is because we are not returning a JSON body. Therefore, `HttpResponse::Ok()` is merely a builder struct. Once we await it, we get a result, and this has to be unwrapped.

We can also see that the `match` statement concludes our return code. This is because we will expect a conflict if someone tries to create a new user with the same username or email. We need to tell the frontend what happened. Again, if the frontend code accidentally double fires a create user request, we would want to know as soon as possible with a `409` response code.

Now that we have built our create view, we need to define our view factory in the `views/users/mod.rs` file, like so:

```
use actix_web::web;
mod create;
use super::path::Path;


pub fn user_factory(app:  &mut web::ServiceConfig) {
    let base_path: Path = Path{prefix: String::from("/user")};

    app.route(&base_path.define(String::from("/create")),
              web::post().to(create::create));
}
```

Again, since we have been building views fairly regularly, none of this should come as a surprise to you. If it does, it is recommended that you read *Chapter 3*, *Handling HTTP Requests*, the *Managing views using the Actix-Web framework* section, for clarity. Now that our factory has been defined, we can utilize it in our `views/mod.rs` file by importing `views_factory` and adding `users::user_factory(app)` to `views_factory` to ensure that our app registers the user views.

Creating and running migration scripts on the database

Now that we have registered our user view, we can run our app and create our user with the `http://localhost:8000/user/create` Postman (**POST**) call, as shown in the following screenshot:

Figure 7.1 – Postman call to our create user endpoint

With this, we should get a `201 OK` response. If we call the exact same call again, we should get a `409 conflict`. With this, we should expect that our new user has been created. With the steps we covered in *Chapter 6*, *Data Persistence with PostgreSQL*, in the *Connecting to PostgreSQL with Diesel* section, we can inspect the database in our docker container, which gives us the following printout:

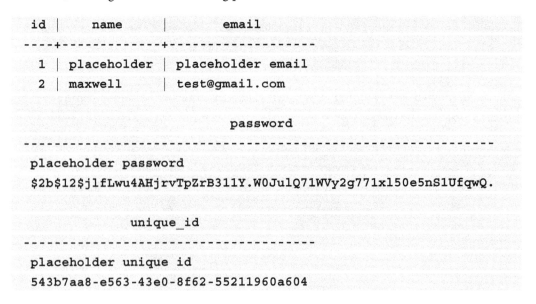

Here, we can see the initial user that was created in our migration. However, we can also see the user we created via our view. Here, we have a hashed password and a unique ID. From this, we can see that we should never directly create our user; we should only create it through the constructor function belonging to the `NewUser` struct.

In the context of our app, we do not really need a unique ID. However, in wider situations where multiple servers and databases are used, a unique ID can become useful. We also have to note that our conflict response on the second one was correct; the third replica create user call did not insert a replica user into the database.

With this, our app is running as normal since there is now a user table with user models linked to the to-do items. Thus, we are able to create other data tables with relationships and structure migrations so that they can be seamlessly upgraded and downgraded. We have also covered how to verify and create passwords. However, we have not actually written any code that checks if the user is passing the right credentials. In the next section, we will work on authenticating users and rejecting requests that do not contain the right credentials.

Authenticating our users

Authenticating our users is a straightforward goal. We want to take the credentials that the user gives us, check them, and then return a true or false regarding whether the user can perform actions based on this. A straightforward way to do this is to constantly include our username and password in our requests. However, this is not safe. If the request is intercepted, then our credentials can be obtained. There is also the risk of internal attackers who might not be able to access the database to directly edit records, though this could be monitoring the server for a limited amount of time. We do not want passwords to be directly available when requests are made. Another thing we have to take into account is that we do not want our user to be typing in their password for every request. Therefore, we are going to have to store their credentials in either the user's browser or cookies. If these are breached, then the attacker has access to the user's raw password.

There are more nuances to security that are outside the scope of this book, but due to the reasons we mentioned earlier, we will be authenticating our users through **JWTs**. This is where we can serialize the password and other bits of data into an encoded token. We grant this once, after the user has successfully logged in. The user then stores the token in their browser and passes it in the header for us to check with each request.
It must be stressed that our approach is not bulletproof. While it is satisfactory for most side project apps, security-focused books will offer more in-depth security solutions if the app contains sensitive information and has different levels of access.

To get started on our authentication system, we have to build our **JWT** struct. Our authentication system is going to grow as time goes on, so it makes sense to build our own `auth` directory to house the JWT. First of all, we have to add the following dependencies to our `Cargo.toml` file:

```
jwt = "0.9.0"
hmac = "0.8.1"
sha2 = "0.9"
```

The `hmac` crate enables us to create a hashed string with a secret key and insert variables into the string before hashing. The `sha2` crate is the hashing algorithm we use, while the `jwt` crate enables us to verify with a key when decoding the hashed token. With this, we can construct the JWT struct for us to utilize when we're authenticating users. In our `src/auth/jwt.rs` file, we must import the required structs with the following code:

```
extern crate hmac;
extern crate jwt;
extern crate sha2;

use hmac::{Hmac, NewMac};
use jwt::{Header, Token, VerifyWithKey};
use jwt::SignWithKey;
use sha2::Sha256;
use std::collections::BTreeMap;
```

Some of the preceding code lines are fairly self-explanatory. However, some are not. `Hmac` is for generating a key and can be used to sign the hashed token. The `BTreeMap` struct is a binary search tree where we can insert keys and values that have been assigned to those keys. This is how we insert data about the user into the token. Now that we have imported the correct structs, we can define our JWT struct with the following code:

```
pub struct JwtToken {
    pub user_id: i32,
    pub body: String
}
```

We want to access the user ID of the token being supplied. We can add other fields later if needed. The body field is the token itself if it's needed again in the future. Now that we have defined our token struct, we can build the encode and decode functions, which allow us to encode the user ID into the token and extract it from a new token that's being passed in, as shown in the following code:

```
impl JwtToken {

    pub fn encode(user_id: i32) -> String {
        let key: Hmac<Sha256> =
        Hmac::new_varkey(b"secret").unwrap();
        let mut claims = BTreeMap::new();
        claims.insert("user_id", user_id);
        let token_str: String = claims.sign_with_key(
            &key).unwrap();
        return token_str
    }
```

Here, we can see that we created a new key with the secret byte string. It can be any byte key, as long as it's the same for the decode function. We should keep this a secret. In *Chapter 10, Deploying Our Application on AWS*, we will cover how to configure these on servers. We then created a new map and inserted the user ID that was provided in the function.

Once we have done this, we sign in with our secret key and return it, since it is the hashed token. We have chosen this approach because we can insert multiple data points into the token by adding more insert lines.

Now that we have our encode function, we can define our decode function in the same block with the following code:

```
    pub fn decode(encoded_token: String) ->
                        Result<JwtToken, &'static str> {
        let key: Hmac<Sha256> = Hmac::new_varkey(
                                    b"secret").unwrap();
        let token_str: &str = encoded_token.as_str();


        let token: Result<Token<Header, BTreeMap<String,
            i32>, _>, > = VerifyWithKey::verify_with_key(
            token_str, &key);
```

```
        match token {
            Ok(token) => {
                let _header = token.header();
                let claims = token.claims();
                return Ok(JwtToken { user_id:
                    claims["user_id"], body: encoded_token})
            }
            Err(_) => return Err("Could not decode")
        }
    }
}
```

Here, we generated a new key with the same byte string. We then used `VerifyWithKey` with the token string and key we created to get the token. While we did not use the header, we can see that the header can be extracted with the standard `header` function.

We can get our map with the `claims` function. We can then generate our struct with the user ID from our claims map. We could just unwrap the verification and then return our struct, which is a similar approach to what the `encode` function does. However, unlike encoding, we do expect the decoding process to fail from time to time as we expect requests to not always have the correct JWT. Due to this, we want to return a result struct so that we can handle the outcome of faulty decoding. Once we have done this, we have to remember to register our JWT struct in our `src/auth/mod.rs` file with the `mod jwt;` line of code. We can then declare it in our `main.rs` file with the `mod auth;` line of code.

Now that we have our JWT defined, we can do some refactoring. Our code in the `src/views/token.rs` file does the following:

1. First, it takes in a reference of a service request.

2. It then passes that to a function that extracts the header, returning an error that's then returned in the function provided in *step 1*.

3. The extract `header` function then passes it to a check password function, which returns a result.

4. The result of the check password function is then returned to the initial function in *step 1*.

The following are essentially three functions that carry out a step and can fail at that step. At a higher level, it can be distilled to the following steps:

1. Get the service request.

2. Extract the header.

3. Check the password.

We can move the `src/views/token.rs` file to `src/auth/processes.rs` since the preceding functions are used to authenticate the JWT. We then need to remove the `pub mod token;` code in the `src/views/mod.rs` file. Once we've done that, we can make all the functions in our `src/auth/processes.rs` file public, and then move our `process_token` function into our `src/auth/mod.rs` file, giving us the following code:

```rust
use actix_web::dev::ServiceRequest;
pub mod jwt;
mod processes;


pub fn process_token(request: &ServiceRequest) ->
                        Result<String, &'static str> {
    match processes::extract_header_token(request) {
        Ok(token) => {
            match processes::check_password(token) {
                Ok(token) => Ok(token),
                Err(message) => Err(message)
            }
        },
        Err(message) => Err(message)
    }
}
```

Here, the `processes` modules are not public. We only want the `process_token` function to be accessible to the processes. We might want to extract the user ID into a view, which is why it is public.

Now, in our `main.rs` file, we must replace the views with `auth`, as shown here:

```
if *&req.path().contains("/item/") {
    match auth::process_token(&req)
    ...
```

After running our app, we can see that our app runs just as well as it did previously. Now, all we have to do is insert the JWT process into the `check_password` function via the following code:

```
use super::jwt;

pub fn check_password(password: String) ->
            Result<String, &'static str> {
    match jwt::JwtToken::decode(password) {
        Ok(_token) => Ok(String::from("passed")),
        Err(message) => Err(message)
    }
}
```

Upon running the app, we will get `token error: Could not decode` as output in the Terminal when we perform item operations. This means that it is working. However, we have not acted on it. All we are doing is printing out to the console that the wrong credentials are being passed to the server. We are going to have to allow the user to log in and store their JWT so that it can be passed for each request. Once we have done this, we can start rejecting unauthorized requests. We will cover this in the next section.

Managing user sessions

For our users, we are going to have to enable them to log in. This means that we have to create an endpoint to check their credentials, and then generate a JWT to be returned back to the user in the frontend via the header in the response. Our first step is to define a login schema in the `src/json_serialization/login.rs` file with the following code:

```
use serde::Deserialize;

#[derive(Deserialize)]
pub struct Login {
    pub username: String,
```

```
      pub password: String
}
```

We have to remember to register it in the `src/json_serialization/mod.rs` file with the `pub mod login;` line of code. Once we have done this, we can build our login endpoint. We can do this by editing the `src/views/auth/login.rs` file we created in *Chapter 3, Handling HTTP Requests*, in the *Managing views using the Actix-Web framework* section, which declares our basic login view. This just returns a string.

Now, we can start refactoring this view by defining the required imports, as shown in the following code:

```
use crate::diesel;
use diesel::prelude::*;
use actix_web::{web, HttpResponse};


use crate::database::establish_connection;
use crate::models::user::user::User;
use crate::json_serialization::login::Login;
use crate::schema::users;
use crate::auth::jwt::JwtToken;
```

At this stage, we can glance at the imports and get a feel for what we are going to do. We are going to extract the username and password from the body. We are then going to connect to the database to check the user and password, and then use the `JwtToken` struct to create the token that will be passed back to the user. We can initially do all this information gathering with the following code:

```
pub async fn login(credentials: web::Json<Login>) ->
        HttpResponse {
    let username: String = credentials.username.clone();
    let password: String = credentials.password.clone();


    let connection = establish_connection();
    let users = users::table
        .filter(users::columns::name.eq(username.as_str()))
        .load::<User>(&connection).unwrap();
```

Once we have loaded the users, we need to check if we got what we expected with the following code:

```
if users.len() == 0 {
    return HttpResponse::NotFound().await.unwrap()
} else if users.len() > 1 {
    return HttpResponse::Conflict().await.unwrap()
}
```

Here, we have done some early returns. If there are no users, then we return a not found response code. This is something we will expect from time to time. However, if there is more than one user with that username, we need to return a different code.

Due to the unique constraints shown, something is very wrong. A migration script in the future might undo these unique constraints, or the user query might be altered by accident. If this happens, we need to know that this has happened right away, since corrupted data that goes against our constraints can cause our application to behave in unexpected ways that can be hard to troubleshoot.

Now that we have checked that the right amount of users have been retrieved, we can get the one and only user at index zero with confidence and check if their password is passable, as follows:

```
match users[0].clone().verify(password) {
    true => {
        let token: String = JwtToken::encode(
            users[0].clone().id);
        HttpResponse::Ok().header(
            "token", token).await.unwrap()
    },
    false => HttpResponse::Unauthorized().await.unwrap()
}
}
```

Here, we can see that we used the verify function. If the password is a match, we then generate a token using the ID and return it to the user in the header. If the password is not correct, we return an unauthorized code instead. Since this view is already registered, we can run the app and make the call with Postman:

Figure 7.2 – Postman call to our login endpoint

Altering the username will give us a `404-response` code, whereas altering the password will give us a `401-response` code. If we have the correct username and password, we will get a `200-response` code and there will be a **token** in the response of the header, as shown in the following screenshot:

Figure 7.3 – Postman response headers from our login endpoint

Now that we have a login endpoint, we need to create a login view for our users. First, we must switch both of our login and logout views in our `src/views/auth/mod. rs` file from GET to POST. With this, we can move toward building our HTML in the `templates/login.html` file. To begin, we will define the meta data with the following code in `head`:

```
<html>
    <head>
        <meta charSet="UTF-8"/>
        <meta name="viewport" content="width=device-width,
                initial-scale=1.0"/>
        <meta httpEquiv="X-UA-Compatiable" content="ie=edge"/>
```

```
        <meta name="description"
            content="This is a simple to do app"/>
        <title>Login</title>
    </head>
```

Once `head` has been defined, we can start styling the view. We can use our BASE_ CSS, which we defined in *Chapter 5, Displaying Content in the Browser*, to inherit our background color and margins based on the size of the screen. We can also inherit the CSS we defined in the `main` file. We do, however, have to define our own login button styling. This is because we do not want the button to float to the right. The other attributes of the button are the same, as shown in the following code:

```
    <style>
        {{BASE_CSS}}
        {{CSS}}
        .loginButtonStyle {
            display: inline-block;
            background: #f7786b;
            border: none;
            padding: 0.5rem;
            padding-left: 2rem;
            padding-right: 2rem;
            color: white;
        }
        .loginButtonStyle:hover {
            background: #f7686b;
            color: black;
        }
    </style>
```

Now that we have defined the styling, we can build our body of the view and house the inputs for username, password, a title, a status message, and a button for submitting the login, as follows:

```
    <body>
        <div class="mainContainer">
            <h2 class="ContainerTitle"
                style="text-align:center;">Login</h2>
```

```
            <p id="loginMessage" class="FeedbackMessage"
                style="text-align:center;"></p>
            <form style="text-align:center;" action="submit">
                <input type="text" value=""
                    placeholder="Username"
                    class="formInputContainer"
                    id="defaultLoginFormUsername"><br>
                <p></p>
                <input type="password" value=""
                    placeholder="Password"
                    class="formInputContainer"
                    id="defaultLoginFormPassword"><br><br>
                <input type="button" value="Submit"
                    class="loginButtonStyle"
                    id="loginButton"
                    style="text-align:center;">
            </form>
        </div>
    </body>
    <script>
        {{JAVASCRIPT}}
    </script>
</html>
```

Here, we can see that we used the `mainContainer` from `BASE_CSS` to define the boarder around the form. We then referenced some other classes and overwrote them so that `text-align` is centered. We then imported the **JavaScript** to manage the login call.

We can define our login functionality in the `javascript/login.js` file. First, we need to create references to our HTML to get data from the form inputs, listen to the login button, and print out progress statements to the user, like so:

```
const loginButton = document.getElementById('loginButton');
const username = document.getElementById(
    'defaultLoginFormUsername');
const password = document.getElementById(
    'defaultLoginFormPassword');
const message = document.getElementById("loginMessage");
```

We must then add an event listener to the login button, which sends the data from the form to the login endpoint. Once the request has been sent, we can update the login message with a note that we are logging in, to inform the user that something is happening; they do not have to click it again.

Once the response is returned, if the status is 200, we can store the token in the local storage and redirect to the home page to manage our to-do items. If it is not a 200-response code, then we can update the login message, telling the user that the login failed and that the user should try again. This can all be encapsulated in the following event listener:

```
loginButton.addEventListener("click", () => {
    let xhr = new XMLHttpRequest();
    xhr.open("POST", "/auth/login", true);
    xhr.setRequestHeader("Content-Type",
        "application/json");


    xhr.onreadystatechange = function () {

        if (xhr.readyState === 4) {
            if (xhr.status === 200) {
                let token = xhr.getResponseHeader("token");
                localStorage.setItem("user-token", token);
                window.location.replace(
                document.location.origin);
            } else {
                message.innerText =
                "login failed please try again";
            }
        }
    };
    let data = JSON.stringify({"username": username.value,
                                "password": password.value});
    xhr.send(data);
    message.innerText = "logging in"
})
```

With this, our frontend is nearly complete. In our `javascript/main.js` file, we need to check if the token is in our storage. If it is not, then we have to redirect the user to the login view. This can be done by putting the following code at the top of the `javascript/main.js` file:

```
if (localStorage.getItem("user-token") == null) {
    window.location.replace(
    document.location.origin + "/login/");
}
```

This stops a user without a token viewing the main items view. We also have to refactor our API call function in this file to also redirect the user to log in if the API call is unauthorized. We also need to get the token from storage and insert it into the header for the request to send it. This refactored function looks as follows:

```
function apiCall(url, method) {
    let xhr = new XMLHttpRequest();
    xhr.withCredentials = true;
    xhr.addEventListener('readystatechange', function() {
        if (this.readyState === this.DONE) {
            if (this.status === 401) {
                window.location.replace(
                    document.location.origin + "/login/");
            } else {
                renderItems(JSON.parse(this.responseText...
                renderItems(JSON.parse(this.responseText...
                document.getElementById("completeNum"...
                document.getElementById("pendingNum"...
            }
        }
    });
    xhr.open(method, url);
    xhr.setRequestHeader('content-type', 'application/json');
    xhr.setRequestHeader('user-token', localStorage.getItem("
                        user-token"));
    return xhr
}
```

With this, our frontend redirects the user to the login view if they do not have a token in storage. It also redirects them to the login view if the token does not pass our checks on the server when we make an API call to any item endpoint. The only thing left for us to do is serve the login and logout views on the server side. Here, we will add the views to the app directory of views. In our `src/views/app/login.rs` file, we can serve the login view using the following code:

```rust
use actix_web::HttpResponse;
use super::content_loader::read_file;

pub async fn login() -> HttpResponse {
    let mut html_data = read_file(
        String::from("./templates/login.html"));
    let javascript_data: String = read_file(
        String::from("./javascript/login.js"));
    let css_data: String = read_file(
        String::from("./css/main.css"));
    let base_css_data: String = read_file(
        String::from("./css/base.css"));

    html_data = html_data.replace("{{JAVASCRIPT}}",
                                  &javascript_data);
    html_data = html_data.replace("{{CSS}}", &css_data);
    html_data = html_data.replace("{{BASE_CSS}}",
        &base_css_data);

    HttpResponse::Ok()
        .content_type("text/html; charset=utf-8")
        .body(html_data)
}
```

This is very similar to the main view. We load the HTML file, and then we replace the JavaScript and CSS tags with the JavaScript and CSS files that were loaded.

In terms of our logout, we are going to take a far more lightweight approach. All we have to do in our logout view is run two lines of JavaScript code. One is to remove the user token from the local storage, and then revert the user back to the main view. HTML can just host JavaScript that is run as soon as you open it. Therefore, we can achieve this by putting the following code in the `src/views/app/logout.rs` file:

```
use actix_web::HttpResponse;

pub async fn logout() -> HttpResponse {
    HttpResponse::Ok()
        .content_type("text/html; charset=utf-8")
        .body("<html>\
                <script>\
                    localStorage.removeItem('user-token'); \
                    window.location.replace(
                        document.location.origin);\
                </script>\
            </html>")
}
```

Here, the HTML and the script are defined in the string. Now, our views can be defined in the `src/views/app/mod.rs` file with the following code:

```
use actix_web::web;
mod content_loader;
mod items;
mod login;
mod logout;
use super::path::Path;

pub fn app_factory(app: &mut web::ServiceConfig) {
    let base_path: Path = Path{prefix: String::from("/")};
    app.route(&base_path.define(String::from("")),
            web::get().to(items::items));
    app.route(&base_path.define(String::from("login")),
            web::get().to(login::login));
    app.route(&base_path.define(String::from("logout")),
```

```
                    web::get().to(logout::logout));
}
```

Here, our app is now ready to run again. Running this app will block us from accessing the main items view if we are not logged in. When we do log in and start creating, editing, and deleting items, we will see the following printout in the console for each item API call:

```
the token is passable
```

If we hit the logout view, we will not be logged in, and will not be able to access the main view. Due to this, we will keep being redirected to the login view. However, we have to remember that our user sessions are only locked down in the frontend. We are not actually acting on a bad token on the server side; we are merely printing out a statement.

Summary

In this chapter, we built user data model structs and tied them to the to-do item data models in our migrations. We then got to dive a little deeper into our migrations by firing multiple steps in the SQL file to ensure our migration runs smoothly. We also explored how to add unique constraints to certain fields.

Once our data models were defined in the database, we hashed some passwords before storing them in our database with the stored user. We then created a JWT struct to enable our users to store their JWT in their browsers, so that they could submit them when making an API call. We then explored how to redirect the URL in JavaScript and the HTML storage so that the frontend could work out if the user even has credentials, before it entertains the notion of sending API calls to the items.

What we have done here is alter the database with a migration so that our app can manage data models that handle more complexity. We then utilized frontend storage to enable our user to pass credentials. This is directly applicable to any other Rust web project you will embark on. Most web apps require some sort of authentication.

However, before we get too excited, we have to remember that we are not actually acting on the JWT on the server side if there is an error in verifying it. If someone were to put our URL into Postman, they would be able to alter to-do items without any tokens, let alone the right one.

In the next chapter, we will explore **REST API** practices, where we will standardize interfaces, redirect requests before they hit the server view if the JWT is not passed via middleware, refresh tokens, and use the JWT in the actual view to link to-do items to particular users. This will allow us to handle multiple users where to-do items that are only linked to the user are displayed.

Questions

1. What are the advantages of defining unique constraints in the SQL as opposed to the server-side code?

2. What is the main advantage of the user having a JWT over storing a password?

3. How does a user store a JWT on the frontend?

4. How could the JWT be useful in the view once we have verified that the JWT is passable?

5. What is the minimal approach to altering data in the frontend and redirecting it to another view when the user hits an endpoint?

6. Why is it useful to have a range of different response codes when logging in a user, as opposed to just denoting that it is successful or not successful?

Further reading

- JWT standard: `https://tools.ietf.org/html/rfc7519`

8
Building RESTful Services

Our to-do application written in Rust technically works. However, there are some improvements that we need to make. In this chapter, we will apply these improvements as we explore the concepts of RESTful API design.

In this chapter, we finally reject unauthorized users before the request hits the view by assessing the layers of our system and refactoring it to handle before and after request data. We then use this authentication to enable individual users to have their own list of to-do items. Finally, we log our requests so that we can troubleshoot our application and get a deeper look into how our application runs, caching data in the frontend to reduce API calls. We also explore nice-to-have concepts such as executing code on command and creating a uniform interface to split the frontend URLs from the backend URLs.

In this chapter, we will cover the following topics:

- What are RESTful services?
- Breaking down the application into layers to map before and after data for each request
- Enabling two possible different futures to execute in the middleware

- Defining a URL path struct to separate the frontend and backend URLs

- Exploring the stateless concept by utilizing the user ID in the JWT to enable our users to get to-do items that only belong to them

- Logging requests and mapping the behavior of our application to highlight silent but problematic behavior of our application

- Caching to-do item data in the frontend to reduce the number of calls to the backend API

By the end of this chapter, we will have refactored our Rust application to support the principles of RESTful APIs. This means that we are going to map out the layers of our Rust application, creating uniform API endpoints, logging requests in our application, and caching results in the frontend.

Technical requirements

In this chapter, we build on the code built in *Chapter 7, Managing User Sessions*. This can be found at the following URL: `https://github.com/PacktPublishing/Rust-Web-Programming/tree/master/Chapter07/managing_user_sessions`.

You can find the full source code used in this chapter here: `https://github.com/PacktPublishing/Rust-Web-Programming/tree/master/Chapter08`.

The CiA videos for this book can be viewed at: `http://bit.ly/3jULCrw`.

What are RESTful services?

REST stands for **representational state transfer**. It is an architectural style for our **application programming interface** (**API**) in order to read (`GET`), update (`PUT`), create (`POST`), and delete (`DELETE`) our users and to-do items. The goal of a RESTful approach is to increase speed/performance, reliability, and the ability to grow by reusing components that can be managed and updated without affecting the system as a whole.

You may have noticed that before Rust, slow, high-level languages seemed to be a wise choice for web development. This is because they are quicker and safer to write. This is due to the main bottleneck for speed in web development being network connection speed. The RESTful design aims to improve the speed by economizing the system as a whole, such as reducing API calls as opposed to just focusing on algorithm speed. With that in mind, in this section, we will be covering the following RESTful concepts:

- **Layered system**: This enables us to add extra functionality such as authorization without having to change the interface. For instance, if we have to check the **JSON Web Token** (**JWT**) in every view, this is a lot of repetitive code that is hard to maintain and is prone to error.

- **Uniform system**: This simplifies and decouples the architecture, enabling whole parts of the application to evolve independently without clashing.

- **Statelessness**: This ensures that our application does not directly save anything on the server. This has implications in microservices and cloud computing.

- **Logging**: This enables us to peek into our application and see how it runs, exposing undesirable behavior even if there are no errors being displayed.

- **Caching**: This enables us to store data in the frontend to reduce the number of API calls to our backend API.

- **Code on command**: This is where our backend server directly runs code on the frontend.

We'll look at the layered system concept in the next section.

Mapping our layered system

A layered system consists of layers with different units of functionality. It could be argued that these layers are different servers. This can be true in microservices, and in big systems, this can be the case when it comes to different layers of data. In big systems, it makes sense to have *hot data* that gets accessed and updated regularly, and *cold data* where it is rarely accessed. However, while it is easy to think of layers as on different servers, they can be on the same server. We can map our layers with the following diagram:

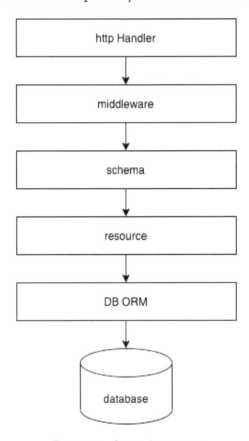

Figure 8.1 – Layers in our app

As you can see, our app follows this process:

1. First, our **http Handler** accepts the call by listening to the port that we defined when creating the server.

2. It then goes through the **middleware**, which is defined by using `wrap_function` on our app.

3. Once this is done, the URL of the request is mapped to the right view and the schemas we defined in our `src/json_serialization/` directory. These get passed into the resource (our views) defined in the `src/views/` directory.

If we then want to update or get data from the database, we use the `diesel` ORM to map those requests. At this stage, all of our layers have been defined to manage the flow of data effectively, apart from our middleware. As pointed out in the previous chapter, *Chapter 7, Managing User Sessions*, we are merely printing out the outcome of the JWT authentication. In order to ensure our API is secure, we have to return an unauthorized response if the authorization fails instead of passing our request to the next layer.

Before we start working on our middleware layer, we have to define the following imports at the top of our `main.rs` file:

```
use actix_web::{App, HttpServer, HttpResponse};
use actix_service::Service;
use futures::future::{ok, Either};
```

In order to ensure that we know that the JWT is authorized, we have to define a flag that we can check later on when deciding whether to process the request or reject it. We can do this by using the following code in our `main.rs` file:

```
.wrap_fn(|req, srv| {
    let passed: bool;

    if *&req.path().contains("/item/") {
        match auth::token::process_token(&req) {
            Ok(_token) => {passed = true;},
            Err(_message) => {passed = false;}
        };
    }
    else {
        passed = true;
    }
    ...
```

From the preceding code, we can see that we declare that there is a Boolean under the name of `passed`. If the authentication passes, then it is set to `true`. If the authentication fails, it is set to `false`, and if the call isn't an item call, then it is set to `true` as we are not checking credentials for other calls.

Now that we have defined a flag, we can use it to dictate what happens to the request. Before we do this, we have to take note of the last lines of `wrap_function` as denoted in this code:

```
let fut = srv.call(req);
async {
    let result = fut.await?;
    Ok(result)
}
```

We are waiting for the call to finish, and then returning the result as `result`. With our JWT, we have to check to see whether the authentication passes. If it does, we then run the preceding code. However, if the authentication fails, we have to bypass this and define another future, which is just the response.

At face value, this can seem fairly straightforward. Both will return the same thing, that is, a response. However, Rust will not compile. It will throw an error based on incompatible types. This is because async blocks behave like closures. This means that every async block is its own type. This can be frustrating, and due to this subtle detail, it can lead to developers burning hours trying to get the two futures to play with each other.

Luckily, there is an enum in the futures crate that solves this problem for us. The `Either` enum combines two different futures, streams, or sinks that have the same associated types into a single type. This enables us to match the `passed` flag, and fire and return the appropriate process with the following code:

```
let end_result = match passed {
    true => {
        Either::Left(srv.call(req))
    },
    false => {
        Either::Right(
            ok(req.into_response(
                HttpResponse::Unauthorized()
                    .finish()
                    .into_body())))
```

```
            )
        }
    };
    end_result
}).configure(views::views_factory);
```

From the preceding code, we can see that we assign `end_result` to the call, or directly return it to an unauthorized response depending on the `passed` flag. We then return this at the end of `wrap_function`. Knowing how to use the `Either` enum is a handy trick to have up your sleeve and will save you hours when you need your code to choose between two different futures.

Running our app will result in a fully functioning frontend where we can update our to-do items. We can see that our new code is not stopping our API calls because of the JWT token that we are sending in the header that we stored in HTML storage. We also note that there is no printing to the console with these API calls. In order to check to see whether we are actually blocking calls without a legitimate JWT in the header, we can call a simple `get` request in Postman with the following URL: `http://localhost:8000/item/get`.

From this, we should get a quick unauthorized (401) response. This shows that our server is now rejecting all item APIs if the authentication fails before the request is even loaded. This protects our server from having to even load the request.

It has to be noted that all requests cannot be locked down, otherwise the user will not be able to access even the login view or any of the app views. However, we might want to add more resources to the auth check in the future. This houses a potential problem. Some views might start clashing with the app views. For instance, our to-do item API views only have the prefix item. Getting all the items requires the `/item/get` endpoint.

It could be reasonable later on to develop a view for the app that looks at a to-do item in detail for editing with the `/item/get/{id}` endpoint. This increases the risk of clashes between the frontend app views and the backend API calls. In order to prevent this, we are going to have to ensure that our API has a uniform interface.

Uniform interface

Having a uniform interface means that our resources can be uniquely identifiable through a URL. This decouples the backend endpoints and frontend views, enabling our app to scale without classes from the frontend views and backend endpoints.

In order to do this, we have to go straight to where the URL for a view is defined, the
Path struct in the src/views/path.rs file. For this struct, we have to add a backend
Boolean field to declare whether the struct instance is for a backend endpoint. If it is, then
we have to alter our define function in this struct to add /api/v1/ to the URL. This is
shown in the following code:

```
pub struct Path {
    pub prefix: String,
    pub backend: bool
}
impl Path {
    pub fn define(&self, following_path: String) -> String {
        match self.backend {
            true => {
                let path: String = self.prefix.to_owned() +
                                    &following_path;
                String::from("/api/v1") + &path
            },
            false => self.prefix.to_owned() + &following_path
        }
    }
}
```

Now that we have modified our path, we have to go through all the mod.rs files in each
view module to add a true value to the backend parameter where the Path struct is
defined in the factory. The only exception is the factory in the app view module, which
will have a false value for the backend parameter.

Once this is done, we will have to go to our frontend to alter the API calls. Because we
defined our own function for these calls, we only have to alter this in two places. In the
javascript/main.js file, we update the API call function with this code:

```
function apiCall(url, method) {
    let xhr = new XMLHttpRequest();
    xhr.withCredentials = true;
    xhr.addEventListener('readystatechange', function() {
        if (this.readyState === this.DONE) {
            . . .
        }
```

```
    });
    xhr.open(method, "/api/v1" + url);
    xhr.setRequestHeader('content-type', 'application/json');
    xhr.setRequestHeader('user-token',
        localStorage.getItem("user-token"));
    return xhr
}
```

The code inside the block that determines whether `readyState` is done is not important as it is completely unchanged, which is why it is denoted with `.  .  ..` We can see that the only change is the adding of `"/api/v1"` in the `xhr.open` function. In our `javascript/login.js` file, we merely update the event listener with the following code:

```
loginButton.addEventListener("click", () => {
    let xhr = new XMLHttpRequest();
    xhr.open("POST", "/api/v1/auth/login", true);
    . . .
```

Now, if we run our app, we can see that our frontend works with the new endpoints. With this, we are getting one step closer to developing a RESTful API for our app. However, we still have some glaring shortcomings. Right now, we can create another user and log in under that user. In the next section, we'll explore how to manage our user state in a stateless fashion.

Statelessness

Statelessness is where the server does not store any state about the client session. The advantages here are straightforward. It enables our application to scale as the session information is cached on the client's side.

It also empowers us to be more flexible with our computing approach. For instance, let's say that our application has exploded in popularity. As a result, we may want to spin our app up on two computing instances or servers and have a load balancer direct traffic to both of these instances in a balanced manner. If information is stored on the server, the user will have an inconsistent experience.

They may update the state of their session on one computing instance, but then, when they make another request, they may hit another computing instance that has outdated data. Considering this, statelessness cannot just be achieved by storing everything in the client. As long as our database is not dependent on a computing instance of our app, we can also store our data on this database, as shown in the following diagram:

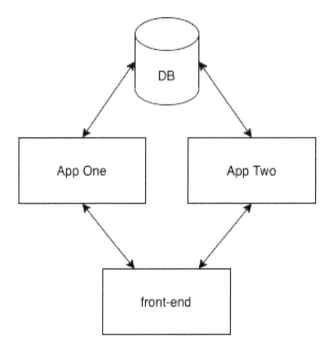

Figure 8.2 – Our stateless approach

As you can see, considering this, our app is already stateless. It stores the user ID in a JWT in the frontend, and we store our user data models and to-do items in our PostgreSQL database. As a result, we do not have to roll back much. However, in the last chapter, *Chapter 7, Managing User Sessions*, we did hardcode a user ID when creating a new to-do item, and we simply got all of our to-do items no matter what user was logged in. In this section, we are going to make the to-do view module user-specific.

First of all, we are going to have to ensure that there are no clashes with the data surrounding the user. Right now, we do not allow any to-do item to be created if a to-do item already has that title. However, with multiple users, it is expected that more than one user might have a pending to-do item that reminds them that the washing needs doing.

Therefore, we are going to have to ensure that the combination of a user ID and a title has to be unique. In order to do this, we can create another migration that ensures this. Creating migrations should be fairly familiar to you by now.

To enable our Rust application to support multiple users, we have to take the following steps:

1. We create migrations for our database, which imposes a UNIQUE constraint for to-do items based on the title and the user ID. Thus, we generate our own migration script with the following command:

    diesel migration generate user_title_constraint

    In our up.sql script in the migration directory, we define the UNIQUE constraint with the following code:

    ```
    ALTER  TABLE to_do ADD CONSTRAINT uc_item UNIQUE (title,
    user_id);
    ```

    Our down.sql script houses the following code:

    ```
    ALTER TABLE to_do DROP CONSTRAINT uc_item;
    ```

    Now that our database is protected against data clashes between users, we can move on to reconfiguring our application logic around this. For all our to-do item views, we are going to have to extract the user ID from the JWT. Therefore, it makes sense to build another function in our src/auth/jwt.rs file that accepts the HTTP request struct, extracts the token from the header, and then calls the decode function in order to avoid repetitive code in all our views that extract the header.

2. Then, we decode the JWT data directly from the request. So, first of all, we have to import the request struct at the top of the file, and then define our decode from the request function in the impl block of the JwtToken struct. This is demonstrated in the following code:

    ```
    use actix_web::HttpRequest;

    . . .


    pub struct JwtToken {
        pub user_id: i32,
        pub body: String
    }
    Impl JwtToken {

        . . .

        pub fn decode_from_request(request: HttpRequest)
        -> Result<JwtToken, &'static str> {
            match request.headers().get("user-token") {
    ```

```
        Some(token) => JwtToken::decode(
            String::from(token.to_str().unwrap())),
        None => Err("there is no token")
    }
  }
}
```

We can see that we simply get the header and match the outcome. If there is not a token, we then call the `decode` function, which returns a result of either the struct or an error message.

3. Now that we have this, we need to add a filter based on the user ID for the `return_state` function. All we have to do is pass the HTTP request into the view and call `decode` from the `request` function to extract and process the token. Before we do this, we are also going to have to alter our `return` function for all the items. We no longer want to get all the items; we want to filter by the user ID. We can do this via the following code in our `src/views/to_do/utils.rs` file:

```rust
pub fn return_state(user_id: &i32) -> ToDoItems {
    let connection = establish_connection();

    let items = to_do::table
        .order(to_do::columns::id.asc())
        .filter(to_do::columns::user_id.eq(&user_id))
        .load::<Item>(&connection)
        .unwrap();

    let mut array_buffer = Vec::new();

    for item in items {
        let item = to_do_factory(&item.status,
            item.title).unwrap();
        array_buffer.push(item);
    }
    return ToDoItems::new(array_buffer);
}
```

From the preceding code, we can see that we took in a reference to the user ID and we added a filter line to the database query in order to ensure that the app does not return items that do not belong to the user.

4. We now have to update all our views as they use the return_state function to load, serialize, and return the to-do items. First of all, we update the create view in the src/views/to_do/create.rs file. We do this by adding the following import at the top of the file:

```
use crate::auth::jwt::JwtToken;
```

Once this is done, we define the token in the view and add an extra filter to the database query based on the user ID from the token. We then pass the user ID in the return_state function as seen in the following code:

```
pub async fn create(req: HttpRequest) -> impl Responder {
    let title: String = req.match_info().get("title"
    ).unwrap().to_string();
    let title_ref: String = req.match_info().get("title"
    ).unwrap().to_string();

    let token: JwtToken = JwtToken::decode_from_request(
                          req).unwrap();

    let connection = establish_connection();
    let items = to_do::table
        .filter(to_do::columns::title.eq(
            title_ref.as_str()))
        .filter(to_do::columns::user_id.eq(
            &token.user_id))
        .order(to_do::columns::id.asc())
        .load::<Item>(&connection)
        .unwrap();
    if items.len() == 0 {
        let new_post = NewItem::new(title,
            token.user_id.clone());
        let _ = diesel::insert_into(
            to_do::table).values(&new_post)
            .execute(&connection);
    }
```

```
    return return_state(&token.user_id)
}
```

From the preceding code, we can see that we extract the title twice from the body. We then get the token from the request. Now that we have everything we need from the request, we establish a database connection and get the to-do items from the database filtered by the title and the user ID.

If the to-do item does not exist, then the length of the results will be zero. If this is the case, we create a new to-do item and insert it into the database. Note that we directly unwrap the token here instead of matching, despite our new function returning a result. This is because the item views all inspect the token in the middleware. If there was an issue, we would not even get to the item view.

5. Now we move on to our delete function in the src/views/to_do/delete.rs file. We initially update our imports with the following:

```
use actix_web::{web, HttpResponse, HttpRequest};
use crate::auth::jwt::JwtToken;
```

With this, we update the delete view with the following code:

```
pub async fn delete(to_do_item: web::Json<ToDoItem>,
                    req: HttpRequest) -> HttpResponse {
    let title_ref: String = to_do_item.title.clone();

    let token: JwtToken = JwtToken::
        decode_from_request(req).unwrap();

    let connection = establish_connection();
    let items = to_do::table
        .filter(to_do::columns::title.eq(
            title_ref.as_str()))
        .filter(to_do::columns::user_id.eq(
            &token.user_id))
        .order(to_do::columns::id.asc())
        .load::<Item>(&connection)
        .unwrap();
    let _ = diesel::delete(
        &items[0]).execute(&connection);
```

```
        return HttpResponse::Ok().json(
            return_state(&token.user_id))
    }
```

From the preceding code, we get the title and extract the token from the request. We then get the to-do item from the database based on the title and user ID. We then delete this to-do item from the database and return the items that exist. Also, we have added an HTTP request to the view parameters, a filter with respect to the user ID. We then pass the user ID into our return state. With this, we are starting to see a pattern.

6. In our `src/views/to_do/edit.rs` file, we update the following imports with these definitions:

```
use actix_web::{web, HttpResponse, HttpRequest};
use crate::auth::jwt::JwtToken;
```

Then, we add an HTTP request to the parameters of the view, define the token, filter the database call using the user ID, and pass the user ID in the `return_state` function. This is seen as follows:

```
pub async fn edit(to_do_item: web::Json<ToDoItem>,
                  req: HttpRequest) -> HttpResponse {

    let title_ref: String = to_do_item.title.clone();
    let token: JwtToken = JwtToken::
        decode_from_request(req).unwrap();

    let connection = establish_connection();
    let results = to_do::table.filter(
        to_do::columns::title
        .eq(title_ref))
        .filter(to_do::columns::user_id.eq(
            &token.user_id));

    let _ = diesel::update(results)
        .set(to_do::columns::status.eq("done"))
        .execute(&connection);
```

```
        return HttpResponse::Ok().json(return_state(
            &token.user_id))
    }
```

7. Finally, we can update the `get` view in our `src/views/to_do/get.rs` file, which is simply defining the token from the request and passing the user ID into the `return_state` function, as seen in this code:

```
use actix_web::Responder;
use actix_web::HttpRequest;
use super::utils::return_state;
use crate::auth::jwt::JwtToken;


pub async fn get(req: HttpRequest) -> impl Responder {
    let token: JwtToken =
        JwtToken::decode_from_request(req).unwrap();
    return return_state(&token.user_id)
}
```

Now, with these uniform, simple alterations for all our views in the item module, our app is now supporting multiple users. You may notice that all the to-do items have been cleared. They have not been deleted, and our code is not wrong.

We have to remember that our migration in the previous chapter, *Chapter 7, Managing User Sessions*, created a default placeholder user. This placeholder user has an ID of 1. When we hardcoded the user ID in the `create` view, we hardcoded a value of 1. Therefore, there are no to-do items registered under our user with an ID of 2.

We also have to remember that our placeholder user cannot be logged in because the password is not hashed, and we hash our passwords when performing a login. Creating and editing to-do items still work fine if we test them out. If we create another user and log in using those credentials, our app will be completely empty. Switching users will result in switching to-do items that belong to the user.

Now that our API endpoints have been updated to accommodate different users, our app essentially functions the way we want it to. If we wanted to ship our application now, there is nothing really stopping us from configuring the build with Docker and deploying it on a server with a database and **NGINX**. However, there are always things we can add. In the next section, we'll look into logging requests.

Logging our server traffic

So far, our application does not log anything. This does not directly affect the running of the app. However, there are some advantages to logging. **Logging** enables us to debug our applications.

Right now, as we are developing locally, it may not seem like logging is really needed. However, in a production environment, there are many reasons why an application can fail, including Docker container orchestration issues. Logs that note what processes have happened can help us to pinpoint an error. We can also use logging to see when edge cases and errors arise in order for us to monitor the general health of our application. When it comes to logging, there are four types of logs that we can build:

- **Informational (info)**: This is general logging. If we want to track a general process and how it is progressing, we use this type. Examples of using this are starting and stopping the server and logging certain checkpoints that we want to monitor, such as HTTP requests.

- **Verbose**: This is information like the type defined in the previous point. However, it is more granular in order to inform us of a more detailed flow of a process. This is mainly used for debugging purposes and should generally be avoided when it comes to production settings.

- **Warning**: We use this type when we are logging a process that is failing and should not be ignored. However, we use this instead of raising an error because we do not want the service to be interrupted or the user to be aware of the specific error. The logs themselves are for us to be alerted of the problem in order to take action. Problems such as calls to another server failing are appropriate for this category.

- **Error**: This is where the process is interrupted due to an error and we need to sort it out as quickly as possible. We also need to inform the user that the transaction did not go through. A good example of this is a failure to connect or insert data into a database. If this happens, there is no record of the transaction happening and it cannot be solved retroactively. However, it should be noted that the process can continue running.

To contrast this with the warning type, this might be if a warning comes up about the server failing to send an email, connect to another server to dispatch a product for shipping, and so on. Once we have sorted out the problem, we can retroactively make a database call to transactions in this timeframe, and make the calls to the server with the right information.

In the worst case, there will be a delay. With the error type, we will not be able to make the database call as the server errored out before the order was even entered in the database. Considering this, it is clear why error logging is highly critical, and the user needs to be informed that there is a problem and their transaction did not go through, prompting them that they should try again later.

We could consider the option of including enough information in the error logs to retroactively go back and update the database and complete the rest of the process when the issue is resolved, removing the need to inform the user. While this is tempting, we have to consider two things. Log data is generally unstructured. There is no quality control for what goes into a log. Therefore, once we have finally managed to manipulate the log data into the right format, there is still a chance that corrupt data could find its way into the database.

The second issue is that logs are not considered secure. They get copied and sent to other developers in a crisis, and they can be plugged into other pipelines and websites such as **Bugsnag** in order to monitor logs. Considering the nature of logs, it is not good practice to have any identifiable information in a log.

Now that we have understood the uses of logging, we can start building our logger:

1. In our `Cargo.toml` file, we add the following crates:

```
log = "0.4.11"
env_logger = "0.8.1"
```

With these crates, we will configure our first logging task, logging the request URL and response status. This requires us to note the URL of the request, and also the status of the response. This means that we are going to have to refactor the `wrap_fn` function in our `main.rs` file.

2. Right now, `wrap_fn` returns a future that is defined by `Either::Right` and `Either::Left`. However, we are now going to have to await the future and get the status result of the call. In order to do this, after our match, we remove end_result at the end, replacing it with the following code:

```
async {
    let result = end_result.await?;
    Ok(result)
}
```

Running the app now will show us that it functions in the same way; however, we also now have access to the result before returning it.

3. Now that we have the result of the calls, we have to ensure that we keep the URL available throughout the server process. We know that once we pass the service request through the call function, the URL associated with it will be destroyed and no longer available. Because of this, we are going to have to clone the request URI path, and then package it in a string before we start anything, as shown in the following code:

```
.wrap_fn(|req, srv| {
    let request_url: String = String::from(
                                    *&req.uri()
                                    .path().clone()
                                );
    let passed: bool;
    ...
```

4. We now have all the variables available to start logging. Initially, we have to utilize the crates that we recently installed at the top of the `main.rs` file with the following code definitions:

```
use log;
use env_logger;
```

5. We then define the logger before we start the server with the following code:

```
env_logger::init();
HttpServer::new(|| {
    ...
```

We then call this logger after the call has been processed.

6. As we need to track calls for general information and high-level system debugging, we should utilize the `info` macro from the `log` crate with the following code in the `async` block:

```
async move {
    let result = end_result.await?;
    log::info!("{} -> {}", request_url,
        &result.status());
    Ok(result)
}
```

Here, we can see that we log our request URL and a reference to the `result` status. It also has to be noted that our `async` block is now an `async move` block. This is because the `async` block could outlive our URL string. The `async move` block moves the ownership of the URL into the block. Now, our app is ready to run.

7. However, you may notice that simply running the `cargo run` command does not do anything. We will not see anything printed out to the terminal no matter how many times we make API calls. This is because we have not defined the environment variable for the Rust log. We can do this with the following command:

```
RUST_LOG="info,parser::expression=info,actix_web=info"
cargo run
```

Seeing as we are using the `actix_web` crate for our server, we might as well allow the info messages to be logged. The parser targets the part of our code that enables the info-level logging. Once this is executed, we get the following output:

```
Finished dev [unoptimized + debuginfo] target(s)
in 16.75s
  Running `target/debug/managing_views`

[2020-11-09T03:42:31Z INFO  actix_server::builder]
Starting 4 workers
[2020-11-09T03:42:31Z INFO  actix_server::builder]
Starting "actix-web-service-127.0.0.1:8000" service on
127.0.0.1:8000
```

From the preceding output, we can see that our application has compiled, which is nothing new. However, the `actix_server` info logs are now telling us that we have started four workers and that our server is listening on localhost at port `8000`. This will come in handy when we are deploying the server as we will actually be able to see what port the application is listening to and that it is running via accessing the logs in the Docker container.

8. Now we need to check out our request logging. If we hit the home page, we get the following output:

```
[2020-11-09T03:42:54Z INFO  managing_views] / -> 200 OK
[2020-11-09T03:42:54Z INFO  managing_views] /api/v1/item/
get -> 200 OK
```

We can see that the logger already timestamps and traces. We also have our response code, status, and URL. The log output is what we expect. The home page is served, and the items are obtained. However, if we log out, we get the following trace:

```
[2020-11-09T04:13:16Z INFO  managing_views]
/logout/ -> 200 OK
[2020-11-09T04:13:17Z INFO  managing_views]
/ -> 200 OK
[2020-11-09T04:13:17Z INFO  managing_views]
/api/v1/item/get -> 401 Unauthorized
[2020-11-09T04:13:17Z INFO  managing_views]
/login/ -> 200 OK
[2020-11-09T04:13:17Z INFO  managing_views]
/login/ -> 200 OK
```

The logout is fine, and so is the redirection to the home page. However, we get an unauthorized `GET` call and then two loads of the login view. This technically works; however, it is not optimal. What the logging has shown is that not having the token in the HTML storage redirects to the login view, and so does not attaching the token to the `GET` call.

If we do not have a token, we ideally do not need to make the GET call. This will reduce an unnecessary API call and redirect. This can be easily solved in our javascript/main.js file. Near the end of the file, we merely call the getItems(); function, meaning that the GET API call will just fire when the script, and thus the view, is loaded. If we remove this and shift the call into the top five lines of the file, we get the following code:

```
if (localStorage.getItem("user-token") == null) {
    window.location.replace(document.location.origin +
                            "/login/");
} else {
    getItems();
}
```

9. At the top, we were already checking to see whether the token is in the storage. If it is not, we then redirect to the login view. Otherwise, we make the GET call. Now, if we do a logout, we get the following trace:

```
[2020-11-09T04:17:05Z INFO  managing_views]
/logout/ -> 200 OK
[2020-11-09T04:17:05Z INFO  managing_views]
/ -> 200 OK
[2020-11-09T04:17:05Z INFO  managing_views]
/login/ -> 200 OK
```

From the preceding output, we can see that our refactor worked! We now no longer have excessive calls.

This example has given us first-hand experience of how logging requests helps us to spot problems while we are developing our application. We have spotted behavior that could be improved and refactored it. If we did not use logging, then it would have been hard to spot.

We can also use logging throughout the application without initializing the logger. To explore this, we can look into logging an error in a different file. In our login view, we remember that we check to see whether there are multiple users with the same username. Now, because of the unique constraints, it is unlikely that this will ever happen, but we need to raise an error log if it does. In order to do this, we have to use our `use log;` crate in our `src/views/auth/login.rs` file inside our login view function with the following code:

```
if users.len() == 0 {
    return HttpResponse::NotFound().await.unwrap()
} else if users.len() > 1 {
    log::error!("multiple users have the username: {}",
               credentials.username.clone());
    return HttpResponse::Conflict().await.unwrap()
}
```

If we were to ever trigger this, we would get the following output:

```
2020-11-09T04:46:49Z ERROR managing_views::views::auth::login]
multiple users have the username: maxwell
```

From the preceding output, we have managed to configure a logger with a range of different levels. This has enabled us to look deeper into how our application is working, exposing hidden problems. With this, we have refactored our API calls to make them more efficient. However, there is still some undesirable functionality in our app that we want to stop.

When we refresh the main items list view, we make another item's GET API call to display to the user. However, we have not altered the to-do items in the database. This is not an error, but it is wasteful. In order to optimize this, we can utilize the REST constraint of caching in the following section.

Caching

Caching is where we store data in the frontend to be reused. This enables us to reduce the number of API calls to the backend and reduce latency. Because the benefits are so clear, it can be tempting to cache everything. However, there are some things to consider.

Concurrency is a clear issue. The data could be outdated, leading to confusion and data corruption when sending the wrong information to the backend. There are also security concerns. If one user logs out and another user logs in on the same computer, there is a risk that the second user will be able to access the first user's items. With this, there has to be a couple of checks in place. The correct user needs to be logged in, and the data needs to be timestamped so that if the cached data is accessed past a certain period, a GET request is made to refresh the data.

Our application is fairly locked down. We cannot access anything unless we are logged in. The main process that we could cache in our application is the GET items call. All other calls that edit the state of the item list in the backend return the updated items. Considering this, our caching mechanism looks like the following:

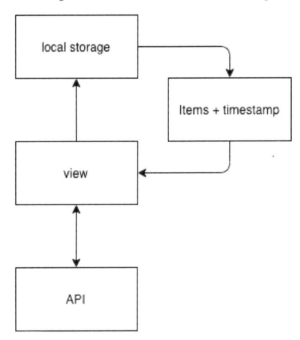

Figure 8.3 – Our caching approach

The loop in the preceding diagram can be executed as many times as we want when refreshing the page. However, this might not be a good idea. Say a user logs on to our application on their phone when they are in the kitchen to update the list, then goes back to their computer to do some work, refreshing the page to update the list. This caching system would expose the user to out-of-date data that will be sent to the backend. We can reduce the risk of this happening by referencing the timestamp. When the timestamp is older than a specified cut-off point, we will then make another API call to refresh the data when the user refreshes the page.

Our caching system will be done entirely in our `javascript/main.js` file. First of all, seeing as we will be rendering the to-to list data from the API call and from a cache, we will have to pull the list of rendering processes outside of the API call function. This can be done with the following function:

```
function runRenderProcess(data) {
    renderItems(data["pending_items"],
                "edit", "pendingItems", editItem);
    renderItems(data["done_items"], "delete",
                "doneItems", deleteItem);
    document.getElementById(
        "completeNum").innerHTML = data["done_item_count"];
    document.getElementById(
        "pendingNum").innerHTML = data["pending_item_count"];
}
```

From the preceding code, we can see the four processes that update four different HTML elements with the data passed in. Now that we have done this, we can lift this code out of the API call function, and also store the date and the data from the API call in the local storage with the following code:

```
function apiCall(url, method) {
    let xhr = new XMLHttpRequest();
    xhr.withCredentials = true;
    xhr.addEventListener('readystatechange', function() {
        if (this.readyState === this.DONE) {
            if (this.status === 401) {
                window.location.replace(
                    document.location.origin + "/login/");
            } else {
                runRenderProcess(
                    JSON.parse(this.responseText));
                localStorage.setItem(
                    "item-cache-date", new Date());
                localStorage.setItem(
                    "item-cache-data", this.responseText);
            }
```

```
        }
    });
    xhr.open(method, "/api/v1" + url);
    xhr.setRequestHeader('content-type', 'application/json');
    xhr.setRequestHeader('user-token', localStorage.getItem(
                        "user-token"));

    return xhr
}
```

From the preceding code, we can see that we have stored the data under the "item-cache-data" key, and we have stored the timestamp under the "item-cache-date" key. We have also called the runRenderProcess function.

Now that our API call function is caching the data, we have to check the timestamp and load from the cache, passing the data to the runRenderProcess function if the cached data is under 2 minutes old. We only do this on loading, as we will refresh our data whenever we edit the state of the to-do items list. This is done in our loading code at the top of the file, as seen in the following code:

```
if (localStorage.getItem("user-token") == null) {
    window.location.replace(document.location.origin +
        "/login/");
} else {
    let cachedData = Date.parse(
                        localStorage.getItem(
                            "item-cache-date"));
    let now = new Date();
    let difference = Math.round((
        now - cachedData) / (1000));

    if (difference <= 120) {
        runRenderProcess(JSON.parse(
                        localStorage.getItem(
                        "item-cache-data"
                        )));
    } else {
```

```
        getItems();
    }
}
```

We can see that with our refactored loading, we do not get repeated GET item calls when we refresh our page, as seen in the following log:

```
[2020-11-11T00:34:47Z INFO   managing_views]
/api/v1/item/get -> 200 OK
[2020-11-11T00:34:51Z INFO   managing_views] / -> 200 OK
[2020-11-11T00:34:54Z INFO   managing_views] / -> 200 OK
[2020-11-11T00:34:55Z INFO   managing_views] / -> 200 OK}
```

And here we have it. We have managed to cache our data and reuse it to prevent our backend API from being hit excessively. This can be applied to other frontend processes too. For instance, a customer basket could be cached and used when the user checks out.

This takes our application from a simple website one step closer to a web app. However, we have to acknowledge that as we use caching more, the complexity of the frontend increases. If this is the case, then it is advised that you use a frontend framework such as **React**, **Vue**, or **Angular**. For our application, this is where the caching stops. Right now, there are no more alterations needed on our applications for the rest of the hour. However, there is one more concept that we should briefly cover, which is code on demand.

Code on demand

Code on demand is where the backend server directly executes code on the frontend. This constraint is optional and not widely used. However, it can be useful as it gives the backend server the right to decide when code is executed on the frontend. We have already been doing this; in our logout view, we directly execute **JavaScript** on the frontend by simply returning it in a string. This is done in the `src/views/auth/logout.rs` file.

Summary

In this chapter, we have gone through the different aspects of RESTful design and implemented them in our application. We have assessed the layers of our application, enabling us to refactor the middleware to enable two different futures to be processed depending on the outcome. This doesn't just stop at authorizing requests. Based on the parameters of the request, we could use this to redirect requests to other servers, or directly respond with a code on demand response that makes some changes to the frontend and then makes another API call. This approach gives us another tool, custom logic with multiple future outcomes in the middleware before the view is hit.

We then refactored our path struct to make the interface uniform, preventing clashes between frontend and backend views. We then explored the stateless concept, passing the user ID throughout the application with the JWT, enabling us to save and serve to-do items that are unique to the user accessing them.

We then explored the different levels of logging and logged all our requests to highlight silent yet undesirable behavior. After refactoring our frontend to rectify this, we then used our logging to assess whether our caching mechanism was working correctly when caching to-do items into the frontend to prevent excessive API calls. Now our application is passable. We can always make improvements; however, we are not at the stage where if we were to deploy our application onto a server, we would be able to monitor it, check the logs when something is going wrong, manage multiple users with their own to-do lists, and reject unauthorized requests before they even hit the view. We also have caching, and our application is stateless, accessing and writing data on a PostgreSQL database.

In the next chapter, we will be writing unit tests for our Rust structs and functional tests for our API endpoints, as well as cleaning the code up ready for deployment.

Questions

1. Why can we not simply code multiple futures into the middleware and merely call and return the one that is right, considering request parameters and authorization outcomes, but instead have to wrap them in an enum?

2. How do we add a new version of views but still support the old views if our API is serving mobile apps and third parties that might not update instantly?

3. Why is the stateless constraint becoming more important in the era of elastic cloud computing?

4. How could we enable another service to be incorporated utilizing the properties of the JWT?

5. A warning log message hides the fact that an error has happened from the user, but still alerts us to fix it. Why do we ever bother telling the user that an error has occurred and to try again with an error log?

6. What are the advantages of logging all requests?

7. Why do we sometimes have to use `async move`?

Section 4: Testing and Deployment

Building our application is one thing. However, it is not very useful if we do not deploy it. Going through the necessary steps to protect the application and deploy it onto a server using Docker so that others can use it. In order to achieve this, we need to build scripts that automate the packaging and deployment of our application, which can be put into pipelines if needed. We also need to run unit and functional tests to ensure that we are deploying an application which works exactly how we want it to.

In this section, we'll build functional and unit tests for our web app. With this, we will be able to see how our components work with a basic Cargo test command, and we'll run our app and run a range of API tests to test the full infrastructure. We then build automated scripts that will package our application into a Docker image, and deploy it onto a server with a database and NGINX in order to protect our application. We then apply what we have learned throughout the book to the Rocket Web Framework. This will show you how our approach won't let the web framework define us, enabling you to confidently apply web concepts to multiple Rust web frameworks.

This section comprises the following chapters:

- *Chapter 09, Testing Our Application Endpoints and Components*
- *Chapter 10, Deploying Our Application on AWS*
- *Chapter 11, Understanding Rocket Web Framework*

9
Testing Our Application Endpoints and Components

Our to-do Rust application now fully works. We are happy with our first version as it manages authentication, different users and their to-do lists, and logs our processes for inspection. However, a web developer's job is never done.

While we have now come to the end of adding features to our application, we know that the journey does not stop here. In future iterations beyond this book, we may want to add teams, new statuses, multiple lists per user, and so on. However, as we add these features, we have to ensure that our old application behavior stays the same unless we actively change it. This is done by building tests.

In this chapter, we'll build tests that check our existing behavior, laying down traps that will throw errors that report to us if the behavior changes without us actively changing it. This prevents us from breaking the application and pushing it to a server after adding a new feature or altering the code.

In this chapter, we will cover the following topics:

- Cleaning up our code

- Testing structs with unit test code in Rust

- Testing functions with unit test code and mocks to check request edge cases in Rust

- Using Cargo to test individual modules, files, and the whole app

- Writing functional API tests in Postman to check how an application runs the whole process end to end

- Creating collections of Postman API tests to facilitate running a series of API tests after each other and exporting them in a file

- Automating the running of all these tests in sequence to test a full workflow using Newman

At the end of this chapter, we will understand how to build unit tests in Rust, inspecting our structs in detail with a range of edge cases. If our structs behave in a way we do not expect, our unit tests will report it to us.

Technical requirements

In this chapter, we'll build on the code built in *Chapter 8*, *Building RESTful Services*. This can be found at the following URL: `https://github.com/PacktPublishing/Rust-Web-Programming/tree/master/Chapter08/caching`.

Node and NPM are also needed for installing and running the automated API tests, which can be found at the following URL: `https://nodejs.org/en/download/`.

You can find the full source code used in this chapter here: `https://github.com/PacktPublishing/Rust-Web-Programming/tree/master/Chapter09`

The CiA videos for this book can be viewed at: `http://bit.ly/3jULCrw`.

Cleaning up our code

Before we write any tests, we need to ensure that our code is clean. If there is code that is not being used, then it makes little sense to spend time and effort writing tests for it. If we run our to-do Rust application right now, you may notice that we get a list of warnings about unused code.

This is because we switched from storing our to-do items in a **JSON** file to using a **PostgreSQL** database. As a result, the code that handled the reading and writing to JSON files became redundant. We can remove this redundant code by deleting the `src/processes.rs` and `src/state.rs` files, and removing `mod state;` and `mod processes;` lines from the `main.rs` file.

Once this is done, we then remove all the functionality from all the traits in the `src/to_do/structs/traits/{pending.done}.rs` directory as the reading and writing of data has been passed onto the database and data model structs. We also have to remove the `mod traits;` line from the `src/to_do/structs/mod.rs` file. Now, let's run our application with the following command:

```
RUST_LOG="info,parser::expression=info,actix_web=info" cargo
run
```

We get the following output:

```
Finished dev [unoptimized + debuginfo] target(s) in 1.34s
Running `target/debug/managing_views`
[2020-11-20T19:44:06Z INFO  actix_server::builder] Starting 4
workers
[2020-11-20T19:44:06Z INFO  actix_server::builder] Starting
"actix-web-service-127.0.0.1:8000" service on 127.0.0.1:8000
```

We get the preceding output without any warnings! Ideally, we should be building tests as we code along. However, if you find yourself having to create tests retrospectively, it is always a good opportunity to truly assess what is being used and what needs to be deleted. Now that we are sure that all the code that we have is actually being used, we can start writing our unit tests for our application.

Building our unit tests

In this section, we will explore the concept of unit tests, and building unit test modules, which contain tests as functions. Here, we are not going to achieve 100% unit test coverage for our application. There are places in our application that can be covered by our functional tests, such as API endpoints and JSON serialization. However, unit tests are still important in some parts of our application.

Unit tests enable us to look at some of our processes in more detail. As we saw with our logging in *Chapter 8, Building RESTful Services*, a functional test might work the way we want it to end to end, but there might be edge cases and behavior that we do not want. This was seen in *Chapter 8, Building RESTful Services*, where we saw our application make two **GET** calls when one was enough.

In our unit tests, we will break down the processes one by one, mock certain parameters, and test the outcomes. These tests are fully isolated. The advantage of this is that we get to test a range of parameters quickly without having to run a full process each time. This also helps us pinpoint where the application is failing exactly with what configuration. Unit testing is also useful for test-driven development, where we build the components of a feature bit by bit, running the unit tests and altering the components as and when the test outcomes require.

In big, complex systems, this saves a lot of time as you do not have to spin up the app and run the full system to spot a typo or failure to account for an edge case. However, before we get too excited, we have to acknowledge that unit testing is a tool, not a lifestyle, and there are some fallbacks to using it. The tests are only as good as their mocks. If we do not mock realistic interactions, then a unit test could pass but the application could fail. Unit tests are important, but they also have to be accompanied by functional tests.

Rust is still a new language, so at this point, unit testing support is not as advanced as other languages such as **Python**. For instance, with Python, we can mock any object from any file with ease at any point in the test. With these mocks, we can define outcomes and monitor interactions with these mocks. While Rust does not have these mocks so readily available, this does not mean we cannot unit test.

A bad craftsman always blames their tools. However, we have structured our code in such a way that we can unit test our code without needing advanced mocking. First of all, we can test our to-do structs. As you'll remember, we have done and pending structs, which inherit a base struct. We can start by unit testing the struct that has no dependencies and is moving down to other structs that have dependencies. In our `src/to_do/structs/base.rs` file, we can define our unit tests for the `Base` struct at the bottom of the file with the following code:

```
#[cfg(test)]
mod base_tests {

    use super::Base;

    #[test]
    fn new() {
```

```
        let title: String = String::from("test title");
        let expected_title: String = String::from("test
            title");
        let status: String = String::from("test status");
        let expected_status: String = String::from("test
            status");

        let new_base_struct: Base = Base::new(title, status);
        assert_eq!(expected_title, new_base_struct.title);
        assert_eq!(expected_status, new_base_struct.status);
    }
}
```

From the preceding code, we can see that we created our `test` module, which is decorated with a `#[cfg(test)]` attribute. Inside the module, we import the `Base` struct from the file outside of the `base_tests` module, which is still in the file. We then test the `Base::new` function by decorating our new function with a `#[test]` attribute.

This is the first time we have covered attributes. An **attribute** is simply metadata applied to modules and functions. This metadata aids the compiler by giving it information. In this case, it is telling the compiler that this module is a test module and that the function is an individual test.

We can see that we essentially created a new `Base` struct, and then checked to see if the fields are what we expected. In order to run this, run the `cargo test` functionality, pointing it to the file we want to test, which is denoted by the following line:

```
cargo test to_do::structs::base
```

The preceding code gives the following output:

```
running 1 test
test to_do::structs::base::base_tests::new ... ok

test result: ok. 1 passed; 0 failed; 0 ignored; 0 measured; 0
filtered out
```

We can see that our test was run, and that it passed. Now we'll move onto writing tests for the rest of the module, which is the Done and Pending structs. In our src/to_do/ structs/done.rs file, we define the tests via the code given as follows:

```
#[cfg(test)]
mod done_test {

    use super::Done;

    #[test]
    fn new() {
        let expected_status: String = String::from("done");
        let title: String = String::from("excel date");
        let expected_title: String = String::from("excel
            date");

        let done: Done = Done::new(title);
        assert_eq!(expected_status, done.super_struct.status);
        assert_eq!(expected_title, done.super_struct.title);
    }

}
```

As we can see, our Done::new function already defines the status as done, so we test to see if this is in our test. We take the same approach in our src/to_do/structs/ pending.rs file with the following code:

```
#[cfg(test)]
mod pending_test {
    use super::Pending;
    #[test]
    fn new() {
        let expected_status: String = String::from("pending");
        let title: String = String::from("washing");
        let expected_title: String = String::from("washing");
        let done: Pending = Pending::new(title);
```

```
        assert_eq!(expected_status, done.super_struct.status);
        assert_eq!(expected_title, done.super_struct.title);
    }
}
```

We run the following command:

```
cargo test to_do
```

This gives the following output:

```
running 3 tests
test to_do::structs::base::base_tests::new ... ok
test to_do::structs::pending::pending_test::new ... ok
test to_do::structs::done::done_test::new ... ok

test result: ok. 3 passed; 0 failed; 0 ignored; 0 measured; 0
filtered out
```

We can see that all of our tests have now run and passed.

Now that we have done some basic testing, let's look at the other modules that we can test. Our JSON serialization and views can be tested in our functional tests with Postman. Our database models do not have any advanced functionality that we have purposefully defined.

Building JWT unit tests

All our models do is read and write to the database. This has been shown to work. The only module left that we'll unit test is the `auth` module. Here, we have some logic that has multiple outcomes based on the inputs. We also have to do some mocking as some of the functions accept `actix_web` structs, which have certain fields and functions. Luckily for us, `actix_web` has a `test` module that enables us to mock requests.

Our first test can be on our `JwtToken` struct in our `src/auth/jwt.rs` file. We define the `test` module at the bottom of the file with the following outline:

```
#[cfg(test)]
mod jwt_tests {
    use super::JwtToken;
    use actix_web::test;
}
```

Our first test inside this module is to check to see if the whole process works if everything is right. We can do this with the following code:

```
#[test]
fn encode_decode() {
    let encoded_token: String = JwtToken::encode(32);
    let decoded_token: JwtToken = JwtToken::decode(
                                encoded_token).unwrap();
    assert_eq!(32, decoded_token.user_id);
}
```

From the preceding code, we have encoded a random user ID number into a token, then decoded it, and checked to see if the user ID could be extracted. If everything is working, then this test will pass. Now we have to ensure that a failure in decoding the token will be handled correctly. This is done by passing a random string into the `JwtToken::decode` function. Once we have done this, we match the outcome. This is done in the following code:

```
#[test]
fn decode_incorrect_token() {
    let encoded_token: String = String::from("test");

    match JwtToken::decode(encoded_token) {
        Err(message) => assert_eq!("Could not decode",
            message),
        _ => panic!("Incorrect token should not be able to be
                encoded")
    }
}
```

As we can see, we expect an error, so if the `JwtToken::decode` function results in anything other than an error, we will raise an error with a helpful message to tell the tester what is going wrong. If the `JwtToken::decode` function results in an error, we then check to see if it is the correct error that we were expecting.

Now we have tested the incorrect token, we can move onto testing our function that decodes from a request. In order to do this, we have to use the `test::TestRequest` struct to mock an HTTP request to see how our function handles it. Initially, we test with a correct token in the header of the request, as shown in the following code:

```
#[test]
fn decode_from_request_with_correct_token() {
    let encoded_token: String = JwtToken::encode(32);
    let request = test::TestRequest::with_header(
        "user-token", encoded_token).to_http_request();
    let out_come = JwtToken::decode_from_request(request);

    match out_come {
        Ok(token) => assert_eq!(32, token.user_id),
        _ => panic!("Token is not returned when it should be")
    }
}
```

From the preceding code, we can see that we encode the token, build a mock request, and add the token to that header. Again, we use the `match` statement to assess the outcome of the function to see if we can get the user ID from the processed token.

We are starting to see a pattern here, that is, building the components needed and passing them through the function being tested using a `match` statement to check the expected result. With this approach, we test the decoding of the request with no token and one with a false token with this code:

```
#[test]
fn decode_from_request_with_no_token() {
    let request = test::TestRequest::with_header("test",
                    "test").to_http_request();
    let out_come = JwtToken::decode_from_request(request);

    match out_come {
```

```
            Err(message) => assert_eq!("there is no token",
                message),
            _ => panic!("Token should not be returned when it is
                not present in the headers"
            )
        }
    }
}
#[test]
fn decode_from_request_with_false_token() {
    let request = test::TestRequest::with_header(
        "user-token", "test").to_http_request();
    let out_come = JwtToken::decode_from_request(request);

    match out_come {
        Err(message) => assert_eq!("Could not decode",
            message),
        _ => panic!("should be an error with a fake token")
    }
}
```

In the preceding code, we can see that we define two tests. In each test, we initially create a fake request that will mimic what we want. We then pass that request into our JWT struct matching the outcome. If the outcome does house the exact content we expect, it will fail. Now that we have built all the tests for our auth token, we can use this approach to test our check_password and extract_header_token functions in the src/auth/processes.rs file. We will use the same approach that we took with the previous code. However, due to the repetitive nature, this is a good opportunity for you to look at these functions and derive unit tests for these functions using the following template:

```
#[cfg(test)]
mod check_credentials_tests {
    use super::super::jwt::JwtToken;
    use super::extract_header_token;
    use super::check_password;
    use actix_web::test;
```

```
    #[test]
    fn correct_check_password() {
        ...
    }
    #[test]
    fn incorrect_check_password() {
        ...
    }
    #[test]
    fn no_token_in_extract_header_token() {
        let mock_request = test::TestRequest::with_header(
                            "test", "test").to_srv_request();
        ...
    }
    #[test]
    fn correct_token_in_extract_header_token() {
        ...
    }
}
```

In order to check that you have written tests along the same lines, you can check out the worked-out tests by accessing the following URL: `https://github.com/PacktPublishing/Rust-Web-Programming/blob/master/Chapter09/unit_testing/src/auth/processes.rs`

Once this is done, we only have to test our `process_function` function in our `src/auth/mod.rs` file with the following template:

```
#[cfg(test)]
mod process_token_tests {

    use super::process_token;
    use super::jwt::JwtToken;
    use actix_web::test::TestRequest;

    #[test]
    fn no_token_process_token() {
        ...
```

```
    }

    #[test]
    fn incorrect_token() {

        ...

    }
    #[test]
    fn correct_token() {

        ...

    }
}
```

You can compare your tests with the tests available via the following URL: https://
github.com/PacktPublishing/Rust-Web-Programming/blob/master/
Chapter09/unit_testing/src/auth/mod.rs

Now we have defined all of our unit tests for our application! We can run all of our tests
using the cargo test command, which gives us the following output:

```
running 15 tests
test auth::jwt::jwt_tests::
decode_incorrect_token ... ok
test auth::jwt::jwt_tests::
decode_from_request_with_no_token ... ok
test auth::jwt::jwt_tests::
decode_from_request_with_false_token ... ok
test auth::jwt::jwt_tests::
decode_from_request_with_correct_token ... ok
test auth::process_token_tests::
incorrect_token ... ok
test auth::jwt::jwt_tests::
encode_decode ... ok
```

```
test auth::process_token_tests::
correct_token ... ok
test auth::process_token_tests::
no_token_process_token ... ok
test auth::processes::check_credentials_tests::
correct_token_in_extract_header_token ... ok
test auth::processes::check_credentials_tests::
incorrect_check_password ... ok
test auth::processes::check_credentials_tests::
no_token_in_extract_header_token ... ok
test to_do::structs::base::base_tests::new ... ok
test to_do::structs::done::done_test::new ... ok
test to_do::structs::pending::pending_test::new ... ok
test auth::processes::check_credentials_tests::
correct_check_password ... ok

test result: ok. 15 passed; 0 failed;
0 ignored; 0 measured; 0 filtered out
```

From the preceding output, our auth and to_do modules are now fully unit tested. Considering that Rust is still a fairly new language, we have managed to painlessly unit test our code because we structured our code in a modular fashion.

The tests crate that actix_web provided enabled us to test edge cases quickly and easily. In this section, in just a few functions, we tested how our functions processed requests with missing tokens, false tokens, and correct tokens. We have seen first-hand how Rust enables us to run unit tests on our code.

Everything is configured with cargo. We do not have to set up paths, install extra modules, or configure environment variables. All we have to do is define modules with the test attribute, and run the cargo test command. However, we have to remember that our views and JSON serialization code are not unit tested. This is where we switch to Postman in order to test our API endpoints.

Writing tests in Postman

In this section, we will be using **Postman** to test our API endpoints. This will test our JSON processing and database access. In order to do this, we will follow these steps:

1. We are going to have to create a test user for our Postman tests. We can do this with the JSON body shown as follows:

    ```
    {
        "name": "test",
        "email": "testing@gmail.com",
        "password": "test"
    }
    ```

2. We need to add a POST request to the URL `http://127.0.0.1:8000/api/v1/user/create`. Once we have done this, we can use our login endpoint for our Postman tests. Now that we have created our test user, we have to get the token from the response header of the POST request to the URL `http://127.0.0.1:8000/api/v1/auth/login` with the JSON request body:

    ```
    {
        "username": "test",
        "password": "test"
    }
    ```

    With this token, we have all the information needed to create our Postman collection. **Postman** is a collection of API requests. In this collection, we can bunch all our to-do item API calls together using the user token as authentication.

3. We can create our collection with the following Postman button, that is, **+ New Collection**:

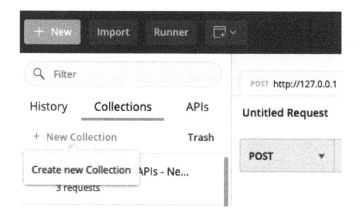

Figure 9.1 – Creating a new Postman collection

4. Once we have clicked this, we have to make sure that our user token is defined for the collection as all to-do item API calls need the token. This can be done by using the **Authorization** configuration for our API calls as seen in the following screenshot:

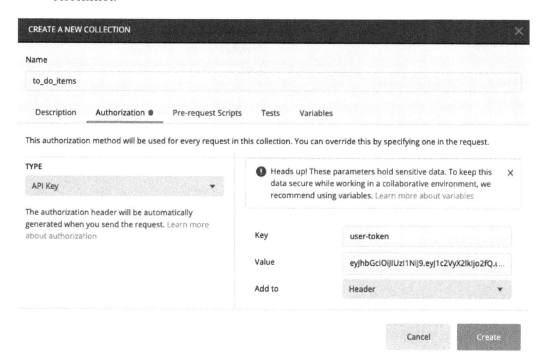

Figure 9.2 – Defining AUTH credentials in a new Postman collection

We can see that we have merely copy and pasted our token into the value with **user-token** as the key, with this to be inserted into the header of the requests. This should now be passed in all of our requests in the collection. This collection is now stored on the left-hand side navigation bar under the collections tab.

5. We can now add requests under the collection by clicking the grayed out **Add Request** button in this screenshot:

Figure 9.3 – Creating a new request for our Postman collection

Now, we have to think about our approach to testing the flow of testing as this has to be self-contained. Therefore, our requests will take the following order:

1. **Create**: Create a to-do item, and then check the return to see if it is stored correctly.

2. **Create**: Create another to-do item, checking the return to see if the previous one is stored and that the process can handle two.

3. **Create**: Create another to-do item with the same title as one of the other items, checking the response to ensure that our application is not storing duplicate to-do items with the same title.

4. **Edit**: Edit an item, checking the response to see if the edited item has been changed to **done** and that it is stored in the correct list.

5. **Edit**: Edit the second item to see if the edit effect is permanent and that the **done** list supports both items.

6. **Edit**: Edit an item that is not present in the application to see if the application handles this correctly.

7. **Delete**: Delete one to-do item to see if the response no longer has this to-do item, meaning that it is no longer stored in the database.

8. **Delete**: Delete the final to-do item, checking the response to see if there are no items left, showing that the **Delete** action is permanent.

We need to run the preceding tests in order for them to work as they rely on the previous action being correct. When we create a request for the collection, we have to be clear about what the request is doing, which step it is, and what type of request it is. For instance, creating our first **create** test will look like the following:

Figure 9.4 – Creating our first Postman create request

As we can see, the step is appended with the type by an underscore. We then put the description of the test from the list in the **Request description (Optional)** field. When defining the request, you may realize that the API key is not in the header of the request.

This is because it is in the hidden autogenerated headers of the request. Our first request has to be a **POST request** with the URL `http://127.0.0.1:8000/api/v1/item/create/washing`.

This creates the to-do item **washing**. However, before we click the **Send** button, we have to move over to the **Tests** tab in our Postman request, just to the left of the settings, to write our tests as seen in the following screenshot:

Figure 9.5 – Accessing the tests script in Postman

Our tests have to be written in **JavaScript**. However, we get access to Postman's `test` library by typing pm into the test script.

First of all, at the top of the test script, we need to process the request, which is done with this code:

```
var result = pm.response.json()
```

With the preceding line, we can access the response JSON throughout the test script. In order to comprehensively test our request, we need to follow these steps:

1. First, we check the basic content of the response. Our first test is to check to see if the response is 200. This can be done with the following code:

    ```
    pm.test("response is ok", function () {
        pm.response.to.have.status(200);
    });
    ```

    Here, we define the test description, then the function that the test runs is defined.

2. Then, we check the length of data in the response. After the preceding test, we define our test to check if the pending item has a length of one via the following code:

```
pm.test("returns one pending item", function(){
    if (result["pending_items"].length !== 1){
        throw new Error(
            "returns the wrong number of pending items");
    }
})
```

From the preceding code, we do a simple check of the length and throw an error if the length is not one as we only expect one pending item in the pending items list.

3. We then inspect the title and status of the pending item in the following code:

```
pm.test("Pending item has the correct title", function(){
    if (result["pending_items"][0]["title"] !==
        "washing"){
        throw new Error(
            "title of the pending item is not 'washing'");
    }
})
pm.test("Pending item has the correct status", function()
{
    if (result["pending_items"][0]["status"] !==
        "pending"){
        throw new Error(
            "status of the pending item is not 'pending'");
    }
})
```

From the preceding code, we throw an error if the status or title does not match what we want. Now we have satisfied our tests for the pending items, we can move onto the tests for the done items.

4. Seeing as our done items should be zero, the tests have the following definition:

```
pm.test("returns zero done items", function(){
    if (result["done_items"].length !== 0){
```

```
        throw new Error(
            "returns the wrong number of done items");
        }
    })
})
```

From the preceding code, we are merely ensuring that the done items array has a length of zero.

5. Now, we have to check the counts of our done and pending items. This is done in the following code:

```
pm.test("checking pending item count", function(){
    if (result["pending_item_count"] !== 1){
        throw new Error(
            "pending_item_count needs to be one");
        }
    })
pm.test("checking done item count", function(){
    if (result["done_item_count"] !== 0){
        throw new Error(
            "done_item_count needs to be zero");
        }
    })
```

6. We can then create the 2_create test with this URL: http://127.0.0.1:8000/api/v1/item/create/cooking. With this, we give the following slightly updated tests for the second crate:

```
var result = pm.response.json()
pm.test("response is ok", function () {
    pm.response.to.have.status(200);
}); pm.test("returns two pending item", function(){
    if (result["pending_items"].length !== 2){
        throw new Error(
            "returns the wrong number of pending items");
        }
}); pm.test("Pending item has the correct title",
    function(){
    if (result["pending_items"][0]["title"] !==
        "washing"){
```

```
            throw new Error(
                "title of the pending item is not 'washing'");
        }
}); pm.test("Pending item has the correct status",
        function(){
        if (result["pending_items"][0]["status"] !==
        "pending"){
            throw new Error("status of the pending item is
                not 'pending'");
        }
}); pm.test("Pending item has the correct title",
        function(){
        if (result["pending_items"][1]["title"] !==
        "cooking"){
            throw new Error("title of the pending item is not
                'cooking'");
        }
}); pm.test("Pending item has the correct status",
        function(){
        if (result["pending_items"][1]["status"] !==
        "pending"){
            throw new Error("status of the pending item is
                not 'pending'");
        }
}); pm.test("returns zero done items", function(){
        if (result["done_items"].length !== 0){
            throw new Error(
                "returns the wrong number of done items");
        }
}); pm.test("checking pending item count", function(){
        if (result["pending_item_count"] !== 2){
            throw new Error(
                "pending_item_count needs to be two");
        }
}); pm.test("checking done item count", function(){
        if (result["done_item_count"] !== 0){
```

```
        throw new Error("done_item_count needs
          to be zero");
      }
  });
```

We can see that we have added a couple of extra tests on the second pending item. The preceding tests also directly apply to the `3_create` test as a duplicate creation will be the same as we will be using the same URL as `2_create`.

The preceding tests require a fair amount of repetition in these tests, slightly altering the length of arrays, item counts, and attributes within these arrays. This is a good opportunity to practice basic Postman tests. If you need to cross-reference your tests with mine, you can assess them in the JSON file at the following URL: `https://github.com/PacktPublishing/Rust-Web-Programming/blob/master/Chapter09/postman_testing/to_do_items.postman_collection.json`.

In this section, what we have done is put in a series of steps for Postman to test when an API call is made. This is not just useful for our application. Postman can hit any API on the internet it has access to. Therefore, you can use Postman tests to monitor live servers and third-party APIs.

Now, running all these tests can be arduous if it has to be done manually every time. We can automate the running and checking of all the tests in this collection using Newman. If we automate these collections, we can run tests at certain times every day on live servers and third-party APIs we rely on, alerting us to when this breaks.

Now, in this book, we will not be covering fully integrated code build pipelines as this is not a **DevOps** book. However, testing our application with **Newman** will give us a good foundation for further development in this area. In the next section, we'll export the collection and run all the API tests in the exported collection in sequence using Newman.

Automating Postman tests with Newman

In order to automate the series of tests, in this section, we will export our to-do item collection in the correct sequence, but first, we have to export the collection as a JSON file. This can be done by clicking on our collection in Postman on the left-hand navigation bar, and clicking the grayed-out **Export** button as seen in the following screenshot:

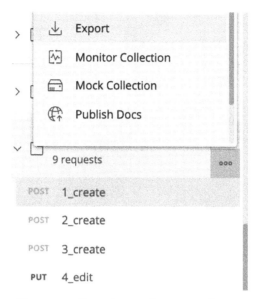

Figure 9.6 – Exporting our Postman collection

Now that we have exported the collection, we can quickly inspect it in order to see how the file is structured. The following code defines the header of the suite of tests:

```
{
"info": {
    "_postman_id": "bab28260-c096-49b9-81e6-b56fc5f60e9d",
    "name": "to_do_items",
    "schema":
    "https://schema.getpostman.com
    /json/collection/v2.1.0/collection.json"
},
```

The preceding code tells Postman what schema is needed to run the tests. If the code is imported into Postman, the ID and name will be visible. The file then goes on to define the individual tests via the code given as follows:

```
"item": [
    {
        "name": "1_create",
        "event": [
        {
            "listen": "test",
```

```
            "script": {
                "id": "128ff3c0-a508-441a-b0b9-da6902a639b7",
                "exec": [
                    "var result = pm.response.json()",

...


"request": {
"method": "POST",
"header": [
        {
            "key": "user-token",
            "value":
            "eyJhbGciOiJIUzI1NiJ9.eyJ1c2VyX2lkIjo2fQ.
            uVo7u877IT2GEMpB_gxVtxhMAYAJD8W_XiUoNvR7_iM",
            "type": "text",
            "disabled": true
        }
],
"url": {
        "raw": "http://127.0.0.1:8000/api/v1/item/create/washing",
        "protocol": "http",
        "host": [
...
```

From the preceding code, we can see that our tests, method, URL, and more are all defined in an array. A quick inspection of the item array will show that the tests will be executed in the order that we want.

Now, we can simply run it with Newman. We can install Newman with the following command:

```
npm install -g newman
```

Now that we have installed Newman, we can run the collection of tests against the exported collection JSON file with this command:

```
newman run to_do_items.postman_collection.json
```

The preceding code runs all the tests and gives us a status report. Each description is printed out, and the status is also denoted by the side of the test. The following is a typical printout of an API test being assessed:

```
→ 1_create
  POST http://127.0.0.1:8000/api/v1/item/create/washing
  [200 OK, 226B, 115ms]
  ✓  response is ok
  ✓  returns one pending item
  ✓  Pending item has the correct title
  ✓  Pending item has the correct status
  ✓  returns zero done items
  ✓  checking pending item count
  ✓  checking done item count
```

The preceding output gives us the name, method, URL, and response. Here, all of them passed. If one did not, then the test description would sport a *cross* instead of a *tick*. We also get the following summary:

	executed	failed
iterations	1	0
requests	8	0
test-scripts	8	0
prerequest-scripts	0	0
assertions	64	0
total run duration: 775ms		
total data received: 1.05KB (approx)		
average response time: 64ms [min: 44ms, max: 115ms, s.d.: 21ms]		

Figure 9.7 – Newman summary

We can see that all of our tests passed. With this, we have managed to automate our functional testing, enabling us to test a full workflow with minimal effort.

Summary

In this chapter, we went through the workflows and components of our application, breaking them down so we could pick the right tools for the right part. We used unit testing so we could inspect a number of edge cases fairly quickly to see how each function and struct interacted with others.

We also directly inspected our custom structs with unit tests. We then used the `actix_web` test structs to mock requests to see how the functions that use the structs and process the requests work. However, when we came to the main API views module, we switched to Postman.

This is because our API endpoints were fairly simple. They created, edited, and deleted to-do items. We could directly assess this process by making API calls and inspecting the responses. Out of the box we managed to assess the JSON processing for accepting and returning data. We were also able to assess the querying, writing, and updating of the data in the database with these Postman tests.

Postman enabled us to test a range of processes quickly and efficiently. We even sped up this testing process by automating it via Newman. However, it has to be noted that this approach is not a one-size-fits-all approach. If the API view functions became more complex, with more moving parts, such as communicating with another API or service, then the Newman approach would have to be redesigned. Environment variables that trigger mocking such processes would have to be considered so we could quickly test a range of edge cases.

Mocking objects will be needed if the system grows as the dependencies of our structs will grow. This is where we create a fake struct or function and define the output for a test. In order to do this, we will need an external crate such as `mockall`. The documentation on this crate is covered in the *Further reading* section of this chapter.

Our application now fully runs and has a range of tests. Now, all we have left is to deploy our application on a server.

In the next chapter, we will set up a server on **Amazon Web Services** (**AWS**) utilizing **Docker** to deploy our application on a server. We will cover setting up the AWS configuration, running tests, and then deploying our application on our server if the tests pass.

Questions

1. Why do we bother with unit tests if we can just manually play with the application?

2. What is the difference between unit tests and functional tests?

3. What are the advantages of unit tests?

4. What are the disadvantages of unit tests?

5. What are the advantages of functional tests?

6. What are the disadvantages of functional tests?

7. What is a sensible approach to building unit tests?

Further reading

- Mockall documentation: `https://docs.rs/mockall/0.9.0/mockall/`

10
Deploying Our Application on AWS

In a lot of tutorials and educational materials, deployment is rarely covered. This is because there are a lot of moving parts, and the process can be fairly brittle. It can be more convenient to refer to other resources when mentioning deployment.

In this chapter, we will cover enough to automate a deployment on a server on **AWS** and then build and connect to a database on there. It has to be stressed that deployment and cloud computing is a big topic. There are whole books written on this topic.

In this chapter, we will get to a point where we can deploy and run our application for others to use. Learning how to deploy applications on a server is the final step. This is where you will turn the application that you have been developing into a practical reality that can be used by others all over the world.

In this chapter, we will cover the following topics:

- Building our own Docker image
- Running a Rust application locally in its own Docker container
- Setting up and configuring an **NGINX** Docker container
- Rerouting requests to different containers with NGINX
- Configuring networks of containers with `docker-compose`

- Creating bash scripts that build and push images to **dockerhub**

- Building an **AWS EC2** instance

- Creating bash scripts that deploy our application to an AWS server

- Configuring traffic rules for the server

- Creating a server on AWS and connecting our application to it

Technical requirements

In this chapter, we will build on the code that we built in *Chapter 9, Testing Our Application Endpoints and Components*. This can be found at `https://github.com/PacktPublishing/Rust-Web-Programming/tree/master/Chapter09/postman_testing`.

You will also need a dockerhub account so that we can package and deploy our application. This can be found at `https://hub.docker.com/`.

You will also be deploying the application on a server. This means that you will need to sign up for an **Amazon Web Services** account. This can be done using the following URL: `https://aws.amazon.com/`.

You can find the full source code used in this chapter here: `https://github.com/PacktPublishing/Rust-Web-Programming/tree/master/Chapter10`.

The CiA videos for this book can be viewed at: `http://bit.ly/3jULCrw`

Running our application locally

So far, we have been running our application with the `cargo run` command. This has been working well, but you might have noticed that our application is not very fast. In fact, it is very slow when we try and log in to the application. This seems to be counterintuitive as we are learning Rust in order to develop faster applications.

So far, it does not look very fast. This is because we are not running an optimized version of our application. We can do this by adding the `--release` tag. As a result, we run our optimized application using the following command:

```
RUST_LOG="info,parser::expression=info,actix_web=info"
cargo run --release
```

Here, we notice that the compilation takes a lot longer. Running this every time we alter the code, and during a development process, is not ideal. However, now that our optimized application is running, we can see that the login process is a lot faster. In order to achieve this, we follow these steps:

1. Create a Docker image for our application.

2. Configure an NGINX container to protect our application.

3. Define the server infrastructure using `docker-compose`.

We'll discuss these steps in the following sections.

Creating our Docker image

Now that we have run our application in a release compilation, we need to package our application in a Docker container. We do this by defining our own Docker file. When we run the Docker file, this creates an image. Once we have this image, we can create containers and run them. We use the following steps to accomplish this:

1. The template for our application image can be defined in a `Dockerfile` file, which is at the root of our application next to our `Cargo.toml` file. At the very top of the `Dockerfile` file, we pull the `rust` image with the following line of code:

    ```
    FROM rust:1.43.1
    ```

2. Using this image, we then install the **C++ compiler** and install the **Diesel** client to manage our migrations to our database using the following code:

    ```
    RUN apt-get update -yqq && apt-get install -yqq cmake g++

    RUN cargo install diesel_cli --no-default-features
    --features postgres
    ```

3. We now have an image that supports a Rust application and enables us to interact with a PostgreSQL database. However, our code is not in the image. We can rectify this by copying our code and inserting it into our image. Once we have done this, we then have to define our directory to be the root of our code. This can be done with the following code:

    ```
    COPY ./css ./css
    COPY ./javascript ./javascript
    COPY ./migrations ./migrations
    ```

```
COPY ./src ./src
COPY ./templates ./templates
COPY ./.env ./.env
COPY ./Cargo.toml ./Cargo.toml
COPY ./diesel.toml ./diesel.toml

WORKDIR .
```

We can see that we have been a bit verbose here. Instead of copying everything, we have actively defined the individual directories we added. This prevents us from adding any undesired files and directories to the image, saving on space and preventing potentially sensitive information from being copied onto the image.

4. Now that we have copied our code, we have everything we need to start running commands on the application. We need to build our application as compiling takes time. It makes sense to compile the application in the image. If we just run the application without precompiling it, we will have to compile the application every time we create a container. This means that we have to compile every time we deploy the application. Something as simple as a server restart would require us to compile the application.

    We also need to expose a port for an entry point and secure a command that gets fired when a container is created from our image. This can be done with the following code:

    ```
    RUN cargo build --release
    EXPOSE 8000

    CMD ["cargo", "run", "--release"]
    ```

In the next section, we'll define our NGINX container.

Defining our NGINX container

Now, while we might be tempted to build this image right now, we are not yet ready. We have to build an infrastructure that works with our application. Once we have built this infrastructure, we will run it locally before running it on a server. We have to ensure that our application is protected and that it can actually engage with the database it has access to. Taking all of this into consideration, our infrastructure should have the following layout:

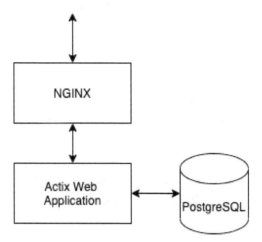

Figure 10.1 – Our server application structure

As you can see, the external traffic has to go through an **NGINX** container before hitting our application container, which then has access to a database. We have already defined a database before, so our next step is to configure our **NGINX** container.

NGINX is fairly important. It enables us to configure how incoming requests are processed. We can handle high traffic, redirect traffic to other servers, use it as a load balancer, configure a timeout and package size, and enable **HTTPS** traffic. We can also do much more. However, NGINX is a book in itself.

In this book, we will be doing the bare minimum to get an NGINX container up and running to pass requests to our application. This will give us enough to allow our application to initially run on a server. We can then seek further reading on NGINX to improve both performance and security.

In order to enable our application to be deployed, we'll follow these steps:

1. We create a `deploy` directory in the root directory. This directory has the following directory tree:

    ```
    ├── deploy
    │   ├── docker-compose.yml
    │   └── nginx
    │       └── nginx.conf
    ```

    Our configuration for the NGINX container will be defined in the `nginx.conf` file. The `docker-compose.yml` file defines the server structure for our application.

2. In our `nginx.conf` file, we initially define our worker processes, error logs, and
    PIDs with the following code:

    ```
    worker_processes   auto;
    error_log  /var/log/nginx/error.log warn;
    ```

    Here, we set the worker processes to `auto`. We can manually define the number of
    worker processes if needed. `auto` detects the number of CPU cores available and
    sets the number to that.

3. We can now move on to defining contexts in our `nginx.conf` file. In the `events`
    context, we define the maximum number of connections that a worker can entertain
    at a time. This is achieved with the following code:

    ```
    events {
        worker_connections   512;
    }
    ```

    The number of workers that we have defined is actually the default number that
    NGINX sets.

4. Now that this is done, we can move on to our `http` context. Here, we define the
    `server` context. Inside this, we instruct the server to listen to port `80`, which is the
    port that listens to outside traffic. Any URL configuration will result in the request
    being passed to the `rust_app` container via port `8000`. This can be achieved with
    the following code:

    ```
    http {
        server {
                listen 80;

                location / {
                    proxy_pass http://rust_app:8000;
                }
            }
    }
    ```

    You can have multiple locations with different configurations. These can then be
    passed to whatever we want.

5. As a side example, let's imagine that we grow our application, and we build a **JavaScript React** container to manage the frontend. Our NGINX container could forward a request to rust_app if the URL starts with /api/. Otherwise, we can direct the request to the front_end container. This can be achieved with the following code:

```
location /api {
    proxy_pass http://rust_app:8000/;
}
location / {
    proxy_pass http://front_end:4000/;
}
```

Here, we can see that NGINX is a powerful tool when used as a gateway to our server structure, although we have only scratched the surface.

In the next section, we'll define our server infrastructure.

Defining our server structure

Now that our NGINX is configured enough to work, we can move on to define our server structure via the deploy/docker-compose.yml file. We begin by defining our rust application with the following code:

```
version: "3.7"

services:

  rust_app:
    container_name: rust_app
    build: ../
    restart: always
    ports:
      - "8000:8000"
    expose:
      - 8000
```

Here, we can see that our configuration is fairly straightforward. Note that our `rust_app` name is the same in our `nginx.conf` file. If it was changed, we would not be able to pass requests from NGINX to our application. Additionally, our `Dockerfile` for our application is outside of the directory that hosts this `docker-compose` file. We have to point to the `Dockerfile` application in the `build` field. Just underneath this, we define our NGINX container with the following code:

```
nginx:
  container_name: 'nginx-rust'
  image: "nginx:latest"
  ports:
    - "80:80"
  links:
    - rust_app
  depends_on:
    - rust_app
  volumes:
    - ./nginx/nginx.conf:/etc/nginx/nginx.conf
```

Here, it has to be noted that our NGINX container is different from our `rust_app`. We are not building our own image through `Dockerfile`. NGINX does a good job of maintaining an official image. Instead, we just pull the latest image and insert our `conf` file into the `volumes` field.

Now that our NGINX has been configured, all we have to do is configure our database. We will keep all the parameters the same as we did in the previous chapters with the following code:

```
postgres:
  container_name: 'to-do-postgres-production'
  image: 'postgres:11.2'
  restart: always
  ports:
    - '5432:5432'
  environment:
    - 'POSTGRES_USER=username'
    - 'POSTGRES_DB=to_do'
    - 'POSTGRES_PASSWORD=password'
```

```
expose:
    - 5432
```

Now that we have defined all of our containers, we are nearly ready to run! All we have to do now is navigate to the root directory and refactor the database URL with the following command:

```
echo DATABASE_URL=postgres://username:password@postgres/to_do >
.env
```

Note that we have changed the URL database location from `localhost` to `postgres`. `postgres` is the name of the container where the database is housed. Now that our application is ready, we can run it by our `-f deploy/docker-compose up` command. Once this has been completed, we need to run our migrations. This can be done with the following command:

```
docker container exec -it rust_app diesel migration run
```

It has to be noted that we did not reference our container ID. Instead, we referenced the name and it still worked. We also have to create a user. This can be done by using `curl` with the following command:

```
curl --header "Content-Type: application/json"
      --request POST
      --data '{
                  "name":"maxwell",
                  "email":"maxwell",
                  "password": "test"


              }'
      http://localhost/api/v1/user/create
```

It has to be noted that the preceding command should be run in one line on your terminal. It is spaced out for ease of reading and format reasons. Now that this is done, we can use our application by merely typing the following URL into the browser:

```
localhost
```

This will hit our port 80, and route through our application rendering page. Here, we have it: a fully functioning web application that has access to a database and is protected using NGINX.

We could copy and paste our code into a server and run the `docker-compose up` command. There is nothing stopping us from putting our code on **GitHub**, manually *accessing our server via SSH*, running a `git clone` command, and then running the `docker-compose up` command. It will work. However, this is fairly manual and not scalable. In the next section, we will build some automated processes when deploying our application on a server.

Deploying our application image on dockerhub

Firstly, we have to manage our expectations. Similar to NGINX, automating deployment processes is a book in itself. In fact, there is a whole profession around it, called **DevOps**.

In this section, we will cover some basic automation processes. However, it has to be noted that this is not state of the art. Just like configuring the NGINX container in the previous section, we will cover enough information for you to get started with automated deployments. We are also just going to be using the `docker-compose` file on the server.

If you want to explore managing multiple containers, and multiple servers, then reading up on **terraform** or **Kubernetes** is advised. By the end of this section, we will have uploaded our application image to `dockerhub`, enabling it to be pulled multiple times from multiple areas. This makes switching to a different orchestration tool that is not `docker-compose` easier. In order to achieve this, we follow these steps:

1. Create a `dockerhub` repository for our to-do application image.

2. Create a bash script that builds our `to-do` application image, which pushes the build to `dockerhub`.

3. Use a `docker-compose.yml` file to pull our to-do application image from our `dockerhub` repository.

Now, let's look at the preceding steps in detail.

Creating a dockerhub repository for our application image

Registering our image on **dockerhub** is fairly straightforward. After logging in, we click on the **Create Repository** button in the top-right corner, as shown in the following screenshot:

docker hub
Explore
Repositories
Organizations
maxwellflitton
Search by repository name...
Create Repository

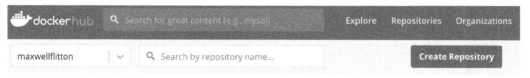

Figure 10.2 – Creating a new repository on dockerhub

Once we have clicked on this, we define the repository with the following configuration:

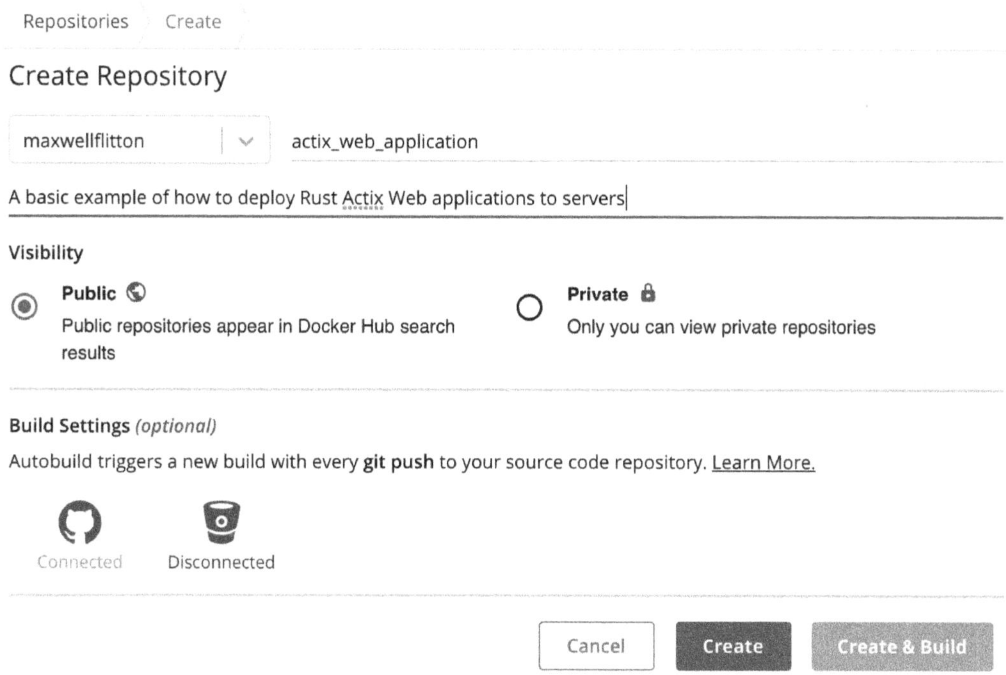

Repositories
Create
Create Repository
maxwellflitton
actix_web_application
A basic example of how to deploy Rust Actix Web applications to servers
Visibility
Public
Public repositories appear in Docker Hub search results
Private
Only you can view private repositories
Build Settings (optional)
Autobuild triggers a new build with every git push to your source code repository. Learn More.
Connected
Disconnected
Cancel
Create
Create & Build

Figure 10.3 – Defining the Docker repository

We can see that there is an option for connecting our repository with GitHub by clicking on the **GitHub** button seen in the preceding screenshot. The **Connected** GitHub status in the preceding screenshot simply means that my GitHub is connected to my dockerhub account. This means that every time a successful pull request gets completed, the image is rebuilt with the code, and then it is sent to the repository. This can be helpful if you are building a fully automated pipeline. However, for this book, we will not connect our GitHub repository. We will push locally.

Creating a bash script for our application

There are a couple of steps that we have to take to push our image on to our repository. We can automate this with a bash script. In the `deploy/push_to_dockerhub.sh` file, we tell the computer that this is a bash script at the top of the file with the following **shebang** line:

```
#!/usr/bin/env bash
```

In our script, we initially navigate to the Dockerfile by changing the directory to where the script is based, and then move back one. This can be accomplished with the following code:

```
SCRIPTPATH="$( cd "$(dirname "$0")" ; pwd -P )"
cd $SCRIPTPATH
cd ..
```

Now that we are in the same directory as the `Dockerfile`, we can build our image, calling it `rust_app`. Then, we can tag it as the latest image and link it to our repository URL with the following code:

```
docker build -t rust_app .
```

```
docker tag rust_app:latest maxwellflitton/actix_web_
application:
```

```
latest
```

Now that we have tagged our image, we need to log in to Docker, and then push our image to the repository with the following code:

```
docker login
docker push maxwellflitton/actix_web_application:latest
```

When this happens, you might be prompted to put in your dockerhub username and password, which is expected. Once you have entered your username and password, Docker will store this safely and you will not be prompted again.

We do not want anyone pushing to the repository. Once you have put in these credentials, they will be stored on your computer, so you will not be asked to present them again in the future. Once the connection is established, the layers of our image will be pushed to the repository. Running the bash script will give the following output when the push has finished:

```
e7ac14f03977: Pushed
69ed0f12bbe5: Pushed
d3f5befc5a60: Pushed
98434bc71833: Pushed
fbd8095465e0: Pushed
8368482e7e46: Pushed
2fed1d14a756: Pushed
d230b3d2f384: Pushed
b953ec408c55: Pushed
eee896fc313e: Pushed
8a05d683e775: Pushed
db4039878dea: Mounted from library/rust
8c39f7b1a31a: Mounted from library/rust
88cfc2fcd059: Mounted from library/rust
760e8d95cf58: Mounted from library/rust
7cc1c2d7e744: Mounted from library/rust
8c02234b8605: Mounted from library/rust
```

We can check whether our image is where we expect it to be by refreshing our `dockerhub` web page, which gives us the following output:

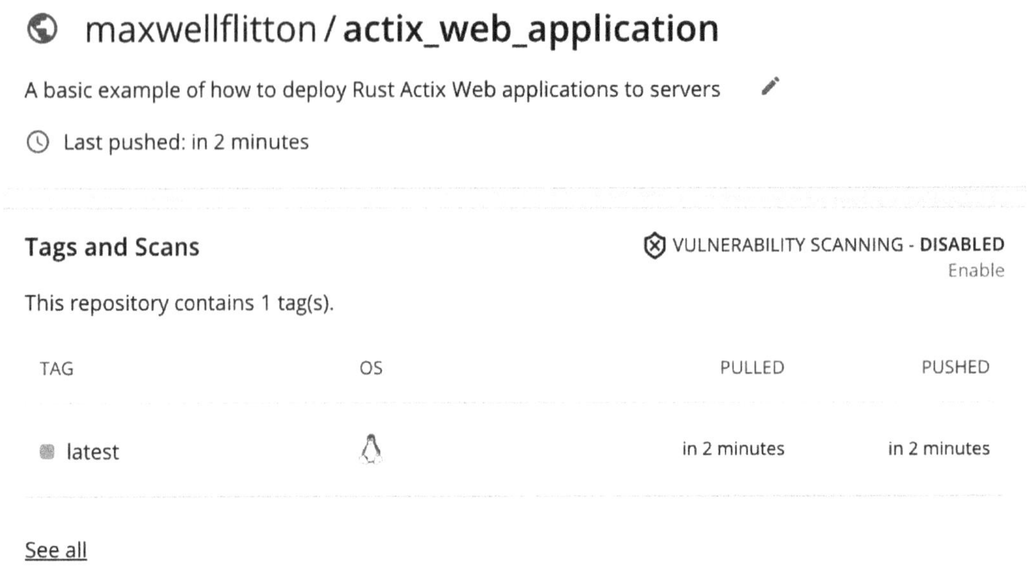

🌐   maxwellflitton / **actix_web_application**

A basic example of how to deploy Rust Actix Web applications to servers   ✏️

🕐 Last pushed: in 2 minutes

Tags and Scans   ⊗ VULNERABILITY SCANNING - **DISABLED**
                                                                                    Enable

This repository contains 1 tag(s).

TAG	OS	PULLED	PUSHED
📦 latest	🐧	in 2 minutes	in 2 minutes

See all

Figure 10.4 – The updated dockerhub repository

We can see that it has been updated (**PUSHED**) in the last two minutes. We can also see that we are using a **Linux** OS.

Using a docker-compose.yml file to pull our to-do application image

Now we can use our image in our `docker-compose` file. All we have to do is change our `build` field to an `image` field pointing to our repository, as shown in the following code, in our `deploy/docker-compose.yml` file:

```
rust_app:
  container_name: rust_app
  image: "maxwellflitton/actix_web_application:latest"
  restart: always
  ports:
    - "8000:8000"
  expose:
    - 8000
```

Running our `docker-compose up` command will run the application again, pulling from the repository if we have deleted our `rust_app` image and container.

We are now able to use our image anywhere. Let's forget that we have actually made a to-do application and imagine that we created a Rust application that logs metrics within a system. When a server performs an action, it posts a message to our application logging the action and datetime.

It is super fast and has low resources to it so that it can handle a lot of traffic. As Rust is still new, other systems may also want to use the server in your organization. All you have to do is document how to use/configure the image in the repo readme on docker hub, give the right people access to the repository, watch them pull down as many copies of your server as they want, and then use them where they want. They do not have to compile; it is already sorted for them in our image. Here, we can see that the benefits of docker hub are fairly obvious.

Another example that is closer to home is that our to-do application is going to be part of a series of microservices. We team up with other developers who are building a contact's service, and this contact's service makes calls to our to-do application as you can assign to-do items to each contact. When developing locally on their computers, their development environment will have a `docker-compose` file pointing to our to-do application Docker repository. Therefore, the contact's developers can develop new features locally with the latest code from the to-do application integrated into their development suite. In the next section, we will be getting a server to pull the latest application image from the docker hub repository.

Deploying our application on a server

Considering that we are now pulling images from docker hub, and that we have got our application running with NGINX and a database locally on our computer with `docker-compose`, it should not come as a surprise that deploying on a server merely refers to orchestrating Docker containers on a server.

As we mentioned earlier, putting our image on docker hub has enabled us to use a range of container orchestration tools such as **Kubernetes** and **terraform**. However, considering this is a simple application and the book is focused on getting a Rust web application up and running as opposed to a **DevOps** book, we will be using `docker-compose` to manage our images and containers on the server. In order to achieve this, we need to follow these steps:

1. Create an EC2 instance on AWS.
2. Configure traffic rules for the AWS server.

3. Write a bash script that SSHs into the server, deploys, and then starts the application.

4. Configure `docker-compose` for the server.

Now, let's take a look at the preceding steps in detail.

Creating an EC2 instance on AWS

First of all, we need to create our server on AWS. We will be doing this through an EC2 instance. An EC2 instance is also known as **Amazon Elastic Computer Cloud**. This is a computing instance that we can create and run. We'll use these steps to create an EC2 instance:

1. In our EC2 instance dashboard, we launch an EC2 instance using the launch wizard, as shown here:

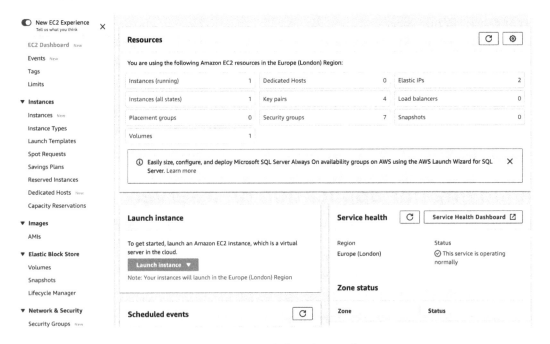

Figure 10.5 – EC2 launch wizard

2. Once we click on the *orange* button (**Launch instance**), we funnel through a series of steps to select an **Amazon Linux 2 AMI**, as follows:

Figure 10.6 – EC2 operating system choices

3. We then select the **t2.micro** option, which is **Free tier eligible**, as shown in the following screenshot:

Figure 10.7 – EC2 size choice

4. Once this is highlighted, we click on the bottom right-hand blue button, labeled **Review and Launch**. We don't have to edit anything in the review. So, we click on the blue button, labeled **Launch**, to launch the computing instance. Once this has been clicked on, we will get a pop-up dialog for a key pair, as shown here:

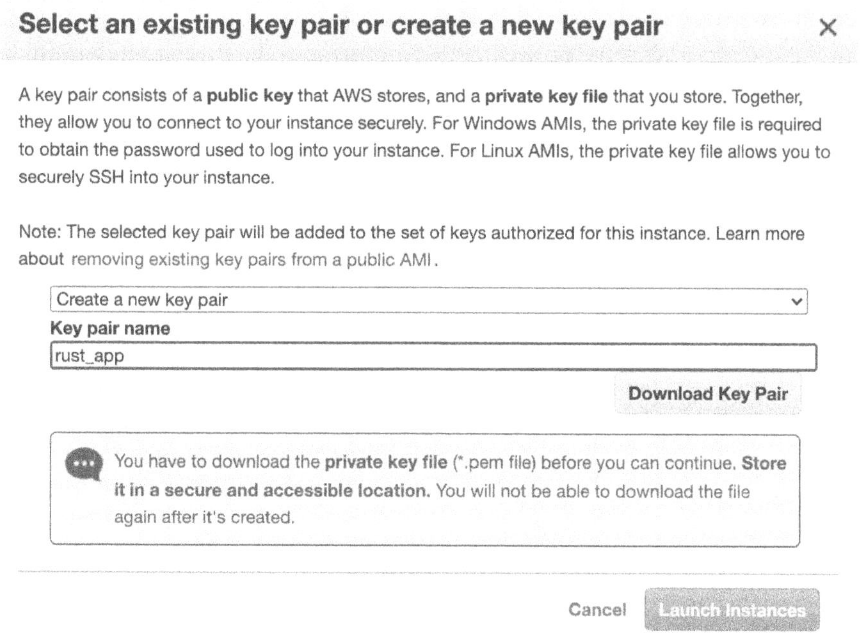

Select an existing key pair or create a new key pair   ✕

A key pair consists of a **public key** that AWS stores, and a **private key file** that you store. Together, they allow you to connect to your instance securely. For Windows AMIs, the private key file is required to obtain the password used to log into your instance. For Linux AMIs, the private key file allows you to securely SSH into your instance.

Note: The selected key pair will be added to the set of keys authorized for this instance. Learn more about removing existing key pairs from a public AMI.

| Create a new key pair   ⌄ |

Key pair name

| rust_app |

                                                                    Download Key Pair

💬   You have to download the **private key file** (*.pem file) before you can continue. **Store it in a secure and accessible location.** You will not be able to download the file again after it's created.

                                                   Cancel   Launch Instances

Figure 10.8 – EC2 key pair configuration

The key is needed to connect to the instance and deploy our application via SSH. It has to be noted that we selected **Create a new key pair** and decided to call it **rust_app**.

We cannot launch the instance until the key pair is downloaded. We have to keep this key pair safe. Once it is downloaded, we cannot get another. We will have to destroy the EC2 instance and create another if we need another key pair. We have to keep the key safe. Make sure you do not upload it to a GitHub repository. If you are using GitHub to track your progress in this book, make sure that all of the .pem files are in .gitignore files.

5. Once we have downloaded the key, we store it in the deploy directory, meaning it has the deploy/rust_app.pem path. It has to be noted that the permissions of the key need to be changed; otherwise, we will not be able to use it. We can alter the permissions of the key using this command:

```
chmod 600 deploy/rust_app.pem
```

6. Once this is downloaded, we click on the **Launch Instances** button. Here, we have to issue a warning. We have now launched an instance. We have to be careful here. When an instance or database is running, you will be charged for this unless you select the free tier option or you have only recently signed up to an AWS account. To be eligible for the free tier option, your account has to be less than a year old.

    If you are not using something, stop and remove it. If you forget to, you could end up receiving a nasty AWS bill at the end of the month. While one EC2 instance is manageable, a couple of instances and databases can quickly result in a bill that is in the hundreds of dollars.

7. Once the instance is launched, we are redirected to the **Instances** dashboard. If we click on the instance that we created, we can see the data around our instance. We can see the **Public IPv4** address, and that our key pair name is called **rust_app**, as shown in the following screenshot:

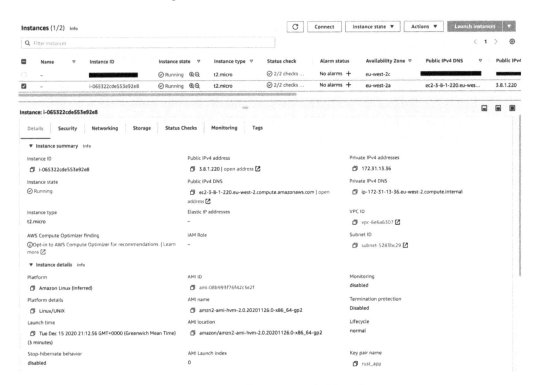

Figure 10.9 – The instances dashboard

As you can see, using the top right-hand selection of buttons, we can connect to the EC2 instance by clicking on the **Connect** button. This sends us through to a **Linux** terminal, which is running on the instance (note that the instance in the preceding screenshot was deleted after writing this book). We start by updating it with the following command:

```
sudo yum update
```

8. If we type docker into the Terminal, we will get an error. This is because Docker is not installed on the instance. We can install it with the following command:

```
sudo amazon-linux-extras install docker
```

9. We then have to start the docker service daemon with the following command:

```
sudo service docker start
```

10. We then add ec2-user to the docker group, so we do not have to use sudo to run docker commands. We do this using the following command:

```
sudo usermod -a -G docker ec2-user
```

11. We then have to install docker-compose, which is achieved by the following command:

```
sudo curl -L
"https://github.com/docker/compose/releases/download/
1.27.4/docker-compose-$(uname -s)-$(uname -m)"
-o /usr/local/bin/docker-compose
```

Note that the previous command is all on one line. If we try and run the docker-compose command, we will get a **permission denied** message. We can fix the permissions using the following command:

```
sudo chmod +x /usr/local/bin/docker-compose
```

In the next section, we'll configure traffic rules for the AWS server.

Configuring traffic rules for the AWS server

Now we have configured everything we need in the EC2 terminal. We are nearly finished configuring our server. The final configuration that we have to define involves the incoming traffic rules. If we do not, then we will not be able to access the application. We accomplish this by using the following steps:

1. We can alter the rules by clicking on the **Security** tab of our EC2 instance, as shown in the following screenshot:

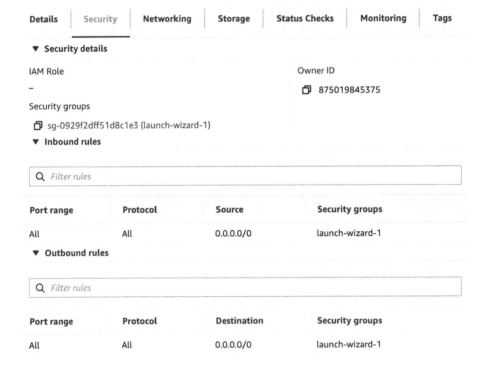

Figure 10.10 – EC2 traffic rules

We can see the **Inbound rules** and **Outbound rules**. We can alter them by clicking on the wizard link under the **Security groups** header.

2. When we click on this, we can see that the inbound type was an SSH. We can edit the inbound rules by clicking on the **Edit inbound rules** button on the right-hand side, as displayed in this screenshot:

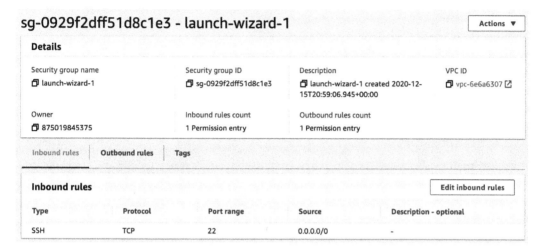

Figure 10.11 – EC2 editing traffic

3. Once we have clicked on the **Edit inbound rules** button, we can click on the **Add rule** button, as shown in the following screenshot. We define the type as **HTTP** with a port range of **80**. We also define the CIDR blocks to be all zeros, allowing the HTTP requests to come from anywhere. The following screenshot shows us what this should look like:

Figure 10.12 – EC2 traffic rules

Now the server is configured and ready for us to deploy our application.

Writing a bash script that connects to the server, deploys and starts the application via SSH

We can build our deployment script, in the `deploy/push_to_server.sh` file, by using these steps:

1. We first change to the directory that the file is housed in with the following code:

    ```
    #!/usr/bin/env bash


    SCRIPTPATH="$( cd "$(dirname "$0")" ; pwd -P )"
    cd $SCRIPTPATH
    ```

    Now that we are in the `deploy` directory, we have access to the SSH key, and the files needed for the deployment.

2. Next, we use the SSH key to copy the `docker-compose.yml` file to the home route of our `ec2-user` in the EC2 user, using the following code:

    ```
    scp -i "./rust_app.pem" ./docker-compose.yml
    ec2-user@3.8.1.220:/home/ec2-user/docker-compose.yml
    ```

    Note that the preceding command is defined in one line of code.

3. Once we have done this, we have the container orchestration file on our server. Considering that the orchestration file is pointing to our image in docker hub for the application, we do not need to copy any Rust code to the server. However, we do have to copy over the NGINX config file to the server, which is achieved by using the following code:

    ```
    scp -i "./rust_app.pem" -r ./nginx
    ec2-user@3.8.1.220:/home/ec2-user/nginx
    ```

    Again, it has to be noted that this command is defined in one line.

4. Now that we have all of the files that we require on the server, we need to SSH into the server and run a series of commands on the server. A simple approach is to run the `docker-compose` file, run a `diesel` migration on our `rust_app` container, and then remove the NGINX files and `docker-compose.yml` file. This can be achieved by using this code:

    ```
    ssh -i "./rust_app.pem" -t ec2-user@3.8.1.220 << EOF
        docker-compose up -d
    ```

```
        docker container exec -t rust_app diesel migration
    run
        rm -r nginx/
        rm docker-compose.yml
    EOF
```

With this, our script for basic deployment is nearly complete. However, we do require a user; otherwise, we will only be able to look at the login screen of the app on the server, and that is not very useful.

5. So, our last command of the deployment script makes the POST API call to the server that has just been spun up with the following code:

```
    curl --header "Content-Type: application/json"
        --request POST
        --data '{"name":"maxwell", "email":"maxwell",
                "password":"test"}'
        3.8.1.220/api/v1/user/create
```

Again, it has to be noted that this command is defined in one line.

6. Now, if we run this deployment script, we can go onto our server by typing in the URL we deployed to and use it! We have a running application on a server. Before we run it, however, we have to change the permissions of the SSH key using the following command:

```
    sudo chmod 600 rust_app.pem
```

This reconfigures the access to the key. If we do not do this, then the connection to the server throws an error under the premise that the key is open as well. It has to be noted that the preceding command has to be done outside of a bash script.

Now that it is running, we just need to make a couple of alterations. Our needs for the deployment script have changed. Instead, we need to stop the Docker containers, remove our rust_app container, and remove our actix_web_application image.

Configuring docker-compose for the server

Once this is done, we then spin up `docker-compose` again, run our migrations, and remove any physical files. This is because automated deploys will happen when we update the code, and thus the image on docker hub. This ensures that the latest code is atomically deployed onto the server when the deployment script is run. This can be achieved by the following code:

```
ssh -i "./rust_app.pem" -t ec2-user@3.8.1.220 << EOF
  docker-compose stop
  docker container rm rust_app
  docker image rm maxwellflitton/actix_web_application


  docker-compose up -d
  docker container exec -t rust_app diesel migration run
    rm -r nginx/
    rm docker-compose.yml
EOF
```

Running the deployment script again shows us that the server pulls the latest image from docker hub.

Even though we are manually running our deployment script, we have built the fundamental building blocks for automation. Building a continuous pipeline is merely porting this script over to a system that runs it based on Webhooks with your GitHub repository. GitHub actions can store SSH keys and sensitive variables, such as the server address, which can be encrypted. Configuring a GitHub action that pushes the new code image to docker hub, and then runs the commands we defined in the deployment bash script will facilitate a continuous integration pipeline. This can also be done with the service **Travis**.

Although our application is technically working on a server and accepting outside traffic, there are some shortfalls to our application. We will solve them in the next section by creating a database that is external to the EC2 instance.

Enabling data persistence on our server

Right now, our application is running a database locally on the EC2 instance. This has a few problems. Firstly, it means that the EC2 is stateful. If we tear down the instance, we will lose all of our data.

Secondly, if we wipe the containers on the instance, we could also lose all of our data. Data vulnerability is not the only issue here. Let's say that our traffic drastically increases, and we need more computing instances to manage it. This can be done by using **NGINX** as a load balancer between two instances, as shown in the following diagram:

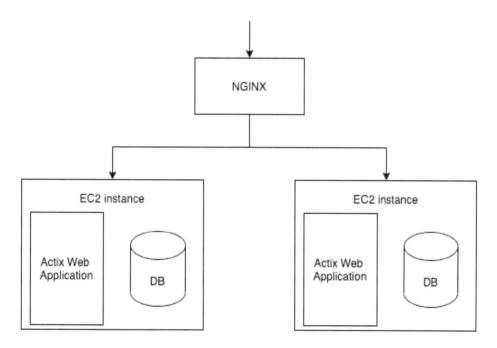

Figure 10.13 – Doubling our EC2 instances for our system

As you can see, the problem here is accessing random data. If user one creates an item, and this request hits the instance on the left, then user one makes a GET request and this hits the instance on the right-hand side, the recently created item would not be present. The user would be accessing random states depending on which instance the request hit.

This can be solved by deleting the database from our `docker-compose` file and creating a database outside, as shown in this diagram:

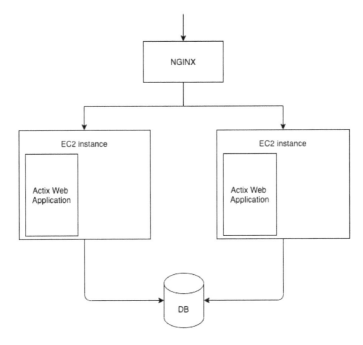

Figure 10.14 – Our new, improved system

Now we have a single point of truth for our data, and our **EC2 instances** are stateless, meaning we have the freedom to create and delete instances as and when we need to.

Creating a database on AWS

Databases are managed through the **RDS service**. We can create a database by clicking on the **Create database** button on the RDS dashboard, as shown in the following screenshot:

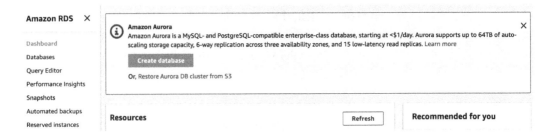

Figure 10.15 – Creating a database

The preceding action gives us the following database creation wizard:

○ **Standard create**
You set all of the configuration options, including ones for availability, security, backups, and maintenance.

○ **Easy create**
Use recommended best-practice configurations. Some configuration options can be changed after the database is created.

Engine options

Engine type Info

○ Amazon Aurora

○ MySQL

○ MariaDB

● PostgreSQL

○ Oracle

ORACLE

○ Microsoft SQL Server

Microsoft®
SQL Server

Version

PostgreSQL 12.4-R1 ▼

Templates

Choose a sample template to meet your use case.

○ **Production**
Use defaults for high availability and fast, consistent performance.

● **Dev/Test**
This instance is intended for development use outside of a production environment.

○ **Free tier**
Use RDS Free Tier to develop new applications, test existing applications, or gain hands-on experience with Amazon RDS. Info

Settings

DB instance identifier Info
Type a name for your DB instance. The name must be unique across all DB instances owned by your AWS account in the current AWS Region.

> todo

⚠ Must contain only letters, digits, or hyphens. Must start with a letter.
The DB instance identifier is case-insensitive, but is stored as all lowercase (as in "mydbinstance"). Constraints: 1 to 60 alphanumeric characters or hyphens (1 to 15 for SQL Server). First character must be a letter. Can't contain two consecutive hyphens. Can't end with a hyphen.

▼ **Credentials Settings**

Master username Info
Type a login ID for the master user of your DB instance.

> username

1 to 16 alphanumeric characters. First character must be a letter

☐ **Auto generate a password**
Amazon RDS can generate a password for you, or you can specify your own password

Master password Info

> ••••••••

Constraints: At least 8 printable ASCII characters. Can't contain any of the following: / (slash), '(single quote), "(double quote) and @ (at sign).

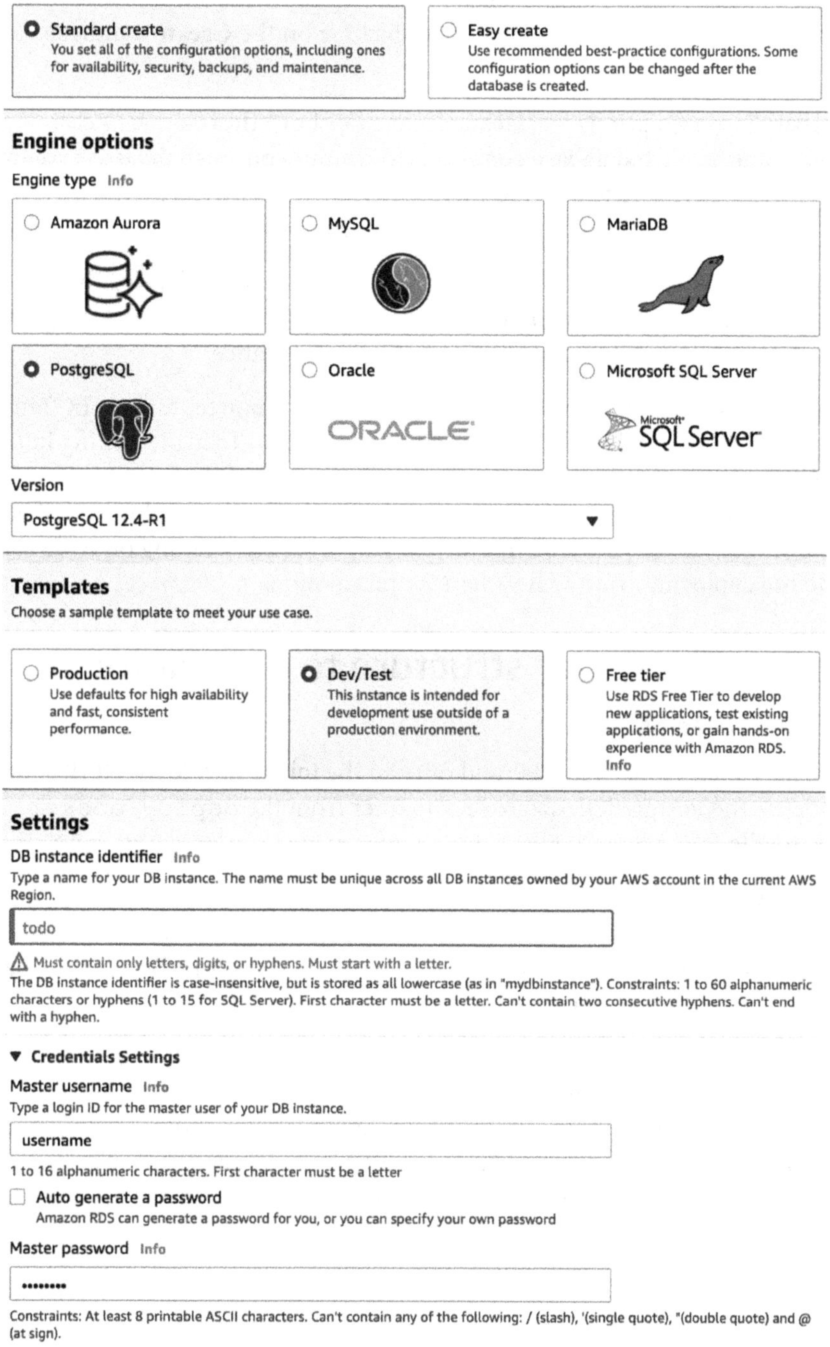

Figure 10.16 – Database creation wizard

You can see that we have selected **PostgreSQL**. We can also select the **Free tier** option if we need to, as this database is going to be taking a very light amount of traffic. Once all the fields are filled in, the database is created by clicking on the **Create database** button at the bottom-right corner of the wizard.

We can see that there are options for backups and snapshots; these are very clear advantages of using an RDS database compared to running our own database containers. Once this is done, we are directed to the database instances dashboard, where we have to remember to set the inbound traffic rules to allow traffic from all IP addresses.

We can also limit it to just the IP of our server. However, it has to be noted that if the EC2 instance is stopped and then restarted, the IP address changes. This can be mitigated by creating an elastic IP address and attaching it to the EC2 instance.

Elastic IP addresses are permanent addresses that you can connect to your EC2 instances, giving you the ability to route traffic as and when you need to. To avoid getting into the weeds of AWS too much, we will just open the database to all traffic for this example since this is a book on how Rust can be implemented in web development. However, if you are unfamiliar with the concepts covered in this paragraph, further reading on AWS services is advised before deploying your own system for production.

Refactoring the server structure to accommodate an outside database

Now that we have created our database and opened the inbound rules to all IP addresses, we need to delete the PostgreSQL database container from the `deploy/docker-compose.yml` file.

Now that this is done, we need to update the database URL. We could do this in our `DockerFile` so that it is baked in the image that gets pushed to docker hub. However, this poses a security risk. If someone pulls the image from docker hub, they then have access to our database. It is also not useful from a development perspective.

When we are developing on our local computers, we need to connect to our local database. If we start to develop another service and it relies on our image, the developed `docker-compose` file at our root will connect to our production database. This is not ideal when trying out new migrations and more. This will just cause havoc on our system. Therefore, it is in our best interests to keep the database URL, in the image on docker hub, pointing to a local PostgreSQL container.

Instead, we can update our database URL in our docker/push_to_server.sh file. This can be done by inserting an update command after we have spun up our docker-compose, as shown in the following code block:

```
ssh -i "./rust_app.pem" -t ec2-user@3.8.1.220 << EOF
  docker-compose stop
  docker container rm rust_app
  docker image rm maxwellflitton/actix_web_application
  docker-compose up -d

  docker exec "rust_app" bash -c "echo 'DATABASE_
URL=postgres://username:password@URL/todo' > .env"

  docker container exec -t rust_app diesel setup
  docker container exec -t rust_app diesel migration run
  rm -r nginx/
  rm docker-compose.yml
EOF
```

In our database URL, you swap the URL after password@ with the URL of your actual database that you created. Once this is done, running this will connect our server to the database that we created. Again, we should not put this URL on GitHub. If we are using this in Travis or GitHub actions, again the URL should be encrypted.

Now we have a fully functioning application that manages users and to-do items. Its deployment process is automated which manages database migrations, and it is running on an AWS server while reading and writing to an AWS database.

It has to be noted that although we have our application running, we have all of our systems open including the database. If you are not going to shut down your instances, it is a good idea to revise the traffic policies for your EC2 instance and database so not all IP addresses can SSH into your EC2 instance. It is also a good idea to restrict IP addresses of incoming traffic to the database to the EC2 instance IP address.

Summary

We have finally come to the end of our journey. We have created our own docker image packaging our Rust application. We then ran this on our local computer with the protection of a NGINX container. We then deployed it onto a docker hub account enabling us to use it to deploy onto an AWS server that we set up.

It has to be noted that we have gone through the lengthy steps of configuring containers and accessing our server via SSH. This has enabled us to apply this process to other platforms as our general approach was not AWS centric. We merely used AWS to set up the server. However, if we set up a server on another provider, we will still be able to install docker on the server, deploy our image onto it, and run it with NGINX and a connection to a database.

There are few more things we can do as a developer's work is never done. However, we have covered and achieved the core basics of building a Rust web application from scratch and deploying it in an automated fashion.

Considering this, there is little holding back developers from building web applications in Rust. Frontend frameworks can be added to improve the frontend functionality, and extra modules can be added to our application to increase its functionality and API endpoints. We now have a solid base to build a range of applications and read further on topics to enable us to develop our skill and knowledge of web development in Rust.

We are at an exciting time with Rust and web development, and hopefully, after getting to this point, you feel empowered to push Rust forward in the field of web development. In the next chapter and appendix, we will be covering the basics of two other Rust web frameworks, **Rocket**, and **Warp**, respectively.

Further reading

- *AWS Certified Developer-Associate Guide, Second Edition*, by Tankariya. V, and Parmar. B (2019), published by Packt Publishing, *Chapter 5, Getting Started with Elastic Compute Cloud (EC2)*, page *165*.

- *AWS Certified Developer-Associate Guide, Second Edition*, by Tankariya. V, and Parmar. B (2019), published by Packt Publishing, *Chapter 10, AWS Relational Database Service (RDS)*, page *333*.

- *AWS Certified Developer-Associate Guide, Second Edition*, by Tankariya. V, and Parmar. B (2019), published by Packt Publishing, *Chapter 21, Getting Started with AWS CodeDeploy*, page *657*.

- *Mastering Kubernetes* by Sayfan. G (2020), published by Packt Publishing.

- *Getting Started with Terraform* by Shirinkin. K (2017), published by Packt Publishing.

- *Nginx HTTP Server, Fourth Edition*, by Fjordvald. M and Nedelcu. C (2018), published by Packt Publishing.

11
Understanding Rocket Web Framework

At this point, we have built a fully functioning to-do application with the **Actix web framework**. In this chapter, we will go through the core concepts so that there will be nothing holding us back if we decide to completely recreate the to-do application in Rocket.

We will not explicitly recreate the application in this chapter, as this would result in pages and pages of repetition. However, there is going to be some repetition here as some of the modules we've created throughout this book are web framework agnostic. We will copy some of the modules we created in the previous chapters for some of the examples provided. Our examples will include constructing basic views, connecting to a database, passing data into the view via the body, and authenticating users using **JSON web authentication**.

In this chapter, we will cover the following topics:

- High-level differences between Actix and **Rocket**

- Setting up and configuring a Rocket server GET API endpoint and running it

- Connecting a Rocket server to a **PostgreSQL** database using Rocket database wrappers

- Passing data into API endpoints

- Authenticating requests with Rocket's own request guards

- Understanding the different types of middleware and implementing it using fairings

- Defining **POST API endpoints** for a Rocket server

Let's get started!

Technical requirements

In this chapter, we will be copying some modules from *Chapter 10*, *Deploying Our Application on AWS*, to augment the Rocket application. These can be accessed at `https://github.com/PacktPublishing/Rust-Web-Programming/tree/master/Chapter10/persist_on_server`.

Note that this chapter will be using a **JWT token** that will not be generated in this chapter. A JWT token has been provided in the root **README** of this book's GitHub repository at `https://github.com/PacktPublishing/Rust-Web-Programming/tree/master/`.

You can find the full source code that will be used in this chapter here: `https://github.com/PacktPublishing/Rust-Web-Programming/tree/master/Chapter11`.

The CiA videos for this book can be viewed at: `http://bit.ly/3jULCrw`

What is Rocket?

Rocket is a Rust web framework, like Actix web. It's newer than Actix web and has a lower user base at the time of writing this book. It also relies on nightly Rust, which is less stable. At the time of writing this book, it is at version **0.4**, though stable Rust is to be supported in version **0.5**, so this is not going to be a drawback for long. Because of its early stages, keeping all of Rocket's components updated can be tricky. This is because breaking changes are often introduced to early crates and frameworks.

However, the framework does have some advantages. Rocket is simpler to write, since its boilerplate code has been taken care of. It also supports **JSON**, forms, and type checking out of the box, which can be implemented with just a few lines of code.

Rocket also has easy to implement handlers and middleware components that do not require you to understand how requests feed through the process. Instead, we just have to implement a trait and function that accepts and returns a request. Depending on your development style, developing applications in Rocket could be faster and is less complicated than Actix in some areas. Its main selling point is its lack of boilerplate code. We will see this when we set up a server in the next section, where we will merely ignite the server in the main function.

Setting up our server

As we mentioned previously, the main difference is that the Rocket framework runs on the nightly build of Rust. Let's get started:

1. First, we will have to switch to the `nightly` build by using the following command:

    ```
    rustup default nightly
    ```

2. Now, we can build our own Cargo project, and then define our dependency on the `rocket` frame with the following dependency in the `Cargo.toml` file:

    ```
    [dependencies]
    rocket = "0.4.6"
    ```

3. Now that this has been defined, we can build our basic server with just one view in our `src/main.rs` file. First of all, we must import what we need with the following code:

    ```
    #![feature(proc_macro_hygiene, decl_macro)]
    #[macro_use] extern crate rocket;
    ```

    The top line of the previous code block may look new to you. This line enables us to use the unstable attributes that are available with the nightly version of Rust. The advantage of this is that we have access to the most cutting-edge features available. However, these features might be unstable or have sparse documentation.

4. We must then import some macros from Rocket that we wish to use. Now that we have imported everything we need, we can define our views by creating some routes, as follows:

    ```
    #[get("/hello/<name>/<age>")]
    fn hello(name: String, age: u8) -> String {
        format!("Hello, {} year old named {}!", age, name)
    ```

```
}
#[get("/bye/<name>/<age>")]
fn bye(name: String, age: u8) -> String {
    format!("Goodbye, {} year old named {}!", age, name)
}
```

We can define the URL and the parameters that have been passed into the view via a URL with a Rocket macro. Like Actix web, the return value of the function is returned to the requester.

5. Now that we have defined our views, we can define our server, mount our views, and then run it. Use the following code:

```
fn main() {
    rocket::ignite().mount("/", routes![hello,
        bye]).launch();
}
```

6. Here, we can see that we mounted multiple views under a prefix, and then launched it. We can launch our server with the cargo run command; we will get the following output:

```
Finished dev [unoptimized + debuginfo] target(s)
in 6.65s
 Running `target/debug/rocket_server`
Configured for development.
=> address: localhost
=> port: 8000
=> log: normal
=> workers: 8
=> secret key: generated
=> limits: forms = 32KiB
=> keep-alive: 5s
=> read timeout: 5s
```

```
=> write timeout: 5s
=> tls: disabled
Mounting /:
=> GET /hello/<name>/<age> (hello)
=> GET /bye/<name>/<age> (bye)
Rocket has launched from http://localhost:8000
```

Here, we can see that logging comes out of the box. We do not have to define anything, unlike Actix web. We also get a note stating what views are mounted and the URL that the server is listening on.

7. We can now call our **hello** view in the browser, which gives us the following output:

```
Hello, 31 year old named maxwell!
```

Figure 11.1 – Result of calling our hello view

Calling this view also gives us the following log:

```
GET /hello/maxwell/31 text/html:
=> Matched: GET /hello/<name>/<age> (hello)
=> Outcome: Success
=> Response succeeded.
```

Here, we can see that the logging is fairly extensive. With this, our server is running. Now, we can move on to the next section, where we will connect our Rocket server to a database.

Connecting to our database

To connect to our database, we will use the diesel crate. We have used the diesel crate throughout this book for connecting to our database. Theoretically, we could just use this, but Rocket does have some functionality that can wrap around diesel. To demonstrate this, we are going to create a simple GET view that accepts a user ID and returns the to-do items that belong to the user with that ID.

Using Diesel crate to connect to our database

Remember that, throughout this book, we have been building isolated modules. We can reuse them. We will need to serialize the database being returned:

1. The modules that we built in the previous chapters are reusable. Because of this, we can copy `src/json_serialization` from *Chapter 10, Deploying Our Application on AWS*, to our `src/json_serialization` directory. We will also be using the same data models. Because of this, we need to copy `src/models` to `src/models`, `src/schema.rs` to `src/schema.rs`, `docker-compose.yml` to `docker-compose.yml`, `src/to_do` to `src/to_do`, and `diesel.toml` to `diesel.toml`.

    Now that we have copied all the essential modules, we just need to remove the actix imports and the `Responder for ToDoItems` code block because we will not be using Actix at all in this chapter.

2. Our modules are ready to be used, but before we can import them into the `main` file, we have to define our own database connection. In the `src/database.rs` file, we will define the database connection with the following code:

    ```
    use rocket_contrib::databases::{database,
        diesel::PgConnection};


    #[database("postgres")]
    pub struct DbConn(PgConnection);
    ```

    Here, we can see that our connection is simpler than when we were implementing the `diesel` crate directly. We are essentially using a Rocket wrapper that manages the boilerplate code.

3. Now that we have done this, we need to define the Rocket database URL dependency in the `Rocket.toml` file with the following code:

    ```
    [development.databases]
    postgres = { url = "postgres://
        username:password@localhost/to_do" }
    ```

4. We must then define the third-party crates that will be needed in the `Cargo.toml` file with the following code:

    ```
    [dependencies]
    rocket = "0.4.5"
    ```

```
serde_json = { version = "1.0",
               default-features = false,
               features = ["alloc"] }
serde = {version = "1.0", features = ["derive"]}
diesel = { version = "1.4.4", features = ["postgres"] }
bcrypt = "0.8"
uuid = { version = "0.8", features = ["serde", "v4"] }


[dependencies.rocket_contrib]
version = "0.4"
default-features = false
features = ["json", "diesel_postgres_pool"]
```

We now have everything ready to rebuild our Rocket application so that we can
manage database connections in our views.

5. Initially, we have to configure the macros in our `main.rs` file with the
    following code:

```
#![feature(proc_macro_hygiene, decl_macro)]


#[macro_use] extern crate rocket;
#[macro_use] extern crate diesel;
use rocket_contrib::json::Json;
use diesel::prelude::*;
```

If we do not configure the macros of the `diesel` crate, then the table schema will
not have the load or filter equal to functions.

6. Now, we have to declare the modules that we copied over with the following
    code block:

```
mod to_do;
mod schema;
mod database;
mod models;
mod json_serialization;
```

With these modules and third-party crates, we can import the database connection, item data model, to-do factory for processing the data, and the JSON serialization for the to-do items when they're returned with the following code block:

```
use crate::database::DbConn;
use crate::models::item::item::Item;
use crate::to_do::to_do_factory;
use crate::json_serialization::to_do_items::ToDoItems;
```

Again, we can see the benefits of coding isolated, well-structured modules. We are able to just copy them into our new application and use them as building blocks for whatever we want. Because they are isolated and have a single purpose, we know what each one does. For instance, if we want to change the structure of the return data, all we have to do is write a new struct while replacing the ToDoItems struct. This can even be done for the factory if we just want to change the processing. Now that we have these building blocks, we can use them in our application views.

Using view parameters

We will keep the hello and bye views that we defined in the previous section.
Let's get started:

1. We can define the get view function with the following code block:

    ```
    #[get("/get/<user_id>")]
    fn get_items(user_id: i32, conn: DbConn) ->
        Json<ToDoItems> {

    }
    ```

    Note that this time, we are passing the database connection into the view via the parameters as opposed to establishing the database connection inside the view.

2. Now, that we have our view, which contains the user ID and database connection, we can filter our to-do items based on the user ID from the database inside the view via the following code:

    ```
    let items = schema::to_do::table
        .order(schema::to_do::columns::id.asc())
        .filter(schema::to_do::columns::user_id.eq(
            &user_id))
        .load::<Item>(&*conn)
        .unwrap();
    ```

Here, we can see that the syntax is the same as what we've been using throughout this book. This is because we are still essentially using diesel. The only difference is that we have `schema` before our `to_do` database table references. This is because we also have a reference to the `to_do` module in the same file. We pass in our connection directly from the params.

Our return data is the same as it is for the Actix web application, where we use the factory to process it, as shown in the following code:

```
let mut array_buffer = Vec::new();


for item in items {
    let item = to_do_factory(&item.status,
                             item.title).unwrap();
    array_buffer.push(item);
}
return Json(ToDoItems::new(array_buffer))
```

The only difference here is that we wrap our struct in the `Json` struct from Rocket. Now, our view is now ready to be used.

Mounting views onto the server

Follow these steps to mount our views onto the server:

1. At this point, we have to mount the views on to the server and also attach the database connection, like so:

```
fn main() {
    rocket::ignite()
        .mount("/", routes![hello, bye])
        .mount("/items", routes![get_items])
        .attach(DbConn::fairing())
        .launch();
}
```

Here, we can see that our `get_items` view URL will be prefixed with `/items`. If we added anymore views to the `routes!` macro, it will also be prefixed with `/items`. There also has to be a warning here. If you do not attach the database connection, your code will still compile, and the server will still run. Any view that uses the database connection will get an unhelpful error stating *"Attempted to retrieve unmanaged state!"*. If you see this, make sure that your database connection is attached and that the docker file defining the database is running.

There is a high chance that your database will be different to mine now.

2. Making a GET request for my application with `localhost:8000/items/get/1` gives me the following output:

```
{
    "pending_items": [
        {
            "title": "code a python password manager",
            "status": "pending"
        }
    ],
    "done_items": [
        {
            "title": "bake pies",
            "status": "done"
        },
        {
            "title": "volunteer at hospital",
            "status": "done"
        }
    ],
    "pending_item_count": 1,
    "done_item_count": 2
}
```

As we can see, this can just be plugged into the frontend code that we have used throughout this book. As we can see, Rocket is living up to its mission statement for reducing boiler code. Our database connection works well with the Rocket application, and there is just one line of code when it comes to defining our database connection.

It may not come as a surprise that the way Rocket does authentication and middleware is also more streamlined. In the next section, we will be authenticating our requests with a **JSON web token (JWT)**.

Authenticating our requests

Throughout this book, we have been intercepting HTTP requests before they've hit the view in order to inspect the header and extract the token. If the token cannot be verified when we were interacting with to-do item views, we rejected the request and gave an unauthorized response to the user.

It is tempting to start constructing middleware for our Rocket views. However, Rocket provides streamlined mechanisms known as request and data guards. In order to implement a request guard, we are going to define our own JWT and apply it to our get items view.

Implementing a request guard

Follow these steps to implement a request guard:

1. We will begin by making a `src/jwt.rs` file and importing the `rocket` dependencies needed for a JWT struct processes with the following code:

    ```
    use rocket::Outcome;
    use rocket::http::Status;
    use rocket::request::{self, Request, FromRequest};
    ```

    The `FromRequest` struct is needed to enable our JWT struct to be implemented before the view is processed. When implementing this trait, we will get the request and extract the token from it when we define the `from_request` function.

    We will also use the `Status` struct to define the status of the returned requests, when extracting and decoding the tokens from the header of the incoming request fails. We use the `Outcome` struct to define whether the outcome of the token's extraction is a success or a failure.

2. Now that we have imported all the Rocket dependencies, we can import what we need to run the processes of the encoding and decoding tokens. These are defined in the following code:

    ```
    use hmac::{Hmac, NewMac};
    use jwt::{Header, Token, VerifyWithKey};
    use jwt::SignWithKey;
    ```

```
use sha2::Sha256;
use std::collections::BTreeMap;
use std::result::Result;
```

The `hmac` crate is used to generate the key for decoding and encoding tokens. `sha2` is the type of algorithm we will use for encoding and decoding. We have to remember to define these dependencies in the `Cargo.toml` file, as shown here:

```
jwt = "0.9.0"
hmac = "0.8.1"
sha2 = "0.9"
```

We now have all the crates needed for the JWT. At this point, we need to build the type of failure if the process fails. We will do this by building our own enum. An **enum** is a data type that consists of a set of names values called elements. Here, we will be defining an enum that denotes a bad count, missing, or invalid outcome.

3. We will be using the bad count if there is more than one token in the header. The missing outcome is to be used when there is no token in the header, and the invalid outcome is to be used when decoding fails. We can do this with the following code:

```
#[derive(Debug)]
pub enum ApiKeyError {
    BadCount,
    Missing,
    Invalid,
}
```

Note that we are using a `Debug` macro here. We need one so that our enum can be used in our `FromRequest` trait.

Building a JWT struct

Follow these steps to build a JWT struct:

1. Now that we have all of the support defined, we can start building our JWT struct. First of all, we must define our struct with the following code:

```
pub struct JwtToken {
    pub user_id: i32,
    pub body: String
}
```

Here, we are storing the user ID in the user_id field and the encoded token in the body field.

2. To populate the body field, we need to define an encode function, which is defined by the following code:

```
impl JwtToken {

    pub fn encode(user_id: i32) -> String {
        let secret_key: String = String::from("secret");
        let key: Hmac<Sha256> = Hmac::new_varkey(
                            &secret_key.as_bytes()).unwrap();
        let mut claims = BTreeMap::new();
        claims.insert("user_id", user_id);
        let token_str = claims.sign_with_key(
            &key).unwrap();
        return String::from(token_str)
    }
}
```

Here, we have defined a key. We then defined a **hash map** and inserted the user ID into this. Once we did this, we inserted the user ID into this map and signed it with our key to produce a token.

3. Now that we can issue tokens, we do not have to decode our tokens for authentication. We can define our decode function with the following function inside the impl block:

```
pub fn decode(encoded_token: String) ->
        Result<JwtToken, &'static str> {
    let secret_key: String = String::from("secret");
    let key: Hmac<Sha256> = Hmac::new_varkey(
        &secret_key.as_bytes()).unwrap();
    let token_str: &str = encoded_token.as_str();

    let token: Result<Token<Header,
        BTreeMap<String, i32>, _>, jwt::Error> =
        VerifyWithKey::verify_with_key(
        token_str, &key);
```

```
match token {
    Ok(token) => Ok(JwtToken { user_id:
        token.claims()["user_id"],
        body: encoded_token}),
    Err(_) => Err("could not decode token")
    }
}
```

Initially, we generated a key using the secret key string. We then received the encoded token that was passed into the function and verified it with a key. However, we did not directly unwrap it. This is because the token could be fraudulent, and the function could fail. Once we received the result of the verification, we matched the outcome, returning an error or our JWT struct.

Now that we have a fully functioning JWT struct that can decode and encode tokens, we can extract and insert the user ID. In order to decode tokens from incoming requests, we need to implement the Rocket FromRequest trait.

Applying Rocket traits to our struct

Follow these steps to apply Rocket traits to our struct:

1. Inside our implication, we have to define a from_request function that will be fired when the request. This can be done with the following code:

```
impl<'a, 'r> FromRequest<'a, 'r> for JwtToken {
    type Error = ApiKeyError;

    fn from_request(request: &'a Request<'r>) ->
        request::Outcome<Self, Self::Error> {
        let keys: Vec<_> = request.headers().get(
            "user-token").collect();
        match keys.len() {
            0 => Outcome::Failure((Status::NotFound,
                ApiKeyError::Missing)),
            1 => {
                let token = JwtToken::decode(
                    String::from(keys[0].to_string()));

                match token {
```

```
                        Ok(token) => Outcome::Success(
                            token),
                        Err(_message) => Outcome::Failure(
                            (Status::Unauthorized,
                            ApiKeyError::Invalid))
                    }
                },
                _ => Outcome::Failure((Status::BadRequest,
                    ApiKeyError::BadCount)),
            }
        }
    }
```

Here, we can see that we have defined a type pattern, `Error`, as our `ApiKeyError` struct. In our `from_request` function, we accept the request as a parameter and return an outcome, which is either an `ApiKeyError` or our `JwtToken`. Inside our function, we extract our token from the header if it is under the key value of `user-token`. If the length of the vector is zero, that means that there is nothing in the header that is under the `user-token` key.

Therefore, we return a missing error. If there is more than one, then something has happened, and we do not know which one is the token. Therefore, we return a bad count. If the number of tokens that's been extracted from the header is one, we can decode the token. Once we've done this, we can match the outcome. If there is an error, we know that our token struct has failed to decode the token, so we return an invalid error message. If it is a success, then we return the decoded token containing the user ID.

2. Now, our `JwtToken` struct is fully capable of guarding our view from invalid or missing tokens. Implementing it is fairly straightforward. All we have to do is pass our `JwtToken` struct into the parameters of the view, just like we did with our database connection. The `src/main.rs` file is defined by the following code block:

```
#[get("/get")]
fn get_items(conn: DbConn, token: jwt::JwtToken) ->
    Json<ToDoItems> {

    println!("get view is firing");
```

```
        let items = schema::to_do::table
            .order(schema::to_do::columns::id.asc())
            .filter(schema::to_do::columns::user_id.eq(
                &token.user_id))
            .load::<Item>(&*conn)
            .unwrap();

        let mut array_buffer = Vec::new();

        for item in items {
            let item = to_do_factory(
                &item.status, item.title).unwrap();
            array_buffer.push(item);
        }
        return Json(ToDoItems::new(array_buffer))
}
```

As we can see, we no longer have to pass the user ID into the URL. Instead, we just reference the user ID field from out token struct. If we test it, we will find that not having a token, or a random false token, will revoke the request before `get view is firing` can be printed to the console.

We are starting to see a theme with Rocket. If we implement Rockets traits in our structs, we can merely pass them into our view parameters, and they will be implemented. With this in mind, it is also worth looking into the **Fairing** Rocket trait.

Defining middleware with fairings

Middleware can be configured using the **Fairing** trait. As you may recall, we used fairings when connecting our database, as shown in the following code:

```
fn main() {
    rocket::ignite()
        .mount("/", routes![hello, bye])
        .mount("/items", routes![get_items])
        .attach(DbConn::fairing())
        .launch();
}
```

The `fairing` trait hooks into the request life cycle, thereby receiving callbacks for incoming and outgoing requests. Fairings can edit or record requests coming in and out. However, what they are not used for is terminating/responding to requests. They also cannot inject non-request data into a request. Note that fairings can prevent a server from launching or a server from being configured. Looking at our database, we can use the `attach` method for the database connection. This is a callback. Rocket fairings have four different types of callbacks:

- **Attach**: This callback alters the configuration of the server while it is launching and can prevent the launch if needed. As we can see, the configuration of the database connection is to be configured for the server when it is launching.

- **Launch**: This callback is called immediately before the server is launched. If we want to fire a process when the server launched, this callback will make it possible.

- **Request**: This callback is fired when the server receives an incoming request. However, again, they cannot abort or respond directly to the request. This is done via request guards, such as the JWT struct that we created in the previous section.

- **Response**: This callback fires when a response is ready to be sent to the user.

In this section, we will create a response that will return a message to the user instead of a not found status. To do this, we have to build a rerouting struct that overwrites the status of the response and the body to a not found message if the URL does not exist. In order to do this, we will create out struct in a `src/not_found.rs` file:

1. First, we must import the crates that we need via the following code block:

```
use std::io::Cursor;

use rocket::{Request, Response};
use rocket::fairing::{Fairing, Info, Kind};
use rocket::http::{Method, ContentType, Status};
```

We will use the `Cursor` struct to wrap the body in a memory buffer for the altered response. We will use the `Request` and `Response` structs to map the request and response through the middleware process. We will use the `Info` and `Kind` structs to define information around the middleware process. We will then use the `Method`, `ContentType`, and `Status` structs to edit `Response` if the response has a `NotFound` status.

2. Now that we have all of our dependencies, we can define our rerouting struct with
    the following code:

    ```
    pub struct ReRouter;
    ```

3. We do not need to define any fields. We need this struct to implement the `Fairing`
    trait. Inside this trait, we will feed the response into the function, as shown in the
    following code block:

    ```
    impl Fairing for ReRouter {

        fn info(&self) -> Info {
            Info {
                name: "GET rerouter",
                kind: Kind::Response
            }
        }


        fn on_response(&self, request: &Request,
                       response: &mut Response) {

            if request.method() == Method::Get &&
               response.status() == Status::NotFound {
                let body = format!("URL does not exist");
                response.set_status(Status::Ok);
                response.set_header(ContentType::Plain);
                response.set_sized_body(Cursor::new(body));
            }
            return
        }
    }
    ```

Here, we have included an `info` function. This merely returns an `Info` struct.
The name field is not really important apart from being used in logging. However,
the `kind` field is important as is gives the server information about what type of
callback is needed.

4. We can chain as many as we want, as shown in the following code example:

```
kind: Kind::Attach | Kind::Launch | Kind::Request |
Kind::Response
```

We must then define the on_response function. This gets fired when the server responds to the user. Here, we feed in the response and request. If the status of the response is not found and the request is a GET method, we must we update the status of OK, set the header of the content type to plain text, and insert a message, stating that the URL does not exist. If this is not the case, then we just return the response.

5. Now that our rerouting struct is ready to be used, we can import the struct at the top of the `src/main.rs` file, as shown here:

```
use crate::not_found::ReRouter;
```

6. Then, we can attach our struct to the server by using the following code:

```
rocket::ignite()
        .mount("/", routes![hello, bye])
        .mount("/items", routes![get_items])
        .attach(DbConn::fairing())
        .attach(ReRouter)
        .launch();
```

We will get the following console output:

```
Configured for development.
   => address: localhost
   => port: 8000
   => log: normal
   => workers: 8
   => secret key: generated
   => limits: forms = 32KiB
   => keep-alive: 5s
   => read timeout: 5s
   => write timeout: 5s
   => tls: disabled
   => [extra] databases:
   { postgres = { url =
```

```
    "postgres://username:password@localhost/to_do" } }
    Mounting /:
    => GET /hello/<name>/<age> (hello)
    => GET /bye/<name>/<age> (bye)
    Mounting /items:
    => GET /items/get (get_items)
    Fairings:
    => 1 response: GET rerouter
    Rocket has launched from http://localhost:8000
```

Here, we can see that `Fairings` has its own section now. The server runs just like it did previously, but if we hit a URL that cannot be found, we get the following message:

```
URL does not exist
```

Figure 11.2 – URL not found response

Now, whatever URL we hit, we can inform the user about what the problem is. There is nothing stopping us from changing the response type's **HTML**, as well as the coding **CSS** and HTML content in the body for the user. However, we have to be careful here. We are telling the user that the URL does not exist because there is a not found status.

If our API endpoint returns a not found status and is a **GET** method, and we return a not found status because we cannot find an entry in the database, the user will be informed that the URL does not exist. Therefore, we have to make sure that we do not return not found statuses in our API endpoints if we want to use this middleware.

Now that we have explored how to secure our API calls though JWT and connected to our database, there is only one more aspect we need to explore: passing data into our views. We will do this in the next section.

Passing data into our views

Passing data into a Rocket application is fairly straightforward. To do this, we will be altering part of the `to_do` module in the `src/json_serialization/to_do_item.rs` file:

1. First, we must define our dependencies with the following code:

```
use serde::Deserialize;
use serde::Serialize;
```

2. We use the `serde` crate to allow our struct to serialize and deserialize the data. This allows the data to be passed into the view or returned from the view. Now, we will add a `Serialize` trait to our `ToDoItem` struct, as follows:

```
#[derive(Deserialize, Serialize)]
pub struct ToDoItem {
    pub title: String,
    pub status: String
}
```

3. Now that our struct has been altered, we can build a simple view that merely takes in the JSON body and returns it. In our `src/main.rs` file, we will define the following dependency:

```
use crate::json_serialization::to_do_item::ToDoItem;
```

4. Now that our dependency has been defined, we can create our input view with the following code:

```
#[post("/input", data="<item>", format = "json")]
fn input(item: Json<ToDoItem>) -> Json<ToDoItem> {
    return Json(item.into_inner())
}
```

Here, we can see that the Rocket macro does more than just define the URL and method. When we define `item` as the data, we know that the data in the body will be denoted as `item`.

We also defined the format as JSON. We do not have to define the format, but if we do, then the view will reject requests in the wrong formats. Now that we have defined the view, we just need to attach it to the server and launch it. If we send a POST request to the view with a body containing the status and title, it will be returned to us. If we add extra fields that are not in our `ToDoItem` struct, the view will still pass, but the extra field will be removed from the data that we are passing through the view.

Note that a theme is starting to develop here. Adding functionality to a view is quick and flexible. We can see this when we combine everything we have covered until now in this chapter. In the next section, we will create a create to-do item view by implementing everything we've covered.

Putting it all together

Now that we have covered authentication, passing JSON body data, and connecting to the database, we can put this all together and create a create API endpoint where we will authenticate our JWT, pass in data about the to-do item we are creating, and check to see if the item already exists. If the item does not exist, we must insert the new item that is being created.

Once we've done this, we need to get all of the items and process them to return the state of all the items in the database in relation to the user. We do not have to build any more dependencies to do this. Initially, we need to import the new item data model with the following code:

```
use crate::models::item::new_item::NewItem;
```

With this, we can start building our create view:

1. First of all, we must define all the data that's needed for the create to-do item process:

    ```
    #[post("/create", data="<item>", format = "json")]
    fn create(item: Json<ToDoItem>, conn: DbConn,
                token: jwt::JwtToken) -> Json<ToDoItems> {
        let title: String = item.title.clone();
        let title_ref: String = item.title.clone();
    }
    ```

    Here, we accepted the to-do item's information from the request body, and we enforced the constraint that the request has to be in JSON format. We also enforced authentication to this view by simply adding the token to the parameters. We also have the database connection included in the view, which we did by adding it to the parameters. We then extracted two references to the title.

    This is a great example of how easily the Rocket framework scales. This is even more compact than using the **Python Flask framework**.

2. Now that we have all the data we need, we will make a database call to see if the new
    to-do item is already is in the database:

```
let items = schema::to_do::table
    .filter(schema::to_do::columns::title.eq(
        title_ref.as_str()))
    .filter(schema::to_do::columns::user_id.eq(
        &token.user_id))
    .order(schema::to_do::columns::id.asc())
    .load::<Item>(&*conn)
    .unwrap();
```

3. If the number of items being returned from the database call is zero, this means that
    the new to-do item needs to be inserted into the database. This can be achieved with
    the following code:

```
if items.len() == 0 {
    let new_post = NewItem::new(
        title, token.user_id.clone());
    let _ = diesel::insert_into(schema::to_do::table)
        .values(&new_post)
        .execute(&*conn);
}
```

4. Now, we need to get the new updated list of to-do items to be returned. This can be
    done via the following database call:

```
let items = schema::to_do::table
    .order(schema::to_do::columns::id.asc())
    .filter(schema::to_do::columns::user_id.eq(
        &token.user_id))
    .load::<Item>(&*conn)
    .unwrap();
```

5. Now that we have our updated data, we can loop through it while processing the loaded items via the to-do factory. This allows them to be serialized. Then, we can append them to a new empty vector. This empty vector is then fed into the ToDoItems struct, as shown here:

```
let mut array_buffer = Vec::new();

for item in items {
    let item = to_do_factory(
        &item.status, item.title).unwrap();
    array_buffer.push(item);
}
return Json(ToDoItems::new(array_buffer))
```

6. Our views are now fully defined. All we have to do now is mount the views with the following code:

```
rocket::ignite()
    .mount("/", routes![hello, bye, input, create])
    .mount("/items", routes![get_items])
    .attach(DbConn::fairing())
    .attach(ReRouter)
    .launch();
```

Here, we have created a view that does everything we need to create a to-do item, inserted it into the database, and returned updated to the user under the condition of authentication. At this point, we have covered the main concepts needed to recreate the to-do application that we have built throughout this book using the Actix web framework.

Summary

In this chapter, we have gone through the main concepts needed to replicate our to-do application. We built and ran a Rocket server. We then defined routes and established a database connection for our server. After that, we explored middleware and built authentication and data processing using guards for our views. With this, we created a view that utilized everything we have covered in this book.

What we gained here was a deeper appreciation for the modular code that we have built throughout this book. Even though some of the concepts we revisited had not been touched since the start of this book, these modules were isolated, did one thing, and did what their label proposed. Because of this, they can easily be copied over and utilized in a completely different framework. Recall the HTML rendering module that we built in *Chapter 5, Displaying Content in the Browser*. It had no dependencies, and it was merely loading the data from HTML, CSS, and JavaScript files, merging them, and returning them to the user. There is nothing stopping us from copying and pasting this into our return statements for some views.

Also, note how simple, boilerplate-free, and scalable the Rocket framework is. While Rocket could introduce breaking changes and still uses **Rust nightly**, it is certainly a framework to keep an eye on. We advise you to build any future projects in Actix web but keep your modules isolated and simple. Therefore, once Rocket reaches maturity, it might be advantageous to start porting the modules over to the Rocket framework.

In the next chapter, which is this book's appendix, we will explore the core concepts of the **Warp** framework so that we can theoretically recreate our to-do application using Warp.

Further reading

- Rocket documentation: `https://rocket.rs/`

Appendix A
Understanding the Warp Framework

In the previous chapters, we built a fully functioning **to-do** application using **Actix web** and the **Rocket** framework.

In this appendix, we'll go through the necessary core concepts so that there will be nothing holding us back if we decide to completely recreate our to-do application in **Warp**. We will not explicitly recreate the application in this appendix, as this would result in pages and pages of repetition.

However, there is going to be some repetition as some of the modules we've created throughout this book are web framework agnostic. We will copy some of the modules we created in the previous chapters for some of this appendix's examples. Our examples will include constructing basic views, connecting to a database, passing data into a view via the body, and authenticating users using **JSON web authentication**.

In this appendix, we will cover the following topics:

- High-level differences between Actix web and the Warp web framework
- Setting up and configuring a Warp server
- Creating basic routes for a Warp server
- Mounting views onto the server

- Understanding the logging of a Warp server
- Using **Diesel** to connect to a database and utilize this through its view parameters

After reading this appendix, we will be able to perform all the core tasks needed to replicate a to-do application by using the Warp framework, and be able to utilize some of the isolated code modules we coded in the previous Actix web chapters.

This means that we will be able to define routes in a Warp server, enable authentication for those routes, connect to a database, if needed, and also get and insert data. We will also be able to accept **JSON** data from the request, and return data to the user. While this appendix will not fully rebuild the application, we will be able to extrapolate the concepts that we will learn about in this appendix and build a fully functioning application if needed.

Technical requirements

In this appendix, we will be copying some modules from the previous Actix web chapter (*Chapter 10, Deploying Our Application on AWS*) to augment the Warp application. This can be accessed at `https://github.com/PacktPublishing/Rust-Web-Programming/tree/master/Chapter10/persist_on_server`.

You can find the full source code that will be used in this appendix here: `https://github.com/PacktPublishing/Rust-Web-Programming/tree/master/Appendix%20A`.

Note that this appendix will be using a **JWT token** that will not be generated in this appendix. A JWT token has been provided in the root README of the following GitHub repository: `https://github.com/PacktPublishing/Rust-Web-Programming/tree/master/`.

The CiA videos for this book can be viewed at: `http://bit.ly/3jULCrw`

What is Warp?

Warp is a Rust web framework like Actix web. It's newer than Actix web with a lower user base at the time of writing this book because of how new the framework is, its community, and how the documentation is not as readily available as Actix web's.

At the time of writing this book, the documentation for Actix web was clearer and more comprehensive. Functionality-wise, however, Warp and Actix web are essentially the same. They both run on stable **Rust** (unlike **Rocket**), and they support the same functionality. However, the way in which Warp goes about configuring views is different. Instead of functions defining views, Warp has what we call filters.

These filters can be used to extract data from the body or the header, run a function, or define a method or URL endpoint. These filters can be chained together, giving us ultimate flexibility in terms of how we map the request and see it being processed in our API endpoints.

In the next section, we'll start setting up our server.

Setting up our server

We need to set up a server in order to listen to requests, process them, and route them to specific views based on their URLs. This server will be the entry point to our application. In order to build our server, we must follow these steps:

1. First, we will build our own cargo project and define our dependency on the Rocket frame with the following dependency, which can be found in the `Cargo.toml` file:

    ```
    [dependencies]
    tokio = { version = "0.2", features = ["full"] }
    warp = "0.2"
    ```

2. Now, we can build our basic server with just one view in out `src/main.rs` file. First of all, we will import what we need with the following code:

    ```
    use warp::Filter;
    ```

    This is all we need to import.

    With this simple import statement, Warp provides us with a lot of tools. To demonstrate this, we are going to define some routes, pass in parameters, return some JSON, and launch a server. Essentially, `Filter` can extract some data from requests. This data can be mutated and combined with other filters, resulting in returning data. Filters can also be chained together, enabling us to reuse parts of our application.

3. Now that we have defined our dependencies, we will define our `main` function with the `tokio` macro, as we did in our Actix web to-do application, as shown in the following code block:

    ```
    #[tokio::main]
    async fn main() {
    }
    ```

4. Inside this `main` function, we will define our views and launch the server. The most basic view that we can define is merely returning a string, as shown in the following code block:

```
let home = warp::path!("home")
    .map(|| "This is a Warp server built in Rust");
```

Here, we assigned a variable to the `path` macro. If `/home` is at the end of the URL, we fire a closure and return the result. In this view, we return a `String` stating that this is a Warp server. We can pass parameters into the `path` macro, and then into the closure, with the following code:

```
let greet = warp::path!("greet" / String / i32)
    .map(|name: String, age: i32| {
        return format!("I am {} and {} years old", name,
            age)
    });
```

Here, we can see that our parameter types are defined and separated with a forward slash.

5. Then, we must pass these parameters into the closure, which returns a string containing our parameters. The parameters have to be in sequential order compared to the parameters defined in the URL. If we were to swap them around, the code would not compile due to the variables not matching. We can also manipulate variables in the closure and return them using JSON, as shown here:

```
let add = warp::path!("add" / i32 / i32)
    .map(|one: i32, two: i32| {
        let result: i32 = one + two;
        return warp::reply::json(&result)
    });
```

Here, we can see that `reply` structs are readily available for us to exploit. Two numbers are passed into the URL, which are then passed into the closure. Inside this closure, we add the two variables and return the result in JSON format.

6. Now that we have defined the views that we need in the `main` function, we need to collect them. We can do this by creating a filter that collects a `get` request and passes it through our views, as shown here:

```
let routes = warp::get().and(
        home
        .or(greet)
        .or(add)
);
```

7. Now, there is nothing stopping us from launching our server in our `main` function alongside our views and collection of views, as shown in the following code:

```
warp::serve(routes)
    .run(([127, 0, 0, 1], 8000))
    .await;
}
```

Here, we serve our `routes` on a local host with port `8000`. Running the `cargo run` command gives us the following Terminal output:

```
Compiling warp_server v0.1.0 (/Users/maxwellflitton/
Documents/github/Rust-Web-Programming/
chapter_twelve/warp_server)
Finished dev [unoptimized + debuginfo]
target(s) in 3.20s
Running `/Users/maxwellflitton/Documents/github/
Rust-Web-Programming/chapter_twelve/warp_server/
target/debug/warp_server`
```

Here, we can see that this is just a compile statement. There is no logging out of the box for Warp. We can establish this by making a call to the add view, which gives us the following output:

9

Figure 12.1 – Result from calling our add view

Here, we can see that we have passed **3** and **6** into the URL and that the response is **9**, which is expected.

8. Checking the console after making the call will show zero logging. We can perform logging, but we do need extra dependencies. In our `Cargo.toml` file, we will add the dependencies we defined here:

```
log = "0.4"
pretty_env_logger = "0.3"
```

9. Now that we have these dependencies, we can import them into our `main.rs` file, as shown here:

```
extern crate pretty_env_logger;
#[macro_use] extern crate log;
```

10. With these imports, we can define the logger inside the `main` function with the following code:

```
pretty_env_logger::init();
let log = warp::log("to_do::api");
```

Here, we can see that we have wrapped the name of a log in a `log` function, which returns the `log` struct. This struct decorates a filter for logging requests and responses.

11. Now that we have done this, we have to attach it to our `routes` so that we can log requests and responses, as shown in the following code:

```
let routes = warp::get().and(
        home
        .or(greet)
```

```
        .or(add)
    ).with(log);
```

We achieved this by appending a `with` function, which accepts our `log`.

12. Now that we have done everything we need for our logger to run, we will run our application with the **Terminal** command defined here:

```
RUST_LOG=to_do::api cargo run
```

Here, we can see that we are pointing to the name of the log we defined in the `main.rs` file. Our application is now running with a logger. When we make a call to the server, we will get a log entry in the Terminal that will look similar to the following:

```
INFO   to_do::api > 127.0.0.1:60612
"GET /add/3/6 HTTP/1.1" 200 "-"
"Mozilla/5.0 (Macintosh; Intel Mac OS X 11_0_1)
AppleWebKit/537.36 (KHTML, like Gecko)
Chrome/87.0.4280.141 Safari/537.36" 145.833µs
```

Here, we can see that the logging process is working.

With this, our server is running. Now, we can connect our Rocket server to our database.

Connecting to our database

In order to connect to our database, we will use the `diesel` crate. We have used the `diesel` crate throughout this book for connecting to our database. We also have to remember that, throughout this book, we have been building isolated modules. We can reuse these.

We will need to serialize the database being returned. Because of this, we can copy `src/json_serialization` from *Chapter 11, Understanding Rocket Web Framework*, to `src/json_serialization`.

We will also be using the same data models, so we will need to copy the following:

- `src/models` to `src/models`
- `src/to_do` to `src/to_do`
- `src/.env` to `src/.env`
- `src/schema.rs` to `src/schema.rs`

- `docker-compose.yml` to `docker-compose.yml`
- `src/database.rs` to `src/database.rs`
- `diesel.toml` to `diesel.toml`

Follow these steps to connect to our database:

1. Our modules are ready to be used. However, before we import them into the `main` file, considering that the previous chapter (*Chapter 11*, *Understanding Rocket Web Framework*) used the Rocket database connection, we have to define our own database connection using just `diesel` in the `src/database.rs` file with the following code:

```
use diesel::prelude::*;
use diesel::pg::PgConnection;
use dotenv::dotenv;
use std::env;


pub fn establish_connection() -> PgConnection {
    dotenv().ok();

    let database_url = env::var("DATABASE_URL")
        .expect("DATABASE_URL must be set");
    PgConnection::establish(&database_url)
        .unwrap_or_else(|_| panic!("Error connecting
            to {}", database_url))
}
```

From the preceding code, we merely get the database URL from the environment. We can then use this URL to establish a database connection for returning the database connection.

2. Now that we have copied over our infrastructure, we can define the dependencies that are needed in the `cargo.toml` file with the following code:

```
serde = { version = "1.0.1", features = ["derive"] }
serde_json = "1.0.4"
futures = "0.3.7"
diesel = { version = "1.4.4", features = ["postgres"] }
```

```
bcrypt = "0.8"
uuid = { version = "0.8", features = ["serde", "v4"] }
dotenv = "0.15.0"
```

All of these dependencies are not needed if we are just directly connecting to the database and nothing else. However, these are needed for the modules that we imported from *Chapter 11, Understanding Rocket Web Framework.*

3. Now that we have all of the dependencies we need for the project, we can define our third-party crates in the `main.rs` file with the following code:

```
#[macro_use] extern crate diesel;
use diesel::prelude::*;
extern crate dotenv;
```

The `diesel` crate and `prelude` enable us to interact with the table definitions in the `schema.rs` file. The `dotenv` crate enables us to get the database URL from the environment from the `establish_connection` function in the `database.rs` file.

4. With the third-party crates imported, we can define our modules from the previous chapters, as shown here:

```
mod schema;
mod to_do;
mod json_serialization;
mod database;
mod models;
```

5. With this, we can import particular structs and functions that we are going to use when loading to-do items from the database and returning the JSON structures to the user, as shown here:

```
use to_do::to_do_factory;
use database::establish_connection;
use models::item::item::Item;
use json_serialization::to_do_items::ToDoItems;
```

6. With these structs and functions, we can now build our view, which accepts the user ID via URL parameters, gets the to-do items from the database, and then returns to-do items using the `json_serialization` module to build the structured response in the `main` function, as shown here:

```
let get_items = warp::path!("user" / i32)
    .map(|user_id: i32| {
        let connection = establish_connection();

        let items = schema::to_do::table
            .order(schema::to_do::columns::id.asc())
            .filter(schema::to_do::columns::user_
                id.eq(&user_id))
            .load::<Item>(&connection)
            .unwrap();

        let mut array_buffer = Vec::new();

        for item in items {
            let item = to_do_factory(&item.status,
                                     item.title).unwrap();
            array_buffer.push(item);
        }
        return warp::reply::json(&ToDoItems::new(
            array_buffer))
    });
```

7. We have to remember that once we have defined the view, we have to register it in our `main.rs` file, like so:

```
let routes = warp::get().and(
        home
        .or(greet)
        .or(add)
        .or(get_items)
    ).with(log);
```

8. We are now ready to run our server with our new view, which connects to our database. There is a high chance that your database will be different. After making a GET request for my application with `localhost:8000/user/1`, I received the following JSON as output:

```
{
    "done_items": [
        {
            "title": "code food only app",
            "status": "done"
        }
    ],
    "pending_items": [
        {
            "title": "learn cricket",
            "status": "pending"
        },
        {
            "title": "read C.O.A.T",
            "status": "pending"
        }
    ],
    "pending_item_count": 2,
    "done_item_count": 1
}
```

This can be directly inserted into our frontend.

There is nothing stopping us from importing the **HTML**, **JavaScript**, and **CSS** directories from the previous chapters and using Warp to serve them. The benefits of using isolated and modular code are clear as the modules can be imported into a range of different frameworks. Now that our database logic works, we have to authenticate our users so that we can get the user ID from the **JSON web token** (**JWT**). In the next section, we will be authenticating our requests by extracting a JWT from the header.

Authenticating our requests

Throughout this book, we have been intercepting the HTTP requests before they can hit the view in order to inspect the header and extract the token. If the token couldn't be verified when we interacted with to-do item views, we rejected the request and gave an unauthorized response to the user.

In Actix, we built middleware that inspected the requests before they hit the server view. In Rocket, we implemented request guards to reject the request if it did not have the authentication needed to make the request.

With Warp, we are going to follow a different approach: we are going to add another filter to our view. In this section, we are going to apply this filter to our GET view in order to get the to-do items that belong to the user. We can achieve this by doing the following:

1. Adding a header extraction filter to our view.

2. Configuring our own JWT to check whether the token that's been supplied is correct.

3. Using the token to dictate how to process and return the data.

In the following sections, we'll elaborate each of these steps.

Adding a header extraction filter

Adding the header extraction filter is fairly straightforward.

We can merely insert an and function just before the map function. This will check if the token is present in the header before the function belonging to that view is mapped. We can then pass the token into the closure in the map function, as shown in the following code:

```
let get_items = warp::path!("user" / i32)
    .and(warp::header("user-token"))
    .map(|user_id: i32, token: String| {
        println!("{}", token);
        . . .
    });
```

From the preceding code, we can see that the rest of the code that gets the to-do items from the database and returns them is denoted by . . . (we covered this in the previous section). Note that although we defined our token parameter as token, we can call it whatever we want.

he closure in the map function maps from left to right in relation from first to last. token is the last addition; therefore, it is the furthest to the right, whereas the parameters defined in the URL is the first, so it is on the furthest to the left.

If we do not include the token parameter, we will get a verbose error message throwing up five errors, complaining about the log, and a long print out of a whole range of filters. If we scroll up enough, we will see that the get_items filter closure only accepts one parameter when it is supposed to accept two.

This is one of the downsides of developing in a new framework. In time, these error statements will be smoothed out. We are printing out the token to the console to see what we are actually passing through. Making a call in the browser will give us the following output:

```
Missing request header "user-token"
```

Figure 12.2 – Result of calling our get_items view with no header

As you can see, this response was provided because our browser's GET request did not contain a header. If we inspect our terminal, we will see that we did not attempt to print out the token. There was no error being thrown on the server side.

This is because the request was rejected by the and function, which was extracting the token from the header before we got to the map function of the view. If we make the request in Postman with a token that has a user ID baked into it, we get the following result:

Figure 12.3 – Result of calling our get_items view with the header for user ID 1

As you can see, the token has a user ID of **1**. If we inspect the console, we will see that the same token has been printed out in the console. With this, we are confident that our GET view rejects the request if the token is not present in the view, and then passes the token into the view if it is present.

In the next section, we will configure our own JWT struct to see if our token is correct, and then extract the user ID from the token if it is correctly decoded.

Configuring our JWT to validate the supplied token

To check that the token being supplied is correct, we must follow these steps:

1. We need to have our own JWT struct that can encode and decode tokens. We can achieve this by copying our JWT struct from `src/auth/jwt.rs` from *Chapter 10, Deploying Our Rust Application on AWS Server*, to `src/our_jwt.rs`.

2. Once we've done this, we need to remove the references from the Actix framework. We can do this by removing the following imports and functions that are defined in the src/our_jwt.rs file, as shown in the following code snippet:

```
use actix_web::HttpRequest;


pub fn decode_from_request(request: HttpRequest)
                        -> Result<JwtToken, &'static str> {
    match request.headers().get("user-token") {
        Some(token) => JwtToken::decode(
            String::from(token.to_str().unwrap())),
        None => Err("there is no token")
    }
}
```

3. Once the functions and imports from the preceding code have been removed, we can define the crates that are needed for our JWT struct by adding the following crates to our Cargo.toml file:

```
jwt = "0.9.0"
hmac = "0.8.1"
sha2 = "0.9"
```

This enables us to encode the token with the jwt crate, store and manage data in the token with the hmac crate, and encode and decode the token using the sha2 algorithm.

4. Now, we can define our JWT module in the main.rs file, like so:

```
mod our_jwt;
```

With that, we have configured our own JWT and it is ready for use. Now, we have to use the JWT to check and extract the user ID.

Processing and returning the data by using our token

There are two outcomes of our token checking process. We know that if the token is not present, the request gets rejected before it hits the view. Therefore, the outcome could either be an unauthorized status as the decoding fails, or an OK status returning the user's to-do items.

Because of this, we have to define our own `async` function. This function manages the token's authentication and returns a rejection or some to-do items, as shown in the following code:

```
async fn get_items_reply(token: String)
            -> Result<Box<dyn warp::Reply>, warp::Rejection> {
    match our_jwt::JwtToken::decode(token) {
        Ok(token) => {
            let connection = establish_connection();

            let items = schema::to_do::table
                .order(schema::to_do::columns::id.asc())
                .filter(schema::to_do::columns::user_id.eq(
                    &token.user_id))
                .load::<Item>(&connection)
                .unwrap();

            let mut array_buffer = Vec::new();

            for item in items {
                let item = to_do_factory(&item.status,
                                         item.title).unwrap();
                array_buffer.push(item);
            }
            return Ok(Box::new(warp::reply::json(
                    &ToDoItems::new(array_buffer))))
        },
        Err(_message) => {
            Ok(Box::new(warp::http::StatusCode::UNAUTHORIZED))
        }
    }
}
```

Here, we can see that the function accepts the token. Here, we defined the return as a `Result` struct that can be either a reply or a rejection. Note that a `Box` struct is used to put the value on the heap with a pointer.

We need this to enable the function to return two different struct types. Without this, Warp will complain that two different types are being returned. We then match the outcome of the decode function using the input token.

If the outcome doesn't contain an error, we can make the database connection, filter the to-do functions from the database by the user ID from the decoded token, package the results using the to-do factory, and then return the to-do items as a reply. If the token decode has failed, we must conclude that the request is unauthorized, and it is returned. We can define our get_items view with this function like so:

```
let get_items = warp::path!("items")
    .and(warp::header("user-token")).and_then(get_items_reply);
```

This defines the URL endpoint as /items. Then, it checks the header and runs our function. This enables us to make a call using the token in the header. This tells the server what user ID is making a call, thus returning the to-do items belonging to the user.

If the token is incorrect or missing, the request gets rejected. Now that we have explored how to get data from the website, we can learn how to pass data via the body of the request.

Passing data into our views

In order to create a to-do item, follow these steps:

1. We need to pass the parameters of the item that we are creating into a view with an auth token as a POST method. Then, we can decode the token that matches the outcome. If the decoding results in an error, we return a rejection. If the token is correctly decoded, we can continue inserting the new to-do item. This process can be defined by using the make_item_reply function, as shown here:

```
async fn make_item_reply(token: String, item: ToDoItem)
-> Result<Box<dyn warp::Reply>, warp::Rejection> {
    match our_jwt::JwtToken::decode(token) {
        Ok(token) => {
            . . .
        },
```

```
        Err(_message) => {
            . . .
        }
    }
}
```

2. Note that we are accepting a `ToDoItem` struct in the function. This is from our `json_serialization` module, and is used to process the body parameters being passed via the request. Because of this, we need to import the struct at the top of the file, as shown here:

```
use json_serialization::to_do_item::ToDoItem;
```

3. Now that we have imported the struct, we can start working on the decode outcomes. We can start with the failed decode result. Here, we will merely return an UNAUTHORIZED status code:

```
Err(_message) => {
    return Ok(Box::new(warp::http::StatusCode:
        :UNAUTHORIZED))
}
```

4. If the decode passes, we can make a connection to the database, and then collect all the data that we'll need to create a new to-do item, as shown in the following code:

```
let connection = establish_connection();

let title: String = item.title.clone();
let title_ref: String = item.title.clone();
```

5. With that, we have made a connection and have all the data we need. Now, we need to check if the to-do item with the title belonging to the user who is making the request is already in the database. If it is, then we do not want to insert a new one. If it isn't, we don't, as shown in the following code:

```
let items = schema::to_do::table
    .filter(schema::to_do::columns::title.eq(
        title_ref.as_str()))
    .filter(schema::to_do::columns::user_id.eq(
        &token.user_id))
    .order(schema::to_do::columns::id.asc())
```

```
    .load::<Item>(&connection)
    .unwrap();

if items.len() == 0 {
    let new_post = NewItem::new(title,
                    token.user_id.clone());
    let _ = diesel::insert_into(
                schema::to_do::table).values(&new_post)
        .execute(&connection);
}
```

Note that the NewItem struct needs to be imported.

6. Now that we have inserted the new to-do item, we need to get all the items for the user and return them:

```
let items = schema::to_do::table
    .order(schema::to_do::columns::id.asc())
    .filter(schema::to_do::columns::user_id.eq(
            &token.user_id))
    .load::<Item>(&connection)
    .unwrap();

let mut array_buffer = Vec::new();

for item in items {
    let item = to_do_factory(&item.status,
                        item.title).unwrap();
    array_buffer.push(item);
}
return Ok(Box::new(warp::reply::json(
                &ToDoItems::new(array_buffer))))
```

Here, we can see that this code is being repeated and that there is an opportunity to refactor this. We can do this by creating a function that gets the to-do items and packages them into a ToDoItems struct.

7. Now that we have our `return` function, we can construct the view. We need to define the URL endpoint, extract the header, extract the data from the body, and then run the `reply` function, as shown here:

```
let make_item = warp::post()
    .and(warp::path("make"))
    .and(warp::header("user-token"))
    .and(warp::body::content_length_limit(1024 * 16))
    .and(warp::body::json())
    .and_then(make_item_reply);
```

Here, we can see that we defined the view as POST and made the URL endpoint `make`. We then extracted the token from the header. If it is not there, we will reject the view.

In the previous chapters, we built some middleware/data guards to decode the token before it hit the view. However, in our POST view, we decode the token inside the `view` function. Middleware is usually preferred because one attack is loading a large amount of data in the body, thereby overloading the server.

However, with middleware, the unauthorized request can be rejected before the large amount of data is opened. In the preceding code, we added a content limit. This ensures that the body is below `16` KB. We want to protect our server against large data payloads before the request hits the `view` function.

8. Now, we must extract the JSON data from the body and feed it into the `make_item_reply` function. Since we defined one of the parameters as a `ToDoItems` struct for the `make_item_reply` function, this is where the fields in the JSON are checked. We can check this with the following call:

```
POST          ▼     http://127.0.0.1:8000/make
```

```
1 ▾ {
2       "title": "eat dinner",
3       "status": "pending"
4   }
5
6
7
8
9
```

Body   Cookies   Headers (3)   Test Results   Status: 200 OK

Pretty   Raw   Preview   Visualize   JSON ▼   ⇥

```
 1  {
 2      "pending_items": [
 3          {
 4              "title": "this is a title",
 5              "status": "pending"
 6          },
 7          {
 8              "title": "cook dinner",
 9              "status": "pending"
10          },
11          {
12              "title": "eat dinner",
13              "status": "pending"
14          }
15      ],
16      "done_items": [],
17      "pending_item_count": 3,
18      "done_item_count": 0
19  }
```

Figure 12.4 – Creating a to-do item with POST

If the header is missing, we get a **400 bad request** response. If any fields are missing in the body, we also get a **400 bad request** response. If the token is incorrect and cannot be decoded properly, then we get a **401 unauthorized request** response.

If all of these steps pass, we get a **200 Ok** status, as well as the new updated to-do items list belonging to the user making the request.

Here, we have created a view that does everything we need to create a to-do item, insert it into the database, and return it updated to the user under the condition of authentication. At this point, we have covered the main concepts needed to recreate the to-do application that we built throughout this book using the Actix web framework.

Summary

In this appendix, we went through a variety of Warp concepts that we need to understand if we wish to replicate the to-do application in the Warp framework. Here, we defined some routes, and then connected these routes to a database. We then chained filters together to map out a range checks, including token presence, body, size, and fields, before processing our view. With this, we created a create to-do view that utilized all of these concepts. Editing, deleting, and creating to-do items can all be done in Warp with the concepts that we have covered.

We also utilized the modular code that we have been developing over the course of this book. It is testament to the power of modular coding that these modules could be merely copied in and plugged into our Warp server to be utilized. As stated in the previous chapter, *Chapter 11, Understanding Rocket Web Framework*, we can copy and paste the rendering module that we built in *Chapter 5, Displaying Content in the Browser*. This is because there are no dependencies for that module. It is loading the data from the HTML, CSS, and JavaScript file, merging it, and returning that data to the user.

Note that the Warp framework enables us to chain filters together, giving us a lot of freedom when it comes to the flow of our views. This also enables us to reuse filters and add extra checks with a small amount of code for a view. We can combine two views together if we want. For instance, if we create a GET items filter, we can merely just tag this onto the end of all the other views to reduce duplicate code.

With that, we have come to the end of this book. Rust is a growing language and there is more to it than what we have covered here. However, we have covered a lot. We've explored the basics of Rust, databases, views, REST APIs, authentication, and deployment on AWS, and then applied these concepts to Actix, Rocket, and Warp. Now, you are ready to get productive with Rust in web development, and start exploring more complex concepts and web architectures with Rust.

Assessments

Chapter 1, Quick Introduction to Rust

Question 1

What is the difference between `str` and `String`?

Answer

A `String` is a reference stored in the stack that points to `str`, which is the data stored in the heap.

Question 2

Why can't string literals be passed through a function (string literal meaning `str` as opposed to `&str`)?

Answer

Because we do not know the size of a string literal at compile time. A `String` reference, on the other hand, is fixed, which is why it can be passed through to the function.

Question 3

How do we access the data belonging to a key in a hash map?

Answer

We use the `get` function, and then unwrap it since the `get` function merely returns an `Option` struct.

Question 4

When a function results in an error, can we handle other processes or will the error crash the program instantly?

Answer

No, results have to be unwrapped before exposing the error. A simple `match` statement can handle unwrapping the result and managing the error when needed.

Question 5

When borrowing, how does Rust ensure that there's no data race?

Answer

A data race condition can happen when we're altering data. Because of this, no other borrows are allowed if a mutable borrow is taking place.

Question 6

When would we need to define two different lifetimes in a function?

Answer

When the result of a function relies on one of the lifetimes and the result of the function is needed outside of the scope, it's called.

Question 7

How can structs utilize inheritance?

Answer

Through composition. The super struct is assigned to an attribute in the child struct. In the constructor function, the super struct is built and assigned to that attribute in the constructor function.

Question 8

How can we slot in extra functionality and freedom into a struct?

Answer

By using traits. Implementing a trait will give the struct the ability to use functions that belong to the trait. The trait's implementation also allows the struct to pass typing checks for that trait.

Question 9

How do we allow a container or function to accept different data structures?

Answer

By declaring enums or traits in the typing or by utilizing generics (see the *Further reading section in Chapter 1, Quick Introduction to Rust*).

Question 10

What's the quickest way to add a trait, such as copy, to a struct?

Answer

By decorating the struct with a derive macro that has the copy and clone traits.

Chapter 2, Designing Your Web Application in Rust

Question 1

What does the -release argument in Cargo do when added to build and run?

Answer

In build, the −release argument compiles the program in an optimized way as opposed to a debug compilation. In run, the −release argument points to the optimized binary as opposed to the debug binary.

Question 2

How do we enable a file to be accessible within and outside a module?

Answer

To enable a file to be accessible to other files in a module, we have to define the file as a module in the mod.rs file in the root of the module. We add "pub" before the definition to make it accessible outside the module.

Question 3

What are the advantages of having traits with a single scope?

Answer

Single-scope traits enable maximum flexibility when defining structs. A good example would be adding an on hold to-do item. With this item, we might only allow it to have an edit trait. We have to edit the on hold back to a pending item before we can delete it or get it for display. If all the action functions were defined in one trait, we could not do that.

Question 4

What steps would we have to take to add an on hold to-do item that will only allow get and edit functionality?

Answer

Define a trait in its own file in traits that inherit from the base struct, which also implements the get and edit traits. Add another option in the factory to enable this struct to be constructed with an on hold string for the status. Add an on hold type to the enum in the factory file. Add another line in the match statement for the entry point in processes that points to a new function processing the on hold item.

Question 5

What are the benefits of the factory?

Answer

The factory standardizes the construction of structs. It also reduces the possibility of building one of a range of structs outside of the module with just one line of code. This stops other files ballooning and does not require the developer to root around in the module to utilize it.

Question 6

How do we effectively map a range of processes based on some parameters?

Answer

We use `match` statements that lead on to other `match` statements. This enables us to code a tree-like effect and there is nothing stopping us from connecting branches later on down the chain.

Chapter 3, Handling HTTP Requests

Question 1

What parameter is passed into the `HttpServer::new` function and what does the parameter return?

Answer

A closure is passed into the function. It has to return the `App` struct so the `bind` and `run` functions can be acted on after the `HttpServer::new` function has fired.

Question 2

How is a closure different from a function?

Answer

A closure can interact with variables outside of the scope of the closure.

Question 3

What is the difference between a process and a thread?

Answer

A process is a program that is executed with its own memory stack, registers, and variables whereas a thread is a lightweight process that is managed independently but shares data from other threads and the main program.

Question 4

What is the difference between an `async` function and a normal one?

Answer

A normal function executes as soon as it is called, whereas an `async` function is a promise, and has to be executed with a blocking function.

Question 5

What is the difference between `await` and `join`?

Answer

`await` blocks the program to wait for the future to be executed, however, the `join` function can run multiple threads or futures concurrently. `await` can also be executed on a `join` function.

Question 6

What is the advantage of chaining factories?

Answer

Chaining factories gives us flexibility on how individual modules are constructed, and how they are orchestrated. The factory inside the module focuses on how the module is constructed; the factory outside the module focuses on how the different modules are orchestrated.

Question 7

What is the advantage of having a utility struct such as the `Path` struct?

Answer

A utility struct reduces the risk of typo errors and makes it easier to maintain and change configurations and simpler to configure factory behavior on the fly.

Chapter 4, Processing HTTP Requests

Question 1

What is the difference between a GET request and POST request?

Answer

A GET request can be cached, and there are limits to the types and amount of data that can be sent. A POST request has a body, which enables more data to be transferred. It also cannot be cached.

Question 2

Why would we have middleware when we check credentials?

Answer

We use middleware to open the header and check the credentials before sending the request to the desired view. This gives us the opportunity to prevent the body being loaded by returning an auth error before loading the view, thereby preventing the potentially malicious body.

Question 3

How do you enable a custom struct to be directly returned in a view?

Answer

For the struct to be directly returned, we will have to implement the `Responder` trait. During this implementation, we will have to define the `responded_to` function, which accepts the HTTP request struct. `responded_to` will be fired when the struct is returned.

Question 4

How do you enact middleware for the server?

Answer

In order to enact middleware, we must enact the `wrap_fn` function on the `App` struct. In the `wrap_fn` function, we pass a closure that accepts the service request and routing structs.

Question 5

How do you enable a custom struct to serialize data into the view?

Answer

We decorate the struct with the `#[derive(Deserialize)]` macro. Once we have done this, we define the parameter type so that it's wrapped in a JSON struct; that is, `parameter: web::Json<ToDoItem>`.

Chapter 5, Displaying Content in the Browser

Question 1

What is the simplest way to return HTML data to the user's browser?

Answer

We can serve HTML data by merely defining a string of HTML and putting it in the body of an `HttpResponse` struct while defining the content type as HTML. The `HttpResponse` struct is then returned to the user's browser.

Question 2

What is the simplest (not scalable) way to return HTML, CSS, and JavaScript data to the user's browser?

Answer

The simplest way is to hard code a full HTML string with the CSS hardcoded in the `<style>` section, and then hard code our JavaScript in the `<script>` section. This string is then put in the body of an `HttpResponse` struct and returned to the user's browser.

Question 3

How do you ensure that the background color and style standards of certain elements is consistent across all views of the app?

Answer

We make a CSS file that defines the components that we want to be consistent throughout the app. We then put a tag in the `<style>` section of all of our HTML files. Then, with each file, we load the base CSS file and replace the tag with the CSS data.

Question 4

How do you update the HTML after an API call?

Answer

After the API call, we have to wait for the status to be ready. We then get the HTML section we want to update using the get element by ID, serialize the response data, and then set the inner HTML of the element as the response data.

Question 5

How do we enable a button to connect to our backend API?

Answer

We give the button a unique ID. We then add an event listener, which is defined by the unique ID. We bind this event listener to a function that gets the ID using `this`. In this function, we make an API call to the backend and then use the response to update the HTML of the other parts of our view that display data.

Chapter 6, Data Persistence with PostgreSQL

Question 1

What are the advantages of having a database over a JSON file?

Answer

The database has advantages in terms of multiple reads and writes at the same time. The database also checks the data to see whether it is the right format before inserting it so that we can perform advanced queries with linked tables.

Question 2

How do you create a migration?

Answer

We install the `diesel` client and define the database URL in the `.env` file. We then create migrations using the client, and write the desired schema required for the migration. We then run the migration.

Question 3

How do we check the migration?

Answer

We use the container ID of the database to access the container. We then list the tables. If the desired table is there, this is a sign that the migration ran. We can also check the migration table in the database to see when it was last run.

Question 4

If we were to create a user data model in Rust with a name and an age, what should we do?

Answer

We define a `NewUser` struct with just the name as a string and age as an integer. We then create a `User` struct with the same field and an extra integer field, which is the ID.

Chapter 7, Managing User Sessions

Question 1

What are the advantages of defining unique constraints in the SQL as opposed to the server-side code?

Answer

Adding unique constraints directly to the database ensures that this standard is enforced, regardless of whether data manipulation is done via a migration or server request. This also protects us from corrupting data if a new feature is added at another endpoint that forgets to enforce this standard, or if the code is altered in later alterations of the endpoints.

Question 2

What is the main advantage of the user having a JWT over storing a password?

Answer

If an attacker manages to obtain a JWT, this does not mean that they have direct access to the user's password. Also, if the tokens get refreshed, then the access the attacker has to items has a limited timeframe. As opposed to our JWT, RFC 7519 defines an expiration claim, which is used to check the expiration time of the token. This is used to invalidate old tokens.

Question 3

How does a user store a JWT on the frontend?

Answer

The JWT can be stored in local HTML storage or inside cookies.

Question 4

How could the JWT be useful in the view once we have verified that the JWT is passable?

Answer

We can store multiple data points in the token when hashing it. Therefore, we can encrypt the user ID. With this, we can extract the user ID to perform operations concerned with the to-do item operations.

Question 5

What is the minimal approach to altering data in the frontend and redirecting it to another view when the user hits an endpoint?

Answer

We return a HttpResponse struct with HTML/text body that contains a string housing a couple of HTML tags. In-between these tags are a couple of script tags. In-between these script tags, we can have our JavaScript commands split with ; between each command. We can then directly alter the HTML storage and alter the window location.

Question 6

Why is it useful to have a range of different response codes when logging in a user, as opposed to just denoting that it is successful or not successful?

Answer

There could be a range of reasons why the data gets corrupted in the database, including alterations in the migrations, if there is an expected error, such as an incorrect auth credential being supplied, and so on. However, there could be an error that has occurred that wasn't the user's fault; for instance, a duplicate username for two different users. This is an error where our unique constraints have been violated. We need to know this has happened so that we can correct it.

Chapter 8, Building RESTful Services

Question 1

Why can we not simply code multiple futures into the middleware and merely call and return the one that is right, considering request parameters and authorization outcomes, but instead have to wrap them in an enum?

Answer

Rust's strong typing system will complain. This is because async blocks behave like closures, meaning that every async block is its own type. Pointing to multiple futures is like pointing to multiple types, and thus it will look like we are returning multiple different types.

Question 2

How do we add a new version of views but still support the old views if our API is serving mobile apps and third parties that might not update instantly?

Answer

We add a new module in the views directory with the new views. These have the same endpoints and views with new parameters that are needed. We can then go in either of two different ways. We can create a new function in the `Path` struct for defining version two or we can add a version parameter in the `define` function. Either way, these new views will have the same endpoints with version 2 in them. This enables users to use the new and old API endpoints. We then notify users when the old version will no longer be supported, giving them time to update.

Question 3

Why is the stateless constraint becoming more important in the era of elastic cloud computing?

Answer

With orchestration tools, microservices, and elastic computing instances on demand, spinning up and shutting down elastic computing instances due to demand is becoming a more common practice. If we store data on the instance itself, when the user makes another API call, there is no guarantee that the user will hit the same instance, getting inconsistent data reads and writes.

Question 4

How could we enable another service to be incorporated utilizing the properties of the JWT?

Answer

The JWT token enables us to store the user ID. As long as the second service has the same secret key, we can merely pass requests to the other service with the JWT in the header. The other service does not have to have the login views or access to the user database and can still function.

Question 5

A warning log message hides the fact that an error has happened from the user, but still alerts us to fix it. Why do we ever bother telling the user that an error has occurred and to try again with an error log?

Answer

When an error happens that prevents us from retroactively going back and sorting out the issue, then we have to raise an error instead of a warning. A classic example of an error is not being able to write to a database. A good example of a warning is another service not responding. When the other service is up and running, we can do a database call and call the service, finishing off the process.

Question 6

What are the advantages of logging all requests?

Answer

In production, it is needed to assess the state of a server when troubleshooting. For instance, if a user is not experiencing an update, we can quickly check the logs to see whether the server is in fact receiving the request or whether there is an error with the caching in the frontend. We can also use it to see whether our app is behaving the way we expect it to.

Question 7

Why do we sometimes have to use `async move`?

Answer

There is a possibility that the lifetime of the variable that we are referencing in the async block might not live as long as the async block. In order to resolve this, we shift the ownership of the variable to the block with an `async move` block.

Chapter 9, Testing Our Application Endpoints and Components

Question 1

Why do we bother with unit tests if we can just manually play with the application?

Answer

When it comes to manual testing, you may forget to run a certain procedure. Running tests standardizes our standards and enables us to integrate them into continuous integration tools to ensure new code will not break the server as continuous integration can block new code merges if the code fails.

Question 2

What is the difference between unit tests and functional tests?

Answer

Unit tests isolate individual components such as functions and structs. These functions and structs are then assessed with a range of fake inputs to assess how the component interacts with different inputs. Functional tests assess the system as a whole, hitting API endpoints and checking the response.

Question 3

What are the advantages of unit tests?

Answer

Unit tests are lightweight and do not need an entire system to run. They can test a whole set of edge cases quickly. Unit tests can also isolate directly where the error is.

Question 4

What are the disadvantages of unit tests?

Answer

Unit tests are essentially isolated tests with made up inputs. If the type of input is changed in the system but not updated in the unit test, then this test will essentially pass when it should fail. Unit tests also do not assess how the system runs as a whole.

Question 5

What are the advantages of functional tests?

Answer

Functional tests are brittle. This tells us essentially how the system will run as a whole, which in some cases, unit tests can miss out on. Functional tests will also show us how systems such as the database will interact with our application.

Question 6

What are the disadvantages of functional tests?

Answer

Functional tests need to have infrastructure in order to run like a database. There also has to be a setup and teardown function. For instance, a functional test will affect the data stored in the database. At the end of the test, the database needs to be wiped before running the test again. This can increase the number of complications and require *glue* code between different operations.

Question 7

What is a sensible approach to building unit tests?

Answer

We start off with testing structs and functions that do not have any dependencies. Once these have been tested, we know that we are comfortable with them. We then move onto the functions and structs that have the dependencies we previously tested. Using this approach, we know that the current test we are writing does not fail due to a dependency.

`Packt.com`

Subscribe to our online digital library for full access to over 7,000 books and videos, as well as industry leading tools to help you plan your personal development and advance your career. For more information, please visit our website.

Why subscribe?

- Spend less time learning and more time coding with practical eBooks and Videos from over 4,000 industry professionals

- Improve your learning with Skill Plans built especially for you

- Get a free eBook or video every month

- Fully searchable for easy access to vital information

- Copy and paste, print, and bookmark content

Did you know that Packt offers eBook versions of every book published, with PDF and ePub files available? You can upgrade to the eBook version at `packt.com` and as a print book customer, you are entitled to a discount on the eBook copy. Get in touch with us at `customercare@packtpub.com` for more details.

At `www.packt.com`, you can also read a collection of free technical articles, sign up for a range of free newsletters, and receive exclusive discounts and offers on Packt books and eBooks.

Other Books You May Enjoy

If you enjoyed this book, you may be interested in these other books by Packt:

Creative Projects for Rust Programmers

Carlo Milanesi

ISBN: 978-1-78934-622-0

- Access TOML, JSON, and XML files and SQLite, PostgreSQL, and Redis databases
- Develop a RESTful web service using JSON payloads
- Create a web application using HTML templates and JavaScript and a frontend web application or web game using WebAssembly
- Build desktop 2D games
- Develop an interpreter and a compiler for a programming language
- Create a machine language emulator
- Extend the Linux Kernel with loadable modules

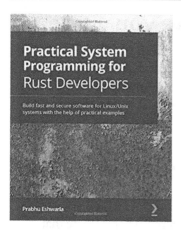

Practical System Programming for Rust Developers

Prabhu Eshwarla

ISBN: 978-1-80056-096-3

- Gain a solid understanding of how system resources are managed
- Use Rust confidently to control and operate a Linux or Unix system
- Understand how to write a host of practical systems software tools and utilities
- Delve into memory management with the memory layout of Rust programs
- Discover the capabilities and features of the Rust Standard Library
- Explore external crates to improve productivity for future Rust programming projects

Packt is searching for authors like you

If you're interested in becoming an author for Packt, please visit `authors.packtpub.com` and apply today. We have worked with thousands of developers and tech professionals, just like you, to help them share their insight with the global tech community. You can make a general application, apply for a specific hot topic that we are recruiting an author for, or submit your own idea.

Leave a review - let other readers know what you think

Please share your thoughts on this book with others by leaving a review on the site that you bought it from. If you purchased the book from Amazon, please leave us an honest review on this book's Amazon page. This is vital so that other potential readers can see and use your unbiased opinion to make purchasing decisions, we can understand what our customers think about our products, and our authors can see your feedback on the title that they have worked with Packt to create. It will only take a few minutes of your time, but is valuable to other potential customers, our authors, and Packt. Thank you!

Index

www.ingramcontent.com/pod-product-compliance
Lightning Source LLC
Chambersburg PA
CBHW062037050326
40690CB00016B/2970